MW00710208

The Power of Vision

The Power of Vision

Here are stories of Christian men who have impacted their generation. They are successful businessmen who follow Biblical principles. As you will see, those same principles have prospered them in their walk with God.

by
Peggy Scarborough with Al Taylor Acknowledgments

As I begin to think of all the people to whom I would like to express my appreciation for their support, suggestions, patience, and hard work in making this book possible, the list continues to grow as did the length of the book.

First, I would like to thank the men of the Board of Vision Foundation for their complete cooperation in this project. They gave freely of their time, even though their schedules were extremely busy. There were many long hours of interviews, consultation, questions, editing, and rewriting. Even though they are all humble men, it was easy to get their stories. I laughed and cried with them as they shared their victories, failures, trials, burdens, and principles of life.

I would like to thank Al Taylor for the many hours of reading, rereading, and consultation. The book could never have come into being without his help and encouragement.

I would like to thank my dear husband, Neigel Scarborough, for creating an atmosphere where I could work at any hour of the day or night and always have his suggestions, understanding, and help.

Kaye Stuman, Paulette Lewis, and Ken Davis, Stewardship Department staff members, were also helpful in various stages of the development of the book. I appreciate so much their help and patience with the many questions and disturbances.

Now, dear reader, grow and grow as you study the lives of these great men of Vision.

Contents

God has always had a people. They are the most special individuals on Planet Earth. They see things differently. They forgive offenses. They give away resources. They serve God and others. Death doesn't intimidate them. Circumstances cannot take away their happiness. How can you explain it? Easy. It only requires one word: Jesus. Jesus loves me; therefore, I love.

What would happen if a select group of faithful Christian men and women were called together and told, "You are free to do anything you feel God is calling you to do. Use your own gifts, experience, and expertise. Work together to assist ministries. Solve problems, start new ministries under the direction of the Holy Spirit." Sounds exciting, doesn't it?

Someone may say, "Well, that is simply what the New Testament has always called us to do." And that would be true. But how rarely is that New Testament opportunity extended to laymen regardless of their abilities? The church has blunted its own potential by trading empowerment of its people for the more coveted control of its people. However, there are some profound exceptions.

Vision Foundation was begun in 1977. Carl Richardson, a preacher of the gospel and a man of keen vision, called together a group of faithful Christians to challenge them with the question: "If you had the freedom to use your own ideas, expertise, and resources, what would you do?" They rallied to the opportunity and established Vision Foundation with the approval of the Executive Committee of the Church of God. It has been an exciting project.

The men and women of Vision focused on Forward in Faith at first. It became the fastest growing Evangelical broadcast. Vision facilitated the purchase of a much-needed building to house the growing ministries. They provided cassette equipment so that millions of preaching tapes could carry the gospel everywhere. Vision gave the land for a new state-of-the-arts recording studio to be built. They purchased television cameras, equipment and then a video production truck. They brought a Christian radio station on the air in 1980. They invested in nationwide television specials, weekly television and overseas crusades. To encourage pastors to use mass media, Vision featured award banquets and gave "golden mikes" for outstanding use of the media, vision awards for outstanding "vision" in ministry and Heritage awards for those who gave us exceptional legacy.

We have invested in Bible schools, prison ministry, stewardship training for ministers and churches, medical missions, Bibles to underground churches, Internet evangelism and discipling, as well as Vision Foundation Lectures.

Is there a future for this concept? We think so. As the church moves into a "last days" intensity of wars, corruption, and anti-Christ-driven opposition, the New Testament paradigm of ministry is more vital than ever. Men and women of vision equipped, empowered, and released to minister under the anointing of the Holy Spirit will demonstrate the plan of Christ and bear much fruit in it.

This book is a collection of individual testimonies by the members of the Board of Vision. Dr. Peggy Scarborough, who compiled these stories, suggested that they are best represented by the title: *The Power of Vision*. I think she has chosen aptly. We offer the book with sincere prayer that God will use it to inspire believers everywhere. You can be one of God's entrepreneurs using your gifts under the anointing of the Holy Spirit to advance the kingdom of God.

Bob Angerer—Making Up for Lost Time

Bob Angerer—Making Up for Lost Time

Becoming Bob

Robert J. Angerer, Sr., (Bob) is an achiever. He is an engineer, lawyer and an oil man, but he was not a Christian until he was 34. Bob has been making up for lost time. God gave Bob the idea for Attorneys for Christ and has now given him the vision for a ministry called Mission Earth.

Becoming an Achiever

Bob was born in Trenton, Michigan; the third son of William B. Angerer and Helen Mary Magiera Angerer. His father was largely of German descent and his mother of Austrian descent. It was from his family that he got his work ethic, enthusiasm, and positive spirit.

Bob grew up on a midwestern farm near Detroit. His father was a general contractor and worked for Ford Motor Company in engine design. Bob's father's family were all hard workers. One of his great grandfathers was General Herkimer of American Revolution fame. His father's family was Methodist, with several Methodist preachers.

Bob's mother had an influence on him. She was an agnostic like her father, but she was a good mother and a hard worker. Her father spoke seven languages fluently and was Henry Ford's interpreter, making a very good salary. When someone accused her father of some misdeed, he was wrongfully fired. As a result, when Bob's mother was just a child, the family moved to a poor farm in Michigan. Her job there was to wash the dead bodies of the people who died while living there. At a very early age she, too, developed a hard-work ethic.

There was no real religious training in the family when Bob was a child. Since his father was raised Methodist and his mother was raised a Catholic, they compromised and decided the family would not to go to church at all. When the children would visit a Methodist church for a wedding or funeral, what they heard was social commentary. When they went to the Catholic church, the services were all in Latin. As a child, Bob received no word from God.

Bob had two older brothers, William and George. Before Bob was born, George died at age 4 while having his tonsils removed. William dated a Church of Christ girl and became a member of that church. He later married and had six daughters. William and his wife often tried to convince Bob to go to church with them. William entered the space program after he completed school and is presently responsible for lifting every shuttle into orbit at the Kennedy Space Center.

As a high school student Bob was a real scholar and leader. In the ninth grade, he had a clinical psychologist as an English teacher. This young teacher had each student do an analysis of the areas in which they were most skilled and for which they had the most preference. The tests revealed Bob's highest skills and interests were engineering and law. Little did Bob know that God would use his gifts in both areas.

Becoming an Engineer and Attorney

Bob studied engineering at the University of Michigan. While in engineering school, he married. His first son, Robert Angerer, Jr., was born in Garden City, Michigan. After Bob graduated with an electrical/electronic engineering degree, he accepted a position as an engineer at a consulting engineering firm designing a major power plant. He began to look at the engineers around him with "big pot bellies" and frowns. These men were only 10 years older than he was. Bob did not want this lifestyle that created such out-of-shape and unhappy people.

Remembering another of his interests was law, he left his engineering career and headed to law school at Florida State University in Tallahassee. After graduation, he took a job with a prominent law firm: Ervin, Varn, Jacobs, Odom, and Kitchen in

Tallahassee. Here he began handling major litigation. During this time a second son, Ronald W. Angerer, was born.

Becoming a Failure

In the middle of success, a major crisis arose. His wife fell in love with his best friend. This was a very painful time for Bob. He tried everything he could to save his marriage. He even went to counselors. They listened to what Bob said and tried to give him some help. They advised, "We think we know what the problem is. Bob, you have a strong work ethic. Maybe you need to change your philosophy to eat, drink and be merry because tomorrow you die." This did not set well with this man who loved his wife, but also had a strong work ethic instilled in him from his family. He chose not to listen to their counsel any longer.

When marriages are falling apart, people often go to church because of this need. Bob talked his wife into going with him to a United Methodist church in Tallahassee for several months. At one point in the pastor's message, he would give people one minute of silent prayer. Bob looked forward all week to that one moment of prayer and peace.

During that time of crisis when Bob was so anxious to find some help, someone knocked on his door. It was a preacher. He asked Bob if he was going to heaven. Bob replied, "I hope so." The concerned but not-too-smart man said, "Read this prayer with me." It was the sinner's prayer. When Bob finished, the preacher asked, "How do you feel?" Bob, who is always positive, said he felt good. The preacher said, "You are saved." This was a step in the right direction for Bob, but not altogether what he needed. His wife remained adamant, and they divorced.

Becoming a Christian

Then God brought Jane Clark, a loving and godly woman into Bob's life in 1980. Shortly after they met, Jane asked Bob if he was saved. Saved? The Baptist preacher who knocked on his door pronounced him saved; he must be. Bob and Jane fell in love on their first date and decided to marry. Jane told Bob that if he loved her he would go to church with her, and he has never stopped.

When he first went to the Church of God, he found the people to be warm and friendly. How he needed this in his life. He was not saved immediately, but the people kept encouraging him to get closer to God. In December 1980, Bob was saved. He had a stirring experience seeing in his mind an image of a notebook with pages flying out and away so that when it stopped, all that was left were clean and new pages. From that point on, his life really began to change.

Jane had two children, Tommy and Shannon, whom Bob adopted, when she and Bob married. Bob had two children. God blessed them with another child, James Michael Angerer. Bob says of his family, "We have five children."

Becoming Close to Christ

Bob had now left the law firm where he worked and started his own firm. He was involved with some of the biggest trial cases one could imagine. These cases involved millions of dollars. During the most stressful part of a trial everyone left him alone in the courtroom and he began to pray. He felt alone. Then he heard the words, "I am here." This gave him a great peace, and he went on to obtain a $20 million jury verdict and judgment.

Becoming a Disciple

Church became very important to Bob. Jane's family decided they wanted to start a new Church of God close to where they lived with Pastor L. R. Johnson, an 82 year-old-man who had been retired. When Jane's family approached the 82-year-old preacher, he shouted, "I'll do it!" He then said, "I'll preach Sunday morning and Sunday night if Bob Angerer will teach the Sunday morning sanctuary class and teach on Wednesday evenings."

Bob was only 35 at the time. What his pastor wanted to do was to disciple him. For three years Bob faithfully taught and found that through teaching, he was learning much about God.

Becoming a Tither and a Giver

Bob did not know anything about tithing. He thought tithing was like membership "dues" in an organization and not a Scriptural doctrine. Jane and God taught Bob that blessing follows obedience in tithing.

One day the church needed some heaters. Bob and Jane took $200 of their tithes and bought space heaters. God taught them a lesson. Their gift was not blessed. They had to spend out money they normally did not have to spend, an amount twice what the heaters cost. The tithe money was not theirs to spend on some need they saw. They quickly learned they should have given the tithe to the church and then given the heaters above the tithe.

Today, when people come to Bob and Jane and ask them to take some of their tithe money to bless someone, they quickly respond, "That sounds good until God teaches you a lesson. The tithe is the Lord's!"

Becoming an Attorney for Christ

Bob became burdened after studying Matthew 25 and the parable about the talents. He was using some of his talents for the Lord, but he was not using his talent as an attorney. He secretly asked the Lord for the opportunity to use this legal talent for Him.

Soon afterwards Bob's pastor's wife asked if he would meet with the Reverend Louis H. Cross, a visiting field representative of the Department of Stewardship. Bob did meet with Brother Cross who explained that the department provided a service in which a representative meets with church members who request it and suggests ideas for estate plans for review and for preparation by the members' attorneys. Cross informed Bob that unfortunately members sometime delay having attorneys draft their wills because of the cost. The delay can result in members and their families not being protected.

Brother Cross shared with Bob that this had been a subject of prayer on his part. Bob saw the answer to both of their prayers. He told Brother Cross that if he discovered members who found themselves in this position, he would prepare their wills free of charge, if they would include the Lord's work in their wills. Within a week Bob received over 50 requests to prepare wills.

Since that time, with Department of Stewardship Director Al Taylor's guidance and staff, attorneys in 25 states have joined with Bob in Attorneys for Christ and prepared several thousand wills for Christians. Many testimonies have been preserved, many families protected, many tax dollars saved and tens of millions of dollars dedicated to the Lord's ministries at all levels. This service and ministry continues today.

By bringing together Bob and Brother Cross, a matched pair of praying Christians, God not only answered their individual prayers, but allowed His answer to spill over to other burdened attorneys, thousands of Christian families, and a host of ministries which have been and will be financially enabled by the gifts included in the Christian wills.

The first Will Center was at the 1986 General Assembly of the Church of God. Every General Assembly since then has included a Will Center. The Will Center has protected many Church of God families and at the same time raised several million dollars for the work of the Lord.

Becoming an Oil Man for Christ

Bob has been representing oil companies since 1976. In the course of all of this he often had to hire experts. Bob's technical background allowed him to understand scientific things easily. He says, "An expert is someone who can take highly technical things and put them in a few words that anybody can understand." So these experts gave Bob an education in the oil business.

Bob was a consultant in Canada in 1987 for another oil company. He could not practice law in Canada, but he directed the litigation. The case was about a 2-trillion-cubic-foot natural gas field in the Yukon Territory in Canada. Four major oil companies had agreed to develop and market gas from his clients' lands as soon as possible in return for two-thirds of the gas produced. They did not do live up to their agreement, so Bob sued them for his client. This required extensive travel to western Canada for over 10 years.

God has divine connections for people. During the course of that litigation, Bob was introduced to Jamil Azad. Jamil is half-Indian and half-Russian, but was trained in Switzerland. He was the chief exploration geologist for the Burma Oil Company, a large English oil company.

When Amoco acquired the Burma Oil Company in the 1970s, Jamil retired and began working with geological interpretation of aerial photography. Oil and gas people have used aerial photography since the 1940s to locate and drill oil reservoirs. The big reservoirs that could be found with the tool were located long ago, but the smaller ones that disappeared in the background noise evaded detection. Jamil developed an analysis that identifies these smaller, but very economic and valuable reservoirs.

Bob was impressed with Jamil and his analysis. He and Bob discussed his technology. He asked Bob, "What would you, Bob Angerer, do with this tool if you had it? It has the potential to increase American reserves by billions of barrels of oil." Bob replied, "Let me think about it." He went away and thought and prayed for a month. He came back and laid out a working plan for Jamil. Now they are equal partners in what has become known as Oil for America.

Since then Bob has gone out and leased land, laid out seismic programs, directed the drilling of oil wells, completed the wells, produced oil and natural gas, and sold the oil. In the past 10 years he has done things that most geologists in the business only envy. Bob maintains America has plenty of remaining oil to be discovered. All that is necessary to end America's energy dependence is to develop new technology, which can reduce the number of dry holes drilled in search of oil. Oil for America has developed and applied this analysis in four oil-producing basins in the United States.

Oil for America's analysis locates these remaining oil reservoirs with pinpoint accuracy. These sites include reefs located in several parts of America including: North Texas, the Williston Basin, the Permian Basin, the Illinois Basin, and the Paradox Basin. Oil for America estimates that its technology can be used to discover and produce over 100 billion barrels of sweet light crude oil in America, more than competitively with world prices. This is more than the oil reserve of Kuwait, Venezuela, Iraq, and five times the existing reserves in the United States.

Becoming a Soulwinner

Over the last 20 years Bob has been blessed to meet and work with some of God's choicest servants. He has been allowed to serve on various boards which have given him the sense he was helping to win the lost. About a year ago, his pastor asked Bob to go with him to Tommy Barnett's Pastor's School in Phoenix, Arizona. Here, Bob realized that he was to be a soulwinner first.

Bob went with a small group soulwinning in the roughest part of Phoenix. Bob and his partner led a hooker and her pimp to the Lord. They took them on a bus back to the church where they watched a presentation of the gospel focused on substitutional sacrifice. Bob watched the hooker fold her arms, not wanting to be there, but as she saw the illustrated message, she began leaning over the rail. When the invitation was given, she walked down the aisle and confirmed Jesus as the Lord of her life.

Bob has led Saturday soulwinning programs in his church. They met at the church and went out to witness to hundreds of families. He has led a homeless person and a person with a master's degree to the Lord. God has given him an image of hills covered with people crying out for help. He has now seen the harvest field around the world that the church has not been able to seize because of lack of money.

Becoming a Man of Vision

Bob is not afraid to share his dream for Mission Earth. This is a ministry that will be used to coordinate, enable, and maximize mission efforts in and out of the United States.

The local church is still very important to the Angerer family. This ministry will be connected with the local church and funded by a foundation financed by the oil revenues from his share of Oil for America.

He and his son, Robert, Jr., are in the law business and the oil business together. His son, James, works in the oil business with him as well. Working with his sons is a great blessing. He is thrilled as he sees his children serving the Lord.

"Don't give up in anything you do. Don't give up on God. Don't give up on yourself. Don't give up on your dreams. Don't give up on anybody else. Don't give up." —Robert J. Angerer

Robert J. Angerer
P. O. Box 10468
Tallahassee, FL 32302

Telephone
850-576-5982

Web site
www.oilforamerica.com

Terry Applegate—A Man With Great Focus

Terry Applegate—A Man With Great Focus

Terry Applegate is the owner and CEO of Applegate Insulation Manufacturing, Inc., headquarted in Webberville, Michigan, with plants in six states serving United States and international customers. A Christian for more than 25 years, with 12 years of service as an elder in his church, Terry continues to be fascinated and captivated by the power and wisdom of God's Word. He is constantly exploring ways to apply the Word in every sphere of life, including the business realm.

The Family Business

Terry Applegate was born in 1952 in Michigan. About the time he was born, his father, Aaron, pioneered the use of electric heating in south central Michigan, in head-to-head competition with the dominant method of heating at the time, natural gas. Natural gas had an incredible advantage at the time—it was virtually free—so the only way Aaron could offer comparable monthly costs was to insulate his electrical heating customers' homes extremely well. This produced a problem and an opportunity for Aaron because no one in the 1950s knew what well insulated even meant. Fuel was so cheap that insulation was an afterthought—if that! However, as Aaron studied the dynamics of heating, cooling, and comfort, he saw the opportunity to create an entirely new business model built around a comprehensive comfortable-home system approach. This integrated system produced a controlled indoor home environment and launched Aaron into the infant insulation industry, running what would become known as the most advanced contracting business in the midwest until he sold it in the mid-1980s.

Terry Became a Businessman at an Early Age

Terry came on board with his father when he was in the seventh grade and remained throughout his high school years, assisting his father by calculating heat loss projections for homes throughout Michigan.

Perhaps because of his father's entrepreneurial example, at age 14 Terry started his own business: eggs delivered directly to the home. His father took him to a local chicken farm where Terry would buy eggs at wholesale prices. Terry then cleaned them off and took them through the neighborhood, developing an understanding of the value of superior customer service and an idea of the hard work it took to earn and maintain a good customer base.

Tough Times for Aaron Applegate

However, even as Aaron's pioneering work with insulation had blossomed into a growing industry, not all was well on the business front. Interestingly enough, Aaron's very success threatened to be his undoing.

High sales and low spirits had their genesis in a presidential speech delivered on April 15, 1977. President Jimmy Carter, responding to the OPEC oil embargo and what he thought to be the start of a declining standard of living, went on national television wearing a cardigan sweater sitting in front of a roaring fire. He implied that Americans should adjust to perpetual energy shortages and declared the moral equivalent of war on high fuel prices. Part of his declaration of war was that he instigated tax credits for insulating in order to save energy. At the time, Terry was managing his father's business, Applegate Heating, Cooling and Insulation.

Applegate Insulation was perfectly positioned to take advantage of the rush to insulate, and early the next day the phones started ringing. Indeed, within days they had to hire and train several additional installation crews as concerned homeowners wanted to insulate with Applegate.

From that April until Thanksgiving, Applegate Insulation made more money than they had ever dreamed they would make. It was phenomenal. They happened to be in the right place at the right time. Unfortunately, they were working with the wrong suppliers.

They Had to Do Something Different

Aaron Applegate not only built his own contracting business from the ground up, but he had been the driving force behind the success of an early cellulose insulation manufacturer. He encouraged and made possible their early expansion by buying and using their insulation himself while also representing them to contractors throughout the region. As demand for cellulose insulation skyrocketed, the manufacturer decided to expand their market share at the expense of Aaron, cutting back on his company's supplies at a critical time and dealing directly with his contracting network. As the owner made clear to Aaron, sales were so strong they no longer needed manufacturer reps but would save money by selling straight to the contractor. Incredible success had apparently rendered Aaron's services of no value to the manufacturer.

Shaking off the bitter taste of betrayal, both father and son once again looked for opportunity and decided to take their future into their own hands. Working with several of their strongest contracting customers, Terry and Aaron formed Applegate Insulation Manufacturing, Inc., to meet their own needs in addition to those contractors who stayed loyal to Aaron. This idea was a gift from God—the solution to their problem.

Their First Insulation Manufacturing Plant

In 1978, Aaron and Terry, now business partners, built their first insulation manufacturing facility in Okemos, near Lansing. While both men had an encyclopedic knowledge of insulation materials, methods, and systems, they had never manufactured cellulose insulation before. Also, because of the incredible demand for cellulose insulation, others had the same idea. There were soon over 50 manufacturers in Michigan alone and over a thousand plants across the country.

Together, Terry and Aaron navigated a hypercompetitive market rocked by dramatic swings in demand for insulation as the nation shook off their doomsday madness, which produced a needed shakeout in the industry. Today only about 35 competitors remain nationwide. Now, with growth coming from a strong demand for housing rather than fear of fuel shortages, Applegate Insulation has become the largest private manufacturer of cellulose insulation in the world. They are also one of the nation's largest producers of hydroseeding mulch and distribute residential lawn repair kits through major retailers nationwide.

Whether in the home construction business or landscaping field, they have achieved their success by giving freely of their time, serving the entire industry by educating contractors and homeowners, and even answering questions from competitors who acknowledge Applegate's unparalleled expertise in their manufacturing areas.

More Plants and More Business

In 1984, Applegate expanded by purchasing a factory in Phoenix, the National Fiber Company, which they kept until 1991 before selling to an Arizona competitor. In 1995, they bought Suburban Insulation in Hagerstown, Maryland, and the next year built one of the most technologically advanced plants in the country in Webberville, Michigan, which increased their capacity by 50 percent compared to their old location. In 1996 and 1997, they acquired manufacturing facilities in Cornelia, Georgia, and Hickory, Kentucky. In 1998, they shut down the plant in Maryland and moved it to Pennsylvania where they bought a plant six times larger. Applegate Insulation acquired Energy Zone Insulation in Buffalo, Minnesota, in 1999, and the following year bought Fibermaster Insulation in Monroe, Louisiana. The company's latest acquisition took place in 2001 with the purchase of a plant in Wisconsin, which they merged into their Minnesota business. The acquisition in Wisconsin cemented Applegate's position as the largest private cellulose insulation manufacturer in the world. Business Reform magazine reports that Applegate has over 200 employees with $25 million in annual sales.

Why Is Applegate so Blessed?

People ask why Applegate Insulation is still in business when almost all their competitors have closed. Terry has an answer:

> "We know our business; we know our customers, and we know how to provide excellent service and good products.

> "This combination has resulted in the establishment of a great reputation. We have always given people the best product available. There is no better product in the world of cellulose insulation than ours, which even our competitors acknowledge. It's a fact we take great satisfaction in, for two reasons. First, as Christians we're called upon to do whatever we do as unto the Lord. We're called to be a workman who is not ashamed; to do unto others, or to serve others as we ourselves would desire to be served.

> "Second, we enjoy our work! God created man to work, to build, to produce, and there's no greater feeling in the world than to fulfill this God-instilled mandate. It may sound funny, but we're passionate about cellulose insulation and hydroseeding mulch. Frankly, in a world of apathy and mediocrity, if you have a passion for your work you have a great chance to succeed."

Take One Day at a Time

Terry Applegate takes one day at a time. There were years of discouragement, but they just kept doing what they were doing. Admittedly, there were many times when they found it hard to see progress, but Terry is adamant that there is incredible value in persevering. Both he and his father just kept showing up. He realizes God has called him to this business, and his responsibility is to put forth the best effort he can on a daily basis.

Terry says, "Many of our competitors would have made it if they just hadn't given up. They got burned out and lost interest. It is rare that people leave what they are doing and go on to something else and become a success. It is better to stick with what you know even if you have to work through times of boredom."

Everything Is a Question of Stewardship

Terry maintains, "Everything is a question of stewardship. God created me for work and worship, and the two are really inseparable. In fact, I am created for good works, and that means all good works, not simply something we now categorize as ministry versus non-ministry. If all of life is understood and viewed in terms of stewardship issues, then everything I do with the resources placed at my disposal is counted as ministry. To engage in business activity, for the Christian, is to be immersed in ministry."

Life and Marriage Falls Apart

During college days, Terry had made a radical departure from Christianity, embracing first one philosophy and then another. But he began to struggle to run a business and keep his marriage together. Suddenly life without Christ did not satisfy him.

His marriage began to fall apart. Even as Terry's wife pursued her own agenda for life, Terry picked up his Bible and began to read it compulsively. He says, "To this day I can attribute it only to the apprehending power of the Holy Spirit and the sovereign will of God who loved me even while I was yet an enemy of Christ." His wife thought he had gone off the deep end. The last thing she was looking for was Jesus Christ. She was too immersed in feminism and too busy trying to find herself. She finally decided she didn't want to be married anymore. She left, filed for divorce, and Terry was devastated.

He had never considered divorce. He sat down in the middle of the floor and wept, trying to figure out what life was all about.

God Restores in Marriage All He Lost

Some time later, Terry met Valerie, who had experienced a similar situation, and they soon fell in love. But they had a difficult time finding a preacher to perform the wedding ceremony. One preacher said he would marry them, if they would attend his church and prove themselves for a year.

Then Terry remembered the church where he had been saved at the age of 13. He had a genuine conversion, but his family was unhappy with him going to that church; so he turned away. Now, years later, he returned to that same church. Garold Boatwright was the pastor. Garold married them in 1980 and immediately both Terry and Valerie recognized they needed something more to base their life on than what they had. They turned to God and started to attend the Faith Fellowship Church of God.

Getting the Revelation About Tithing

One night Terry was sitting in an easy chair reading the Church of God Evangel. He saw an article on tithing. Pastor Boatwright had taught and preached about tithing—you might say he laid the foundation for what was about to happen—but it had never clicked until this particular moment. It hit him, "We are supposed to be tithing. We have to start doing it."

Times were tough in the 1980s. The insulation business everywhere had come almost to a halt during the hostage crisis. Oil problems, along with high interest rates, had forced many out of business. Applegate Insulation was not doing well and money was tight. Terry said, "Business was dead. You could not give it away." This was not a good time to get this revelation. How could they possibly get by on 10 percent less? His feeling was, "We have made a commitment to God and here this article clearly set forth the fact according to Scripture that tithing was something God expected and required His people to do."

Valerie pointed out to Terry that tithing would be the equivalent of committing economic suicide. Valerie's parents always told her tithing was the stupidest thing a person could do with their money, but she shrugged her shoulders and told Terry to lead the way and she would follow. That is when things turned around for them. They tithed totally from a perspective of obeying God.

God Is Faithful

While it did not happen overnight, Terry and Val discovered that God is faithful. Never once did God let them down, but instead He always provided during those tough times, and Terry's faith continued to build.

Here Terry was giving 10 percent right off the top and while it was tight, it was no more so than before he tithed. However, as the future unfolded, Terry and Valerie experienced a steady progression in their financial condition. There was definite progress.

Tithing presented Terry with the challenge of submitting his will and his thinking to the Word of God. His confession was that God was the Creator, God of the universe, and that He owned it all. God was telling Terry that He had a rightful claim to 10 percent off the top. Tithing proved to be the concrete way Terry could prove that he really believed that. In other words, it was a matter of ownership. Did God own everything or not?

As Terry and Val learned to obey God concerning tithing, they also found it easier to obey Him in other areas as well. Many of the blessings promised to covenant believers in Deuteronomy 28 started to appear in their lives. When they read the Bible, they found out that God wanted to prosper them. Terry found that God really meant what He said when He promised:

"Now it shall come to pass, if you diligently obey the voice of the Lord your God, to observe carefully all His commandments which I command you today, that the Lord your God will set you high above all nations of the earth. And all these blessings shall come upon you and overtake you because you obey the voice of the Lord your God ... the Lord will command the blessing on you in your storehouses and in all to which you set your hand, and He will bless you in the land which the Lord your God is giving you" (Deuteronomy 28:1-2).

Their Company Was a Testimony

Terry's company became a testimony to the reality of God keeping His promises. He and Val were the recipients of "blessings overtaking them." Customers they never called on or even considered approaching have literally walked into their offices requesting Applegate products.

Top salesmen from competitors have walked in and stated they wanted to work for no one but Applegate and that all their customers would follow them. One salesman even told his customers they would soon be buying from Applegate even before he came and talked to Terry. Why was this? Was it because Terry was suddenly smarter or more charismatic in the personality sense? No! Terry was the same person who had been just getting by a little earlier. The difference was that God, in His sovereign will and plan, was sending blessings to overtake Terry because he had simply been obedient to His Word. The Holy Spirit opened Terry's eyes to the truth, made him live in obedience to that truth, and now was blessing him for his obedience.

He Uses the Business as a Tool in the Hands of God

The incredible life story of John D. Rockefeller, a devout Christian man who used his business to expand the opportunities to declare and demonstrate the power of Christ, challenged Terry to take what he does seriously and to do it to the very best of his ability. Terry uses his business as a tool in the hands of God just as Rockefeller did.

Incredible Ministry Opportunities

Terry believes that as a businessman he has incredible ministry opportunities before him. He tries to use every platform he has for the Kingdom purpose. His customers are accustomed to seeing all his products filled with Scripture references. Whether it is written on his products, in his actions, or in his speech, Terry continually proclaims the gospel of Jesus Christ to the business world. He has hundreds of semi-trailers. Scripture verses are painted on the trailers, utilizing them as another ministry platform.

Applegate Communications, a marketing arm of his business, publishes two journals: The Cellulose Insulation Journal and The Professional Hydroseeding Journal. Millions of papers are distributed to builders, contractors, prospects, etc. In these papers, he sees that there are articles about how the Word and law are applied to business. He also has published many antiabortion articles utilizing this forum. He is amazed at how Scripture plays out before his eyes as he is reminded of Paul's writing in 2 Corinthians 2:16, "To the one we are the aroma of death leading unto death; and to the other the aroma of life leading to life. And who is sufficient for these things?"

"Many call professing a new faith in Christ or simply that they have been encouraged and blessed by the articles, and then there are those few who have declared their hatred for us, God, and life itself," says Terry.

A Child's Life Is Saved

Many times there are glorious stories to tell. Other times there is a price to be paid. Once he received a phone call from California. A girl called to say thank you for having run an ad decrying abortion in 1995. She said, "Because of that ad, I did not have a planned abortion. Today I have a 4-year-old son. I was just looking at him and wanted to call to say thank you."

Principles to Live By

Some of the principles Terry lives by are: Be consistent. Stay focused. Do one thing well. Don't quit.

Our Work Is as Precious as Life

Terry has a strong work ethic. He believes, "Our work is as precious as life itself, because both are God's gifts to us." He writes in the Business Reform magazine, December 2001: "Without work we cannot take dominion for Christ. Without work we disobey and dishonor God. Without work we find ourselves in the place of rebels. As Christians we should love our work. Our work is the theater in which we play ourselves; the canvas on which we can create that unique individual God thought of as me. Our vocation gives our life meaning and is the vehicle for fulfillment as we pursue God's purposes in a productive and contributive manner."

He Serves the Community

As owner and CEO of Applegate Insulation, Terry has had the privilege of serving as chairman of the ASTM task group for cellulose insulation, and he is currently on the board of directors of the Cellulose Insulation Manufacturers Association. Additionally, he is on the Board of Citizens for Traditional Values, was a founding board member for Free International Missions, and has been in jail for rescuing preborn children at abortion mills.

Valerie has served on the school board for Lakeside Christian School and as cochairman of the Shiawassee County Republican Party. Both Terry and Valerie have served as members of the Republican County Executive Committee. Terry was a delegate to the National Convention of the Constitution Party in 2000. The Applegates are members of Okemos

Christian Center in Okemos, Michigan, where he serves as an elder.

Terry and his pastor, Craig Dumont, work closely together to touch the business world for God. Writer Joe Johnson said, "Together, like iron sharpening iron, they have challenged each other's Christian thinking while growing in the Lord."

In his booklet, *A Christian View of Vocation,* Terry writes: "Our plant has grown from one plant to five (now six) and from $1.5 million a year in sales to sales significantly higher than that. Along the way, our products have continued to improve in quality and yet we have been able to lower our prices. Our company is more profitable today than 20 years ago. Our customers have a better product and a lower price; hence, they are better off than they were 20 years ago. We buy thousands of tons of newsprint from churches, schools, and community groups, along with commercial paper brokers. Therefore, because our company continues to operate at a profit, stay in business and expand, others profit as well. Wealth generation cannot be limited to simply one level or one company or even one community. The Christian businessman is ministering financially to many people he will never meet."

Terry Applegate
1000 Highview Drive
Webberville, MI 48892

Telephone
800-627-7536

Autry Dawsey—The Seer and Hearer

Autry Dawsey—The Seer and Hearer

What kind of man is this? Autry Dawsey can look at a piece of property and see whether or not it has potential. He can tell you immediately what kind of business might thrive or not thrive there. The gifts of the Spirit operate for him in the business world. He hears the voice of God clearly. It's like he has a clear-cut connection to God. Yet, he is a businessman, not a preacher. Further, whatever he touches is blessed of God. What makes this kind of man?   Is this kind of spiritual depth possible in the business world? Let's find out!

What Kind of Family Produces This Kind of Man?

When God wants to do something great, He starts with a child. Autry was born in 1936 in Bolton, North Carolina. He and his three brothers—A. B. Dawsey, Jr., J. W. Dawsey, and P. E. Dawsey—had a unique childhood. They were sons of A. B. Sr., and Gladys Dawsey.   Their childhood was spent on the farm.

Their mother, Gladys Dawsey, was a very influential woman. She was the daughter of a Pentecostal Freewill Baptist pastor in eastern North Carolina. She was a deeply spiritual woman. Not only did she have deep feelings for people, she acted upon her feelings. Her heart broke with the things that break God's heart. She never worried about whether a woman was supposed to be involved in ministry. She just found a need and filled it. She found a hurt and healed it. She acted on her deep feelings and concerns and found solutions for the problems of people.

The Boys Home of North Carolina was actually started in the Dawsey home. Gladys brought disadvantaged children, ages 9 to 15, into the home and cared for them as she would care for her own children. She made them a part of the family. She taught them the Word of God. She taught them character building. She taught them how to go back into the world and be successful. Her message to these unfortunate children was, "You can make it!"

She also taught her family to love hurting people. The entire family got involved. This close-knit, Baptist family were all humanitarians with a great desire to help people.

Much of what all of this family is, they attribute to their Proverbs 31 mother. Nobody questioned her influence. She walked in an aura of anointing in whatever she did. She had found herself and wanted to help others find themselves.

Autry became a Christian about the age of 6. His mother led him to the Lord Jesus Christ at home. There was no great drama connected with his conversion. In his childlike way, Autry came to the Lord Jesus knowing that He would not turn him away.

Their mother taught Autry and his brothers the power of taking the Word of God as it actually is. They were trained that God's Word does not have to be accompanied by great emotion. Just believe what God said. They learned early that the Word of God works in every situation of their lives.

The Little Boy With the Million-Dollar Voice

Autry became a singer shortly after he was saved. He became known throughout the area as the little boy with the million-dollar voice. At the age of 7, he was singing on the radio every Sunday morning with his pastor, J. Homer Butler. He knew at this young age the thrill of lifting people from the everyday problems of life to experiencing the presence of God through the use of his anointed voice.

His brothers were all called to the ministry about the same time. Why was Autry not called? He was unique. It seemed that music was Autry's gifting and calling. At the time he did not know it, but God was calling him to a different destiny from his brothers. His calling was a great call.

The Boys Home Moves

Finally, it became evident the Dawsey home was no longer adequate for the family and the boys. A. D. Peacock, Hap Collier, Crowell Black, and some other businessmen got involved and started the first Boys Home Cottage in Lake Waccamaw. (This is the present location for the Boys Home of North Carolina). The family moved to Lake Waccamaw.

The boys taken into the home were from abusive and problem families or from homes where the father was absent. Thus, there was always stress. Eventually A. B. Dawsey Sr., had a heart attack and needed to get out of the stressful environment. The decision was difficult for Gladys because the Boys Home was the love of her life.

College Days and Early Career

During this time, Autry's brothers went to Lee College to further their education in the ministry. They joined the Church of God. A. B. went to Whiteville and started a Church of God on Lee Street. It was at this time that Gladys, their mother, also joined the Church of God.

Autry left home in 1954 to go to Lee College where his brothers had gone earlier. While there he sang in a quartet with Al Taylor, Henry Harrington, Bobby Willerson, and Johnny Childers (pianist). This was an exciting time for Autry because he loved ministering in churches every weekend. Autry also became a member of the Church of God.

Meeting His Soul Mate

While at Lee College, Autry met and married Faye. He found his soul mate. This was a marriage made in heaven. She was, and still is, everything he could want in a wife and companion. The love they have for each other is a miraculous gift. Richard Bach said, "A soul mate is someone who has locks that fit our keys and keys to fit our locks." This describes their relationship. Faye shares Autry's deepest longings and his sense of direction.

Together, they left Lee College and went to Peabody College in Nashville to continue Autry's education. This was a time of growth for the newlyweds. They found their love growing deeper every day.

After completing Peabody, Autry was hired as general manager of Pan American Tire Company in Miami and worked there for seven years. This was a great job for a young man, and Autry loved his work.

The Beginning of the Nursing Home Business

One Christmas when the boys were home, their father had a serious talk with them. He said, "Sons, my health is demanding that we get out of the Boys Home. The doctors in this area want me to start a nursing home. I don't know how you feel about it. I want to do it; but I can't do it alone. If I do it, I will have to have your help."

All five of the men—the four brothers and their father— agreed they would be a part of the new family project. They were all miraculously able to borrow $12,500 each and make their contributions. All the boys were in the ministry except Autry. They could not leave their churches and did not feel called of God to the business world. They felt that Autry should come home and administer the nursing home. The brothers who were preachers took their vacations and helped with the construction. God helped them to quickly put up a beautiful facility.

On the opening day of the Dawsey Nursing Home in Whiteville, in 1966, about 50 patients transferred into the home. The Dawseys were on their way as humanitarian businessmen.

Building More Nursing Homes

One thing led to another, and eventually they built five homes in North Carolina. Autry and his brothers built all of them. They subcontracted some of the work out.

A. B. was the president of the corporation. In every home, Autry and his family saw the hand of God. Autry was the administrator for each of the facilities until they hired someone else. He moved when a new one opened and stayed until the home was running smoothly. When Autry became involved with the nursing homes, he had no idea where it would lead. Unbelievable doors opened.

God Leading Into New Business Ventures

Soon the family became involved with motels in Knoxville. Further, they bought convenience stores and auto dealerships.

Autry ran the business, and his brothers were preachers. Every week he sent a check to his brothers. He began to understand that business was his calling.

Sorrow Comes to the Family

One of the most heartbreaking things that ever happened to Autry was when he got word that his brother, J. W., had died suddenly at age 52 on October 10, 1982, while building a new church in Knoxville, Tennessee. J. W. had just finished preaching a message in his church, the Lovell Heights Church of God. As he was walking down the steps of the church, he was struck with a massive heart attack.

This came as a shock to the family. Up until that time, J. W. had been in good health. In fact, he was the healthiest member of the family. The brothers thought he would outlive all of them. J. W. loved the outdoors and was an excellent preacher and prayer warrior. Autry had leaned heavily on him for advice in running the family business. It was the most upsetting thing that had ever happened to their family and to Autry personally. But it made Autry realize that time was short.

Sixteen months later, on February 27, 1984, Autry's other brother, A. B., died suddenly of a heart attack. A. B. had gone to Gallup, New Mexico, to preach on the Indian reservation. He had a heart attack and was rushed to the hospital in Gallup. Within a short time he died.

Family Adjustments Changed the Business Plan

There were now family adjustments. Autry loved being in the family business, but it seemed necessary, after the loss of two brothers, to divide up the family estate. From then on, Autry and Faye were on their own.

God Blesses Everything He Touches

God did not fail Autry. One door opened another door. He walked through the doors he felt were of God. Some of the businesses he bought or became a partner in are listed:

- *Owner and executive director of Lake Waccamaw Convalescent Center, Lake Waccamaw, N.C., since 1978.*
- *Best Western Premier Inn (Whiteville, N.C.) along with several other motels, apartments, and commercial and residential properties.*
- *Founder and director of Waccamaw Bank*
- *President and chief executive officer, Premier Management Company, Inc. (Management company for other companies listed)*
- *President, K.A.R. Enterprises, Inc. (motel)*
- *President, B&D Enterprises (real estate)*
- *President, Dawsey Investment Co, Inc (fast food)*
- *President, Premiere Construction, Inc. (construction company)*
- *Managing partner, Premiere Enterprises of Whiteville, LLC (real estate)*
- *President, Premiere Hospitality Group, Inc. (motel)*
- *Managing Partner, Dawcut Hospitality, LLC (hotel)*
- *President, 701 Associates (real estate);*
- *President, 374 Operating Co (real estate)*
- *President, Premiere Point (housing development)*

- President, Premiere Living, Inc. (Nursing home; substantial operations sold in 1998)
- D&H Foods (Sonic)

He served with distinction in several professional capacities including:

- Governor's Advisory Council on Comprehensive Health Planning (1973-77).
- Board of Governors, American Nursing Home Association, Region O, Health Planning Council.
- Chairman, North Carolina State Board of Examiners for Nursing Home Administrators, Region 3
- President's Council, Lee College, Cleveland, Tenn.
- Member, Board of Vision Foundation
- Executive Committee — Southland Leadership & Resource Center
- President of North Carolina Nursing Home Association

God Gives Him Supernatural Strength

People often ask Autry how he manages so many businesses. God gives him supernatural strength because of a powerful prayer life and principles by which he lives.

Do Right

Autry and Faye live by, and have instilled in their children, the principle of "Do right." They maintain that if you have integrity and treat people as you want to be treated, you will always succeed.

They live by the philosophy: Do what is right regardless of circumstances or repercussions. If you do what is right, it will hurt you at times; but in the long run, you will win.

He Listens for the Voice of God

Most business people are too busy to be quiet for long. Likewise, this is not the hour in which men take kindly to an exhortation to listen, for listening is not a part of our culture. Even Christians have accepted the philosophy that noise, size, and activity make one successful. Faye and Autry have listened to what God says, "Be still, and know that I am God" (Psalm 46:10).

Faye and Autry are intercessors. They believe that if anyone seeks to walk with God, He will walk with them. They believe whoever will listen will hear the Father speaking. Sometimes God wakes Autry at 2 a.m. and speaks to him. When he is awakened with thoughts on his mind, he assumes God placed them there. He gets much of his direction like this. Being a reserved person by nature, Autry does not always tell other people what God is saying to him.

Autry and Faye are prayer warriors. Autry prays while walking. Every morning he walks and prays for 45 minutes. God also speaks to and through Faye. She has a very precious and close relationship with her Lord. When she wakes up in the morning, she often says, "Good morning, Lord."

Faye has a set time and place to pray every day. Her time is 10 a.m. This appointment with God is as important as an appointment with the doctor, the lawyer, or friends. She taught her children not to wait until the end of the day to pray, but to start in the morning. She has learned that when you get in the presence of God, something happens that does not happen anywhere else. She loves the presence of the Lord that she senses in her daily prayer life. At this time, she brings to the Lord the family, the business, their fears, and their concerns.

Faye believes a mother must learn to hear the voice of the Lord. They have two wonderful children, Kimberly Honeycutt and Autry Dawsey Jr., and seven grandchildren. At the time of the births of the grandchildren, doctors did not have the benefits of ultrasounds to tell you the gender of the unborn baby. God revealed to Faye the gender of all of the grandchildren before the births.

Kimberly did not tell her mother on one occasion she was pregnant. She said to her husband, "God will show Mama." Sure enough, one morning Faye goes to Kimberly and Russell's home and declares, "God has shown me that you are going to have a baby." It was a fact.

God gives them much revelation about their business. On one occasion Faye and Autry were in San Francisco, ready to sign a contract with a man there. On Sunday evening before Autry had a meeting on Monday, Faye was in a store when the Lord spoke to her to get out of the shop and get back to the motel room. She obeyed. At that point in time, she did not understand that God wanted to talk with her. She wondered why it was so urgent for her to go back to the motel, but she has learned to be obedient to the still small voice.

When she arrived at the motel, God began to speak to her. The voice of the Lord, which she heard, said, "Do not do business with the man you have come to see. He is a crook, and you must not deal with him." Autry already had papers ready to sign; but when he heard his wife's counsel, he decided to return home without any further business plans. By the time they arrived home, they got the information that the man did not even own his office. He was merely renting the space, and this was not a good business deal at all.

So many times God speaks to Faye and Autry in this manner. On another occasion, Autry was getting ready to go into business with two men in Raleigh. He took Faye with him to meet the men. Again God spoke to Faye that they must not do business with these men. This time Autry did not want to take her advice. He argued with his wife, "I don't think you are hearing clearly this time. This man that you are afraid of is the son of a governor." She uttered, "God won't allow it." Soon Autry learned that his wife was right again. The man proved to be dishonest and ended up taking his own life.

God Endows His Children With Gifts

God endows His children with gifts. Autry has an unusual gift for looking at property and knowing what will succeed or not succeed on that piece of real estate. It seems that the three "To Know" Gifts of the Spirit—Word of Wisdom, Word of Knowledge, Discernment of the Spirits—operate through him. Most of the time when he gets these impressions, he is right. God just places him at the right place at the right time. His business has been blessed because of it. Autry laughingly says, "If I am right 51 percent of the time, I am on the winning side."

They Give and God Rewards

One of the reasons Autry and Faye have such a powerful prayer life is because they are tithers and givers. They have made God a financial partner. They know giving to the Lord is also one of the highest forms of worship.

They believe that one dime out of every dollar belongs to the Lord. It is a bill they owe. They believe the Lord when He says, "Bring ye all the tithes into the storehouse, that there may be meat in mine house, and prove me now herewith, saith the Lord of hosts, if I will not open you the windows of heaven; and pour you out a blessing that there shall not be room enough to receive it" (Malachi 3:10).

They go far beyond the 10 percent for which God asks. The tithe gets the window open and the gifts get the blessings coming. Autry maintains, "If you give, God rewards." When they give, they expect the power of God to be released on their behalf.

Sometimes they give on credit. They actually borrow money and give to God's work. There have been lean times in business when they borrowed money to live on; but during those lean times, they gave more to God's work than mere tithes. Autry further says, "God has honored me because I have honored Him and His work." They both will tell you that it is unbelievable the way God blesses them. Giving has increased their capacity for receiving from God.

He Prays and Then Obeys

The life of this great man of God is a life of praying and obeying. "And it shall come to pass, if thou shalt harken diligently unto the voice of the Lord thy God, to observe and to do all his commandments which I command thee this day, that the Lord thy God will set thee on high above all nations of the earth: And all these blessings shall come on thee, and overtake thee, if thou shalt hearken unto the voice of the Lord thy God. 'Blessed shalt thou be in the city, and blessed shalt thou be in the field. Blessed shall be the fruit of thy body, and the fruit of thy ground, and the fruit of thy cattle, the increase of thy kine, and the flocks of thy sheep. Blessed shall be thy basket and thy store. Blessed shalt thou be when thou comest in, and blessed shalt thou be when thou goest out.' ... The Lord shall command the blessing upon thee in thy storehouses, and in all that thou settest thine hand unto; and he shall bless thee in the land which the Lord thy God giveth thee. ... And the Lord shall make thee plenteous in goods ... And the Lord shall make thee the head, and not the tail; and thou shalt be above only, and thou shalt not be beneath; if that thou hearken unto the commandments of the Lord thy God, which I command thee this day, to observe and to do them" (Deuteronomy 28:1-13).

Autry Dawsey
P. O. Box 396
Whiteville, NC 28472

Telephone
910-640-3111
910-642-5170

Fax
910-640-2187

P. E. Dawsey—The Soulwinner

P. E. Dawsey — The Soulwinner

P. E. Dawsey is experiencing the greatest miracles of his entire life. When others are retiring, he has refired. He has always been successful in everything he has attempted. He has evangelized, pastored, and turned dead churches around. He is an outstanding businessman. He has experienced five heart attacks. He needed a heart transplant; but there was no heart to be found. The doctors had planned to take him off the life support system within a few hours, and he would be dead. In the last moments, God gave him the heart of a 46-year-old cowboy. P. E.'s work was not finished. God had more situations for him to turn around. His heart's desire now is to win the lost in China. He is turning situations around in that country every time he lands there. He is now experiencing that for which he was born.

The Making of This Soulwinner

P. E. is the brother of Autry Dawsey, the Seer and Hearer. There were four boys who grew up together in Whiteville, North Carolina. All of them had unique personalities and callings. They grew up together on a farm as a very close-knit family. P. E. says, "If one of us had a dollar, it belonged to all of us. We were just that close."

The family had spiritual, but strict rules. The boys were not even allowed to play ball on Sunday. Often when they were out playing during the day, their mother would call them inside and say, "Boys, it's time to pray." Prayer time came before anything else in that home.

Love for People Was Learned Early in Life

Love for people was learned early in life by all the Dawsey boys. Their mother and father brought underprivileged boys into their home whenever they found a kid with a need.

The farm was a good place to help the boys find themselves and God.

P. E. recalls when a boy staying with the Dawseys decided to run away from their home once. Dad Dawsey went looking for him and brought him back home. The boy soon realized that if he did not stay in the Dawsey's home, the welfare department would put him in a reformatory. However, that night Mr. Dawsey stood outside the boy's room and heard him praying, "Lord, I know I've done wrong; but I have a feeling that when Mr. Dawsey was my age he may have done worse than me."

The boys who were taken in by the Dawseys were so happy with the family that they seldom wanted to leave. They were treated with love and respect by all the family, regardless of their background or problems.
The boys all went to a Freewill Baptist church when they were children. There was not much in Columbus County to make them go astray. The most exciting thing in the week was listening to the Grand Ole Opry on Saturday night with neighbors and friends.

All the Brothers Were Saved and Called of God at an Early Age

All the Dawsey boys were saved at an early age at home. P. E., A. B., J. W. and their cousin Bill Ellis were all called to preach about the same, when P. E. was 15. The pastor of that little Freewill Baptist Church was B. W. English. The evangelist was Ray Rumbsey.

This great pastor, Dr. B. W. English, taught the boys much of what they know about the ways of God. He set a special time for them every Sunday evening. He taught them the Bible, how to preach, how to motivate people, and anything a young preacher needed to know about the ministry.

The boys preached in Freewill Baptist Churches all around the eastern North Carolina area. God blessed them, and many souls were saved. Often P. E. would preach and the others sing.

Then, Millard Maynard came to Whiteville for a tent revival. This handsome Indian stayed in their home and had a great influence on the Dawsey boys. During this time, he shared with the boys about Lee College in Cleveland, Tennessee.

P. E. and J. W. went first to Lee College. Later Autry went. A. B. decided God was leading him to the University of North Carolina.

The Family Moves to a New Boys Home in Waccamaw

Finally, there were simply too many boys to care for on the farm. Some businessmen bought an old abandoned hotel in Waccamaw for the Boys Home. So the Dawsey family moved there. These became wonderful, but hard days for Dad Dawsey. He had to do much of the work for the family of boys. There was not enough money to hire the work out, so Dad Dawsey was up every day at 1-2 a.m. He could not lean on his boys, because they had already left home.

The Soulwinning Pastor

P. E. came home to pastor a Freewill Baptist church in Rosehill, North Carolina. Those were precious days. Here he learned much about being a shepherd. But there was more for him.

G. W. Lane invited him to preach a revival in Ohio. G. W. was a shouting preacher. P. E. loved this great man of God. The revival was a great success, and P. E. felt it was time to become a member of the Church of God.

He loved the people of his congregation. The thought of leaving them was a tough one, but he had to tell his congregation that he had joined the Church of God. It was conference year. The people requested that he remain with them until the conference.

The Soulwinner Becomes a Team Player

G. W. Lane felt that P. E. should come to Ohio to be his associate pastor, minister of music, and director of Christian education. This was a new beginning for P. E. Those years were exciting years. The glory of God came down service after service. His music and G. W.'s preaching made a great ministerial combination. God used him and G. W. as a powerful team. They were on WNOP every Sunday morning and WCKY every Sunday night with the Voice of Calvary radio broadcast. They could be heard all over the nation.

A New Vision to Help More People

Dad Dawsey had a heart attack, and it became necessary for him and Gladys to leave the Boys Home. The doctor felt that the stress was too much, so the family bought a home on the lake until Dad had regained his health.

The boys always scheduled their Christmas vacations to be at home with the family. These were always memorable times. After Christmas dinner one year, Dad Dawsey said, "Boys, Gladys and I want to talk to you in the living room." When they were all assembled, Dad began: "Boys, you know the county commissioners have closed down the old aged home in this area. The people who sacrificed to make this area what it is have been sent out of the county where their friends can't visit them and where they don't know anybody. The county commission has said that if I will build a home, they will bring these old folks back and pay the welfare price that they are now paying in other counties. It would be an instant income."

The boys all wanted to help these elderly people who felt such a loss being moved out of the county away from family and friends. But none of these brothers had any money. They all sat and talked about the dilemma of the seniors from the nursing home, feeling helpless. However, they had learned early in life that obedience is better than sacrifice.

Finally, P. E. spoke up and said, "Let's give it a try. Let's see if we can all borrow some money from different banks. A. B., you take First National; J. W., you take Columbus National

Bank; I'll take Waccamaw Bank. Autry, you find another bank." The brothers were known in the area; maybe that would be a plus in borrowing money. They knew they would be borrowing on faith. They did it then and have done it many times since.

P. E.'s cousin, George, was president of Waccamaw Bank. P. E. went to the bank to see his cousin. George saw P. E. waiting for him and said, "P.E., what can I do to help you?"

"I need to borrow $5,000."

"You don't have an account with us; plus, you don't live here. In addition, you don't any anything for collateral."

"George, don't be silly. I've got the same thing you have—godly parents who taught us that a good name is rather to be chosen than great riches."

With that, George picked up the phone and told someone to open up an account for P. E. and put $5,000 in the account.

When P. E. arrived home, his other three brothers had been successful, too. Together they had $20,000. After they rejoiced together, they went to their father. "Dad, get the blueprints, and we will pour the foundation. We will all ask for a two-week vacation at the same time." They did it. They put the home up in a short time, and they were ready for the old people. Soon the county brought the people back and placed them in the Dawsey Home. This was a happy time for the elderly and for the Dawseys. They were doing what God had called them to do.

Dad and Mom Dawsey set out to work hard. The boys kept their ministries and jobs. Their dad would sleep one shift, and their mother would sleep another shift. One of them was always up in order to see that those precious elderly people got their medicine on time and had their needs met. They were still reaching out to hurting people. They were born for this kind of ministry.

Finally, Dad's health would not permit him to continue going at that pace day in and day out. The brothers who were preachers could not leave their ministries, so Autry agreed to leave his job in Miami and come home. During this time, the brothers supplemented Autry until there was enough for him to live on. Later, Autry did the work so they could be in ministry and sent them money.

A New Vision to Be State Evangelist

A. M. Phillips asked P. E. to come to Florida to be a state evangelist. During this time, he helped build a church in Homestead, Florida. After the pastor retired, the church asked P. E. to stay as their pastor. P. E. stayed for seven years— finished the building and parsonage and developed the grounds.

Back to Ohio for an Even Greater Ministry

P. E. then moved back to Oxford, Ohio, bought 10 acres of ground, built a new parsonage and another new church was erected. P. E. loved pastoring, but he got tired. He felt that he had to be on the job 24 hours a day. When he took a vacation, P. E. always left on Sunday night after church so he would not miss a Sunday service.

One of P. E.'s greatest abilities is that of taking hopeless situations and turning them around to make something good out of them. H. B. Ramsey called and asked P. E. to meet him at Shoney's in Franklin, Ohio. The overseer told Dawsey that he had a problem with a church in Franklin. The pastor had been in this church for 30 years, but had gone independent and the church was in his name. There were only five people left. All of the others had gone with the pastor.

P. E. accepted this challenge and turned the circumstances around. The church had room for one parking space and was on a one-way street.

P. E. knew he had to do something. He and his brothers had been working with convenience stores and independent gas stations, so he contacted Starr Oil Company. They bought the church, thus enabling P. E. to purchase 10 acres of land next to the interstate and to build a new church building. He developed the property and soon had a self-supporting church.

The superintendent of schools was a friend to P. E. He revealed to P. E. how to build the rooms to school specifications. The church leased out five rooms to the school board. The payments on these five rooms gave the church enough money to make the payments on the entire church.

L. H. Aultman next asked P. E. to be promotion and development director for the entire state of Ohio. This was another time for him to stretch. God used him to bless churches all over Ohio. State Overseer Aultman sent P. E. to Princeton Pike Church of God to pastor.

The Soulwinner Handles Crisis Times

While serving at Princeton Pike, P. E. had two heart attacks, six weeks apart. It became necessary for him to take a leave of absence. He went to Florida to recuperate. For weeks the church continued sending him his check. It finally became apparent that he needed to resign because of health. The church needed a full-time pastor. After he recuperated, he went back to North Carolina.

One of the most tragic things that ever happened to the Dawsey family was when J. W. and A. B. went to be with the Lord. J. W. had just finished preaching a sermon, walked down the steps, had a fatal heart attack and died.

A. B. was overseer of New Mexico. Sixteen months after J. W.'s death, A. B. was preaching on the Indian reservation, had a heart attack and died, also.

This was an upsetting time for P. E., as well as Autry. Further, there were decisions that had to be made about the estate. Autry and P. E. made the decision to give the cash flow to the members of their deceased brothers' families. They kept the properties that had to be managed.

The Greatest Soulwinning Ministry of His Life—China

P. E. began recalling that God had shown his mother that he would carry the gospel. The Lord had broken P. E.'s spirit, and he was weeping. The night God called him to preach, he knew his call to the ministry was different from the call upon his brothers. He went to his mother weeping: "Mom, I believe my ministry will be overseas. I won't be home as much as my other brothers." This had not been a reality in the earlier days of his ministry. But it now was.

In 1995, God opened the doors for P. E. to go to China. He had served on Vision Foundation with Carl Richardson. They had been friends for a long time.   Carl said, "P. E., I am going to China. Come go with me."
P. E. responded, "I've got to go with you."

Approaching the time to leave, Carl was unable to go. P. E. asked, "Do you know anybody else who can go?" Carl told him about a man in Virginia Beach, Virginia—Gary Russell with China Harvest. P. E. contacted Gary, went to the university and stayed with Russell three days and nights. Gary taught him the things to do and not to do in China.

On their first trip to China, Gary observed, "P. E., you are born for this ministry and for this time."

They went to China and several provinces together. P. E. realized that smuggling Bibles into the country was serious business, but he felt this was the greatest thing that ever happened to him in his entire ministry.

What P. E. saw when he got to China broke his heart. He saw a group of people starving for a word of hope. They had no hope. They had been taught they came from nothing. They knew only what the Communist party had told them.

P. E. feels this is why he was born. His heart and life is in China. He quickly saw that you are not allowed to preach there, but you can work with the underground church through the born-again believers. You can witness one-on-one. It is exciting to work with the underground church. They are so happy to see you. When they hug you, you know they have passed from death to life.

When you give someone a Bible, you know that at least 50 people will turn from communism to Christianity. P. E. was shocked when he learned that there were 200,000 preachers who preach 12 to 15 hours a day but do not have Bibles. There are 80 million Christians who do not own Bibles. Yet, in spite of this, there are 20,000 to 30,000 converts every 24 hours. P. E. could give a person a Bible for $8.

P. E. met LeAnn, a brilliant young lady who was saved while doing research and came across a Bible. Her father was a doctor. Her mother was a highly educated person. Yet, they lived in a small place three stories high. As LeAnn began to read the Bible, she began to feel something. "What is this?" she asked. She felt something changing in her life. She found Jesus as the Lord of her life. It was seven years before she met another believer.

P. E. determined to help this young lady get to the United States to study. It took four years, but it finally became a reality. She has completed her studies in Cleveland, Tennessee, at the Theological Seminary. At the time of this writing, she is working, preparing to go back to China to work among her people.

LeAnn translated her first book from English to Chinese and sent it home to her mother by P. E. LeAnn told P. E., "If anyone can win my mother, you can. She respects you so highly because you helped me come to the United States to study."

When P. E. arrived in China, he and Gary Russell sent for LeAnn's mother. At 1 a.m., she arrived at the little place where they were staying. He gave her the soft copy from her daughter. Then, they began talking about the Lord. That morning, Brother Russell and P. E. led her and her cousin to Jesus. Then, LeAnn's mother called LeAnn in Cleveland. She wept on the phone, "LeAnn, honey, I know your Jesus now." What a time of rejoicing they had in that little humble home in the wee hours of the morning.

P. E. and Brother Russell gave each of them a Bible of their own. In China, a Bible is in the hands of the person for only 24 hours to copy, then it is passed on to someone else. They took those Bibles, wrapped them, rewrapped them and rewrapped them in tissue and put them in their suitcases. They left about 2:30 a.m.

P. E. began talking to Christians who had spent time in prison. Some had spent 22 years in prison with hard labor, some beaten three times a day. Their keepers threw their food to them on the floor. Many of these Christians die in prison. The prison keepers burn their bodies and use the ashes on the farms. In the year 2000, 160,000 Christians were executed.

One young lady, who ran a small mission in her home, was told to deny Christ. She refused. First, they took an ax and chopped her piano to pieces. Next, they burned her house down. Still, she did not deny Christ. Then they tied her hand down. They took the end of an axe and beat her hand until the hand was completely gone. Now someone has to care for her all the time.

On one occasion the police found about a dozen people worshiping. They took their belongings outside and burned them. The police then told the Christians to deny Christ. They refused. The officers went outside and urinated in a pan made in the shape of a cross. They forced the Christians to drink their urine. While the Christians were drinking that horrible urine, the police shot them in the back of their heads.

When P. E. heard these testimonies, he was never the same man or preacher again.

One of the things he enjoys most is helping get Christians out of prison. Money is the name of the game in China. If he gives the underground leaders money, they can get a Christian released from prison. When the prisoner is released, the underground Christians take him immediately to another province in China. Otherwise, he would be arrested again before nightfall.

P. E. met an interesting young man named Lionel. P. E., Lovell Cary, and Gary Russell had helped get Lionel into Indonesia, because he was in major trouble with the police in China. They had already imprisoned his father and were making plans to execute him, if they caught him. From Indonesia, Lionel went to the Philippines where he is now teaching in the Bible school. His plans are to go back to China one day.

P. E. weeps when he talks about the dedication of these people. They are willing to literally lay their lives down for the gospel.

One morning about 1 o'clock, a knock was heard at the door of the small, humble room. The last thing you want to hear in China is a knock on the door at 1 a.m. There stood a woman who looked 70 years of age. P. E. later learned that she was only 50. She had a terrible odor. Her hair was not combed. She said, "Is this the man of people who has a Bible for me?" Isaac Lee from Korea, who helps smuggle in Bibles, wondered if she were a spy.

She told them her story. She had been traveling for about a week and had never been to this place. She had slept under trees, drank out of creeks, ate out of garbage cans. God led her to this very house. She did not ask anybody where the foreigners were staying. The first door she knocked on was this house. She had been fasting and praying for 12 years. God had shown her in a vision that they had a Bible for her. He said to her, "Get up and go. They have a Bible for you." The Holy Spirit had led her to this very door. She had been through many villages and did not even stop or slow down. She did not stop because not one of the places was the place God had shown her in her vision. This was the place and this was the house.

Brother Lee gave her a Bible. It was a dramatic moment. She knelt down and wept, holding the Bible on her heart. Thousands in China are coming to Christ in this manner. God is using this method instead of crusades and great evangelistic meetings.

P. E. enjoys working with Brother Lee. Brother Lee's mother was so interested in her son getting trained to help his people in North Korea that she even offered to sell her eyes so that he could come to America to study.

On one occasion two people from North Korea went to Seoul looking for food. Brother Lee led both of them to the Lord. Before they left to go back home, they said, "Don't just fill our bags with natural food; but give us the bread of life." Lee filled part of their bags with Bibles and the rest with rice. As they crossed the river going back into North Korea, soldiers apprehended them.

The soldiers poured the rice onto the ground and found the Bibles. They beat the two men severely. The soldiers said, "Tell us where you got the Bibles, and we will stop beating you." They refused to tell. Finally, they were placed in prison and beaten unmercifully. The soldiers beat one of the men on the head until the man's skull was split. The new Christian died instantly.

The other man was almost killed. The soldiers thought he would die, so they threw him into the streets. However, he suddenly became conscious. He got up and rushed to a friend's home, where he was nursed back to health. Today, this man is still smuggling Bibles into North Korea. P. E. feels honored to be associated with this kind of Christian—a man willing to give his life for the sake of the gospel.

On another occasion, P. E. sat in a room with a man who had tears streaming down his face. He talked about his closest friend. The friend's son went out one day to locate believers to come to a prayer meeting. Soldiers stopped him. They said, "We know you are a believer. If you will tell us where the other believers are, we won't harm you." He would not tell. They cut his ear off. The boy lifted his voice and sang, "Oh, how I love Jesus!" Then they cut off his other ear. Again he sang, "Oh, how I love Jesus." They removed his head from his shoulders. The soldiers took him home to his father and placed the boy in his father's arms. Then they grabbed the 2-year-old grandson. They said, "If you will tell us where the other believers are, we will not kill this child." The man would not tell. The soldiers took the child, placed him in a bag, poured gasoline on him and burned him alive. The grandfather heard the child screaming. He had just seen his son brought home dead, and now his grandson was dead.

Another man had just gotten out of prison. He had been there because of the gospel. His wife tried to get him to say he would never again mention the name of Christ, but he would not do it. He knew that if he were caught again talking about Jesus, they would execute him. At the time of this writing, this man is on the run in China. He doesn't even own a Bible. All he knows is that he must serve God.

Winning Souls as a Police Chaplain at Home

When P. E. Dawsey comes home from China, he works for the Lord in his community. He is chaplain for the Whiteville Police Department. Here he becomes the chief counselor to the chief and his officers. He does weddings, funerals, or whatever he is called upon to do. Often he has to deliver death notices to families.

When you leave home in the morning as a police chaplain, you never know what you are going to face that day. The police officer may be asked to raid homes where there are drugs, prostitution, etc., and P. E. goes with him. He has run into robberies, domestic violence, and so forth. It is difficult to help a member of a family you feel is being abused, because they can turn against you. He has even had frying pans thrown at him!

Helping the Suffering in the Home Land

There was a terrible hurricane in the year 2000 which devastated North Carolina. P. E. took funds out of his organization to help hundreds of hurting people. He rented a large truck, went to Wilmington on two occasions, bought food and other essentials for those who were suffering. At Christmas, he filled the trucks with food and toys for the children. He took the mayor with him to deliver the goods paid for by his ministry.

The Soulwinner Is Given Another Chance to Win More Souls

Two weeks after one of P. E.'s trips to China in 2001, he had another heart attack. This was his fifth attack, which made it extremely serious. He had gone to the emergency room of the hospital. He was in great pain, but the doctor had not brought him any pain relievers. Autry, his brother, went to the doctor three times to tell him that P. E. had to have some help. The doctor responded to Autry, "I told you I would take care of your brother, and I will." The family was very upset with the lack of concern from the doctor.

About that time, a doctor from Duke Hospital who knew P. E. walked through the emergency room. He saw Autry in the waiting room and asked, "What is wrong?" Autry told him the situation. In just a few moments, the doctor came back and told Autry, "I have sent for a helicopter to airlift P. E. to Duke Medical Hospital." Shortly, P. E. was in the hospital at Duke. They determined he was to have a heart transplant. This seemed an impossible situation. Doctors said P. E. had only 24 hours to live. In fact, they planned to pull the plug on the life support system the next day, if a heart was not found.

The next day Autry was told by the doctor, "We have located a heart in Texas. A team of doctors is on a Lear jet now to harvest the heart of a 46-year-old cowboy. A horse kicked him, and he is brain dead. As soon as they get back with the heart, we will proceed." The doctors arrived at 3 a.m.

Eight hours later, doctors tapped P. E. on the shoulder and said, "You have your second chance." God was not through with P. E. Dawsey. Now he believes he must work the works of God while there is still time.

Back to the Harvest Field

Four months later, P. E. told the doctors he was going to make his trip to China as planned. The doctors said, "No way! God has given you a second chance, so you need to be careful." They reminded him that in the States he had good doctors. In China, the doctors did not have the ability to take care of him in a crisis situation.

Finally, when they understood that P. E. was determined to go to China, they wrote him a letter to give to a doctor there, if necessary. Further, they sent him out with an ample supply of medicine in case he could not get home. In October 2002, P. E. left for mainland China again.

Autry said, "I am afraid for you to go." P. E. reasoned, "I looked at the map today. It's about as close to heaven from China as from Columbus County." He went to China, and God used him again in a powerful way.

P. E. says, "I am in the will of God. I am an ambassador—chosen and appointed by God to work among the people in China. Not everybody is standing in line for my position."

While he is in the United States, he travels much in order to raise the budget to go to China, as well as to take Bibles to China. He organized his 501-C3 organization, which he calls Vision of the World. He has a map of China on a three-plate glass window in his office, which is located near the courthouse.

At one time P. E. was president of the Medical Center in Lake Waccamaw. He and his brothers donated the property on which it was to be built. He resigned as president, but still serves on the board. The board sees that the office, as well as doctors and nurses, serve the community well.

P. E. earned doctor of ministry and doctor of divinity degrees from Covenant Theological Seminary in Wilmington, North Carolina. Further, he serves on the board of directors. Dr. English, his first Freewill Baptist pastor, is president of the school.

P. E.'s goal for the rest of his life is to go often to China. He comes home long enough to raise his budget and then returns. He wants to be there winning the lost whether he lives or he dies. Afraid? No! He would be just as happy to go home to heaven from China as from the United States.

P. E. Dawsey
P. O. Box 147
Whiteville, NC 28450

Telephone
910-646-3511

Fax
910-640-2187

H. Bernard Dixon—God's Entrepreneur

H. Bernard Dixon—God's Entrepreneur

When God wants to show the world how to overcome obstacles and become successful, He uses a person who has done it. This is Hal Bernard Dixon. This financier was born in poverty, but he rebelled against it. Hal made a decision to be everything God created him to be. Thus, he moved from being a "poor boy" to being an influential player in God's kingdom. He is a leader in church, community, and business. The body of Christ would not be nearly so blessed if he had not rebelled against indigence and paid the price to be who he is today— God's entrepreneur.

Hal Dixon was not born into a wealthy family. He was born in 1928, a child of the Great Depression, to Dudley and Cynthia Lou Crowder Dixon, in a small mill town in eastern North Carolina. When Hal's mother and father married, they were quite young. His mother was only 15, and his dad was 22. His dad quit school in the third grade, and his mom quit in the fifth. His dad was 11 years old when he started to work. His dad and mom worked in the cotton mill on separate shifts. It was hard work with little pay. Because they were young, uneducated, and untrained, Hal's parents were not prepared for marriage and family.

Hal was the oldest of five children. The family of seven lived in one of the 88 four-room houses in the little mill village. Some of the time his father was not able to provide for the needs of the family. His mother's parents helped out when they could. Since there was no such thing as baby-sitters in those days, one of the parents tried to be home with the children while the other worked.

Life was difficult for the parents and the children. However, despite the troubling family background, the children were able to adjust most of the time. Out of his childhood experiences, Hal formed this philosophy:

"It's not what happens to you that counts. It is the way you take it. It is your response to what happens to you that can either help or hurt." As Eleanor Roosevelt observed, "No one can hurt you without your consent." Hal refused to be harmed by the incidents that were occurring in his life.

Perhaps because of his own family background, Hal's father was not able to tell his children that he loved them. Instead, he was sometimes overbearing in his discipline of the children. There was the constant worry of never having enough money. As a very young child, Hal associated unhappiness and frustration with poverty, causing him to rebel against poverty. Some people think money is the root of all evil. Hal discovered at an early age that the lack of money could be a very real root of evil, heartache, and sorrow.

Achievement Began Early

One of the positive lessons Hal's dad passed on to him was a high work ethic. He advised his young son that when he worked for someone, he should do more than what was expected—to work harder and longer. In addition, God gifted Hal Dixon with an entrepreneurial initiative. Hard work and achievement became a part of his life from a very early age. His father gave the children 10 cents a week for allowance.

Boy Scouts were big in those days. Hal wanted to be a Boy Scout, but he had to have a Boy Scout manual which cost 50 cents. Hal's dad could not afford to buy the manual. On Hal's 10-cents-a-week allowance, he could go to the picture show. He could buy an RC Cola and a candy bar. But for five weeks he saved for that Boy Scout manual. He set a goal and was willing to pay a price. He saved that allowance until he had enough to buy a Boy Scout manual. He joined the Boy Scouts because at that early age, he wanted to be a part of a moving, successful organization.

Hal looked for ways to make money. Sometimes he traded things. He would sometimes buy a pig, raise it, and then sell it to somebody for a profit. He bought candy bars in 24-per-box counts and resold them individually. He worked a paper route at the age of 12. He worked at the theater. At the age of 14, he operated a projector in a movie house. At age 16, he was working long hours at the college soda shop. To help the family, Hal gave his dad half of everything he made.

He was determined to be successful. He saw what was going on in his mother's and father's lives and resolved that his life would be different. Some of his classmates were the sons and daughters of professors and staff members of the local college. They had a dramatic influence on his life. They encouraged him through association to have an ambition for an education, for success; to make something of himself.

Since Hal's dad was a section leader at the mill, Hal was able to get a job delivering boxes of spool thread from one level to another. He soon realized that this entire culture was not for him. He determined not to be swayed by the lifestyle of the mill workers.

During the war years there were not many men around. Hal attended the small local public schools. His high school had no one to coach the football team—in fact, there was no football team. That did not deter Hal. He was an aggressive leader even then, and he had persistence. He went to the Wake Forest College football coach and asked for football uniforms for the high school team. Hal got the college to donate the equipment and uniforms, and then he became the football coach until someone else could help out.

He did the same thing for the baseball team. He was captain of the basketball team and president of the Monogram Club, an athletic club.

Following high school graduation Hal tried a lot of things. Some worked; some did not. He even tried to be a beach bum right after graduation, but that didn't work. He returned home and decided to talk to the dean of Wake Forest about the possibility of attending the college. Apparently the dean saw potential in Hal and gave him a 50 percent scholarship. Hal was then able to talk his illiterate grandfather into lending him $60, the balance needed for tuition and fees. Hal's grandfather wanted his grandson to have what he never was able to achieve.

College Life

Hal dreamed a lot. He was in the movie theater often. This helped stir his imagination. He was never satisfied to remain where he was. He was always reaching out to something more. Sometimes he dreamed of being a great athlete, but that was short-lived because God had bigger plans for him.

When he first went to Wake Forest College, Hal was trying so hard to be accepted that he did not study as he should have. He began a major in pre-med, but found that to be very difficult due to his young age and lack of preparation. When he took "quantitative analysis" he decided not to be a doctor.

He always enjoyed extracurricular activities. Hal became part of a fraternity and made friends. After the first year, he settled down to a study schedule and began to make good grades.

Since Hal was subject to the draft, it seemed the acceptable thing to go into the U. S. Army. He enlisted for 18 months, following the war, with the occupational forces in Japan. This delayed his college training, but the GI Bill paid the rest of his college tuition.

When Hal returned from military service, Wake Forest College had initiated a good business school. Hal took a few business courses and found that he liked it. It seemed to fit him. He realized he had to pay the price day in and day out if he wanted to master the subjects he studied. As a result of his dedication, Hal developed a keen business mind. He graduated with a major in business and a minor in French.

The Developing Entrepreneur's Conversion

Hal had always gone to Sunday school and liked the people at the Wake Forest Church of God, but he had never really taken church seriously. While he was a senior in college at age 22, he committed his life to Christ. A former Sunday school teacher, Ernestine Babb, held a revival in their church and came to visit him personally. On Sunday morning, April 14, 1950, instead of walking out after Sunday school, Hal walked to the back row of seats in the church. He stayed until she gave the altar invitation. Hal was holding on to the back of the seat. His heart was beating hard and fast. Suddenly he found himself out of the seat, walking down the aisle. Some wondered how long it would last, but his grandmother believed in him and was happy to see him make a move towards God.

This was the single most important decision of Hal's life. As a result, his life and lifestyle changed dramatically. Hal testifies: "From that point on, it was as if a curtain came down on my former life and a whole new scenario developed. I was totally made over again. Not only inside, but also my outward expressions and practices were totally different from what they were before. I gave up all my extracurricular activities at the college and devoted my energies to the church." His paradigm shifted. He saw things differently. He felt things differently. He thought differently. He behaved differently.

Development of Business Skills for the Entrepreneur

Before Hal's conversion, he could not stand and express himself before people. It was just impossible. However, the Lord gave him the desire and ability to immerse himself in the activities of the church. He became a leader in the Wake Forest Church of God.

- *Within three months he was elected superintendent of the Sunday school.*
- *He initiated several Sunday school enlargement campaigns.*
- *He was director of the Vacation Bible School.*
- *He raised money for the poor in the community.*

- He visited in the homes of the elderly and shut-ins.
- He attended cottage prayer meetings.
- He started a Boy Scout troop and served as a scoutmaster.
- He served as president of a community foundation made up of representatives of Wake Forest Church of God, Glen Royal Baptist Church, and Southeastern Theological Seminary.
- He served as a youth leader of the church.

Although Hal graduated from Wake Forest with a B.S. degree in business administration, he wanted to be a minister. The people he knew who were most productive were ministers. But he never got a call. God just did not call him to be a minister.

The Marriage of Hal and Starr

One of the families in the Wake Forest Church had their niece, Starr Stone, come and visit with them. That was when Hal and Starr met. Hal had involved a cousin of Starr's in the youth group he led, so the family was already impressed with this dynamic young man. At the time they met, Starr had recently left college and was the caregiver for her baby sister. Her mother had just died a few days after giving birth to the baby.

After Hal met Starr he attended a fellowship meeting in Zebulon, North Carolina, which is between Wake Forest and Middlesex, where Starr lived. Soon Hal and Starr started dating (always with a chaperone). These were interesting visits, because Starr was from a large family. It was not long before they realized they were in love. Hal and Starr were married in September 1951, and moved to Raleigh, 17 miles from home, into a two-room apartment. They shared the bathroom with another couple.

Hal became acquainted with the GE appliance distributor through his uncle who worked in a hardware store. After graduation Hal was able to secure a job at the GE distributorship in Raleigh. The company was large enough to have several stand-alone departments. It was in the audit function that he gained an understanding of how the different departments worked together. In other words, he learned how a business operates. This was an invaluable experience for him later in life.

Divine Destiny

The desire to be involved in ministry was still in the back of Hal's mind. He thought, "I'll go to seminary, even if I don't have a call to preach. Perhaps I can teach." He made application to Duke University Divinity School. He even went for an interview. He wanted to go one semester and then transfer back to Southeastern at Wake Forest. Duke did not like this idea at all. Before he could make concrete plans, he received a call of destiny from Cleveland, Tennessee.

Because of Hal's involvement with the church on the local level, and his acquaintance with leaders on the district and state levels, State Youth Director E. C. Thomas took note of him. When Thomas left North Carolina, he took a job as credit and sales promotion manager for the Church of God Publishing House in Cleveland, Tennessee. When he was promoted to business manager, he recommended Hal to come to Cleveland to replace him. Hal interviewed with the publications board and was hired. He began work on June 1, 1955. Hal's philosophy is: "Success comes from preparation, persistence, and timing."

Arriving in Cleveland, Hal thought he had reached "heaven." He had the best of both worlds. He had business, which he thoroughly enjoyed, and he had the North Cleveland Church in which to share his ministry gifts. Further, he was able to go back to school at the University of Chattanooga and Cleveland State Community College and further his education.

At first in the Publishing House, there was so much to be done: credit system, collection letters, advertising and marketing, budgets, etc. Hal loves to analyze data, reports, budgets, etc. He has a special ability to get to the important issues, to cut through (or see through) fluff to what's really pertinent. He pays attention to details, as well as sees the big picture.

The relationship between E. C. Thomas and Hal Dixon became a life-long friendship. They were opposites in some respects. E. C. never got in a hurry; Hal was always in a hurry. Hal was impetuous, brimming over with ideas; E. C. was deliberate and cautious. He was a people person and an excellent strategist. They complemented one another. Hal made things happen that E. C. wanted to happen.

When Hal arrived at the Publishing House, there was one Pathway Bookstore in Cleveland and one in Tampa. He developed a bookstore chain (which is no longer in existence today). The Chattanooga store was the first to open. After that, Hal initiated a franchise program for the bookstores. There were seven bookstores overall before he left.

- *He developed a trade department.*
- *He initiated advertising and resources such as catalogs, brochures, and other strategies to enhance sales.*
- *He built a book club membership to 2,000 plus, sheet music club (with Connor Hall) and a record club (with Connor Hall).*
- *He was active in Christian Booksellers Association and at various times served as director, speaker, secretary, workshop leader, and emcee for banquets.*
- *He was active in National Sunday School Association; President Clate Risley invited him to speak in some of the workshops.*

After the Dixons moved to Cleveland in May 1955, they began attending the North Cleveland Church of God. At that time most all of the executives and staff of the Publishing House, Lee College, and General Headquarters attended North Cleveland. Floyd Timmerman was the pastor. Almost immediately Hal became involved in the church. He led a Sunday school enlargement campaign the following fall. Hal was president of the Unity Class and then became Sunday school superintendent about 1957.

Since the church did not have a Christian education department at the time, the superintendent served in that capacity for the Sunday school. Hal initiated and conducted the church training course and held teachers' meetings on a regular basis. Attendance ran 400 to 500. During Doyle Stanfield's tenure as pastor, several boards were organized in the church. J. Martin Baldree was elected chairman of the Christian education board, and he and Hal worked together for several years. Serving in this capacity, Hal was most successful, and the church became successful. Hal brings out the best in others and holds them accountable for doing the job.

During the 45 plus years Hal has been a member of North Cleveland, he has worked in many capacities. During the T. L. Lowery and Ronnie Brock years, they had a chapel ministry and bus ministry. Attendance averaged from around 1,300 to as many as 3,700. Hal was given the state honor of Tennessee Sunday School Superintendent of the Year for 1959, 1960, 1971-72, 1988-89.

Other contributions he made through the years to North Cleveland include:

- *The purchase of a church building presented as a gift to North Cleveland.*
- *Member of the Church and Pastor's Council and the Finance Committee for many terms.*
- *Chairman of the Building Committee for the present facility (1972), the North Cleveland Towers (1974) and the Family Ministries Center completed in 1999, as well as a new 2,400-seat sanctuary and Prayer Center scheduled to be completed in 2004.*
- *Chairman of the North Cleveland Towers Boards since it was first organized in 1971-72.*
- *Chairman of the Historical Commission with much involvement in the 75th anniversary celebration of North Cleveland.*
- *Superintendent of the Year several times.*

Hal has always believed you can get a lot done if you don't care who gets the credit. That's the way he operated at the North Cleveland Church. However, Hal can be impatient with those who waste his time. People who are not real workers do not hang around him for long.

Birth of Hal, Jr.

When they first arrived in Cleveland, Hal and Starr moved into a trailer on Montgomery Avenue owned by Alda B. Harrison. Here, their only son was born on Easter morning, April 1, 1956. After months of anticipation, they were thrilled at the birth of their firstborn. They named him Hal Bernard Dixon, Jr.

As the months passed and Hal, Jr., grew, they began to see a difference in his progress and that of other children. The more he grew, the more noticeable the difference. It became apparent he faced multiple mental and physical challenges. He had cerebral palsy with severe physical handicaps.

After the birth of their second child, Valerie Starr, in 1962, they became concerned for her safety around Hal, Jr. He was very strong for his age, and because of his mental condition, he could not understand that some of the things he did hurt the baby. Eventually, his physical size and mental condition proved too much for them to handle. They went through many months of agony, trying to decide what would be best for the family and Hal, Jr.

Finally, the decision was made to admit him to an institution where he could receive appropriate therapy and treatment. He was profoundly mentally retarded and confined to a wheelchair for the remainder of his life.

As a family they visited Hal, Jr., taking him presents and special treats. During one of their visits, as they sat with him while he opened his gifts, Hal was struck with a thought that made a profound impact on him: "Hal, Jr., will never be able to support himself or make a meaningful contribution to society. That means that I must do the work of two, and make a contribution for him."

In time the Dixons were blessed with two more additions to the family. In 1966, Candace Starr was born, followed by Vanessa Starr in 1970. Hal has always had a great appreciation for the beautiful name "Starr." Not only do his wife and three daughters bear the name, there are four "Starr" granddaughters and numerous "Starr" companies, such as Starrco, StarrChex, StarrManagement, Inc., Starr I, Inc., and many others.

Business Liaisons

As a result of being at the Publishing House, Hal became involved in business ventures with E. C. Thomas and Lewis Willis.

- *He was able to locate about seven acres of land on the northeast quadrant of I-75 and 25th Street. He approached Thomas and Lewis about purchasing the property with him. They borrowed enough money to buy this tract of land for about $60,000. After six months, they sold the property for $150,000. Today, two motels, a service station and a Cracker Barrel are located on the land.*
- *In 1963, Hal joined Thomas and Lewis in buying the Diplomat Motor Lodge, a new motel in Cleveland for $450,000. After 21 months, they sold the motel.*

The profit from these business ventures was a tremendous amount of money for Hal. His starting salary at the Publishing House was only $400 a month. He doesn't remember making more than $16,000 annually during the 19 years and nine months that he worked there, early on.

Working with E. C. Thomas was a great blessing to Hal. It was at this time Hal realized his call was to be a businessman. Business is the foundation on which he has built his entire life. He accepted business as a basis of his way of operating in this world to bring glory and honor to the Father. He loved business. He would get an idea and plan it. He would put all the pieces together and implement it. He loved to make a deal.

Involvement in Lay Ministries

Hal, Stan Butler, Paul Duncan, Joshua Thomas, Donald Rowe, and Dudley Pyeatt became concerned about the Church of God needing to utilize its laity more effectively. They petitioned the general church to form a lay department, which now functions as the Department of Lay Ministries.

Setting Goals and Paying the Price

Setting goals and paying the price to reach those goals is a practice of Hal's life. In 1969-70, he made the decision to invest in a McDonald's franchise. He wanted to provide for his family those things he never had for himself. His desire was that he could make things easier and more meaningful for his family. At the Publishing House he could not see any prospects for making more money or for more advancement. He believed that whoever had talent, abilities, and resources was obligated to use them for a worthy cause.

In 1969, he started looking for ways to make money. He talked to owners of Hardees and others. Ultimately, he went to Atlanta to talk to the regional franchise director of McDonald's who was also a graduate of Wake Forest and had been a member of the same fraternity. After this meeting of destiny, Hal and his brother Jerry formed a partnership for the development and operation of McDonald's restaurants in North Carolina. In April 1970, they opened their first restaurant in Goldsboro, North Carolina. Within a couple of years, they opened two more stores in Wilson and Kinston. They lost money the first two years, but after opening the Kinston store, things began to look a lot better.

The Businessman and Banking

In 1973, Red Mullinax said, "Let's start a bank." Red, Hal, and eight other friends got together and started First Citizens Bank in Cleveland. They raised $1.5 million by selling stock. It proved to be one of Hal's most valuable resources.

Leaving Pathway Publishing House

In 1974, McDonald's initiated a new policy to grow and expand new stores that required on-site location of the franchisee. Hal made one of the most difficult decisions he ever had to make. He left the Publishing House, took an apartment in North Carolina, and began his role as an active McDonald's operator.

Hal commuted back and forth for about six years, until they finally had a total of 10 restaurants. It was not a pleasant six years. It was unfair to Starr and their three daughters. But Hal's philosophy is: "You do what you have to do."

However, during that time, he had an almost unbroken record of reading the Word and praying each morning and night. He would fly out of Chattanooga on Monday at 6:50 a.m. and return Friday at 10:30 p.m.

Remarkably, he maintained his involvement in North Cleveland Church of God as superintendent of Sunday school, as a member of the Bradley County Board of Education, and as a member of the board of directors of First Citizens Bank during those six years.

Family Life Is a Great Priority

In 1990, Hal sold his part of the business to his brother Jerry and to another franchisee. It was time to spend more time with Starr and the girls.

All three of Hal's daughters graduated from Lee College and then went on to other colleges or universities. One of them has a Ph.D., one has an MBA, and one has a degree in physical therapy. They are full-time mothers and housewives. Valerie is married to a lawyer. Candace is married to a minister. Vanessa is married to a doctor. Hal and Starr have 10 grandchildren. North Cleveland Church of God honored the Dixons as "Family of the Year" in 1987. Hal, Jr., went to be with the Lord in 1990. Virtually all of Hal's dreams have been fulfilled in his children.

Hal maintains, "If I had not made that sacrifice, I would not have been able to provide for my children as I wanted. But also, I would not have been able to do what the next level indicates, which was to take advantage of gifting opportunities."

Gifting Opportunities

When Ron Brock was pastor of the North Cleveland Church of God, he approached Hal about a chapel in East Cleveland that he wanted to buy. Hal went over and looked at it and decided to buy it for the church. They put air conditioning in the sanctuary and completely renovated the building. He named it after his grandmother, India Crowder. She was a principal founder of his local church in Wake Forest. They dedicated the building April 27, 1980. Hal was able to pay tribute to his grandmother for her faithfulness to the Lord. The building was known as Crowder Memorial Chapel Church of God.

Church of God School of Theology

When Hal and other local church leaders were looking for possible sites for the North Cleveland Towers, they bought several tracts on both sides of Walker Street. However, they decided instead to build the Towers on Magnolia Street behind the church. When the seminary was looking for a permanent site in the late 1970s, Hal talked with Seminary President Cecil Knight and General Overseer Ray Hughes, Sr., about the Walker Street property. They agreed it would be a good location for the seminary.

Hal went to the North Cleveland Council and asked that the seminary be given perpetual use of the parking lot across from the church and adjacent to the seminary.

Hal has been able to accomplish much for the kingdom of God because of his initiative. The difference between people who exercise initiative and those who don't is the difference between success and failure. It takes initiative to be a leader in God's kingdom.

While Hal was developing the McDonald's franchise in North Carolina, he worked in the development area on an "as-needed basis" with General Overseer Cecil Knight. Hal returned to Cleveland about the time Knight was appointed as president of the seminary. Hal was asked to serve as the first development director of the Church of God School of Theology. Further, he was chairman of a committee in charge of laying out the details for the Pentecostal Resource Center.

During the two years Hal was at the School of Theology, he followed up on the completion of the seminary building and the design and construction of the PRC. It was during this time they established the idea for the Hall of the Prophets and the Hall of the Faithful.

Pentecostal Resource Center

When plans were being made for the Pentecostal Research Center, the idea was conceived to incorporate into the resource center a place for housing important documents relating to the Pentecostal experience. This would be a place where scholars from all over the world would have access to resources by and about Pentecostals.

Hal was asked to serve on the oversight committee for the building of this edifice. He served with Chairman Robert Hart, Frank Culpepper, Paul Patton, and other key leaders. Hal was the major non-architectural person in the design of the PRC and the first "Clerk of the Works."

Dr. Ray Hughes, Sr., asked Hal to make a contribution toward the Pentecostal research segment of the PRC building. This was an exciting project for Hal and Starr. They both had rich Pentecostal legacies. Starr's grandfather and Hal's grandmother were both pioneers in the Pentecostal Movement. They were elated to be able to participate in establishing the Pentecostal Research Center so that future generations could learn about the rich history and heritage of the Pentecostal faith.

Dr. Hughes suggested to Hal the possibility of naming the center in memory of Hal, Jr. The idea of naming the center for his son seemed to be a fitting memorial.

The inscription at the bottom of the picture of Hal Bernard Dixon, Jr., at the Pentecostal Research Center reads . . . A voice through which God spoke . . . a hand through which God helped. Hal Bernard Dixon, Jr., April 1, 1956.

The plaque close to the picture reads:

Hal Bernard Dixon, Jr.

Pentecostal Research Center dedicated as a tribute to Hal Bernard Dixon, Jr., by his parents who have a great desire to perpetuate Pentecost through research. May 5, 1987.

. . . God hath chosen the weak things of the world to confound the things which are mighty (1 Corinthians 1:27b).

At the dedication outside the PRC building, Hal was asked to speak but declined. When the group moved into the research center, Hal was asked again to speak. This was an emotional moment. Hal was greatly anointed and spoke with authority and passion as he expressed his feelings.

Hal and Starr have been pleased they were able to help perpetuate the Research Center in the name of Hal, Jr. One reason they did so was to demonstrate that the Lord can use the halt, the maimed, the weak, and the crippled in order to provide something beneficial to mankind and that will bring honor and glory to God.

After the death of Hal, Jr., in 1990, Hal went to the mountains for a time of prayer and solitude. This was again a time of great emotion for Hal. He wrote letters to family and friends, and the words seemed to flow onto the paper. This was a deeply moving and spiritual experience.

Making a Master Plan

In 1978, Hal called together President Charles Conn of Lee College, Pastor Ronnie Brock of the North Cleveland Church of God, General Director of Publications O. C. McCane, and others from different church entities. He presented the observation that they were all searching for properties in the same general area and, in some instances, might be competing for the same property. His idea was that the property should be developed cooperatively.

Hal talked with Steve Carroll and his partner, both architectural school graduates, about the concept of shared development. He got the city fathers to meet with the heads of the church departments and the architects. They bought into the plan to develop the core infrastructure for future growth and development.

One of the professors from the architectural school worked with them to develop a master plan. The area covered by the master plan was from the First Baptist Church to 15th Street and from Ocoee Street to the railroad. The group applied for an Urban Development Action Grant (UDAG) to assist in funding the plan. However, their request was turned down. Some say it was because of church involvement.

Despite the decision by UDAG, the plan proceeded and progress has continued with the church entities doing their own "urban renewal." During the 24 years since the master plan was formed, much of the area has been developed, at least in the physical area. The Church of God Theological Seminary, Lee University, and the North Cleveland Church of God have played a major part. During the 16 years of Dr. Paul Conn's presidency at Lee, there have been 16 buildings added to the campus. Those involved in the formation of the master plan so many years ago could not have dreamed that Paul Conn would come along and extend the Lee University boundaries to 20th Street.

The completion of the current North Cleveland Church of God sanctuary project and Prayer Center will be the

culmination of that dream. Man dreams, gets a bit of a vision
for what might be or what he might do, then pursues and
sticks with the dream, and the Lord seems to finally bring the
vision into reality. The realization of the dream for the
development of the master plan is probably as meaningful to
Hal personally as the money he has made or recognition he has
received. Hal's concern that the total area be utilized and
maximized through a cooperative effort is still being realized.

Working With Lee University

After Hal left the seminary in 1982, he was appointed to
the Lee College Board of Directors. He was placed on the
facilities and development committee, and appointed chairman
when the post became vacant.

During the entire tenure of Paul Conn at Lee University,
Hal has served on the facilities and/or construction surveillance
committee.

The Dixon Center

One day Paul Conn, the then new president of Lee
University, approached Hal. He was starting a whole new fund-
raising campaign. He said, "Hal, I want to build a number of
buildings on the Lee campus. I want to start with a theatre/
communications center. I want it to be a building that is useful
to the community—a place for concerts, recitals, musicals,
dramas, and other theater presentations, as well as a television
studio. Special speakers could be brought in for an audience of
about 500 people. State-of- the-art communications equipment
would be utilized in the presentations and in training students in
that area."

Dr. Conn wanted Hal to make a substantial gift from
which he could launch out. Hal had given to the college through
the years, but not as a lead donor in a campaign. At the time
Hal had just sold several businesses. "Okay, I'll do it, Paul.
And I want this to be named in honor of my wife."

Paul said, "No, you've been very active in Cleveland and especially at the college both with your time and money. I think it would be more appropriate in your name. You are known here and you've been in politics." Hal had a little problem with that.

Hal went to the mountains to pray. Coming to the conclusion to let his name go on that building was a problem. While in the mountains, he realized that whenever someone's name is on a building, it indicates a commitment on the part of that person for some positive good for that college, church, or whatever it is. By that fact alone, it brings honor and glory to God because someone has committed himself either to give money or to perform services to be entitled to that honor. So Hal returned home and gave permission for his name to go on the building.

Community, Civic and Social Organizations

Hal believes in being involved in the community. He was a member of the Bradley County Board of Education (13 ½ years) and the Bradley County Commission (16 years). He served as chairman of the school board for two years and the commission for four years.

While a member of the school board, he and the other members built incentives for those involved in administration to complete graduate training. At the time Hal went on the board, only two school principals had a master's degree. As an incentive, pay increases were given to those who completed advanced degrees. They also built into the system compensation for athletic coaches.

Hal was on the building committee that constructed one of the largest comprehensive high schools in the state of Tennessee. Also, during Hal's tenure, they built one elementary school and one middle school, and the old high school was converted into a middle school.

When Hal served on the commission, the county budget and taxes were major items of concern. Despite money being tight, they authorized the money for a new high school to be built in the northern end of the county. The commission dealt with many controversial issues involving the county nursing home, the hospital, and the needs of the various departments that made up the county government. During his years of service to the community, Hal always strived for integrity in the political process.

Some of the community, civic, and social organizations in which Hal holds and/or held membership are:

- *Member, Cleveland Rotary Club, 1970—*
- *Member, Cleveland Country Club 1977-*
- *Member, Bradley County Commission, Bradley County, Tenn., 1982-98*
- *Chairman, Bradley County Commission Finance Committee, 1982-98*
- *Member, Bradley/ Cleveland Chamber of Commerce Economic*
- *Development Council, 1982-94; 1995-98*
- *Member, Bradley County Nursing Home Board, 1996-98*
- *Member, Cleveland/Bradley Business Incubator, 1996-98*
- *Member, Bradley County Commission Landfill Committee, 1984-1991*
- *Member, B.P.O.E. #1944, Cleveland, Tenn., 1989-90*
- *Member, Walden Club of Chattanooga, 1981-99*
- *Member, Bradley County Commission Agricultural Committee, 1989-90*
- *Chairman, Bradley County Commission, 1986-90*
- *Member and former chairman, 1970-72, Bradley County Board of Education, 1969-82*
- *Member, Hermes Board of Directors, 1981-84*
- *Member, Bradley County Regional Planning Commission, 1982-84*
- *Member, Bradley County Commission Road Committee, 1982-84; 1994-98*

As evidence of Hal's involvement in business, community, and church, his name will be found on dedication plaques and buildings throughout the community.   His name is included with those having a role in the process of planning, approving funds and building of a bank, church, eight-story apartment tower, schools, hospital, nursing home, Lee University, the courthouse annex, etc.

Church-Related Organizations

Local Church

Present:

Member, North Cleveland Church of God, 1956-present
Chairman, Historical Committee, 1978 —
President and Director, North Cleveland Towers, 1971 —
Chairman, Building Committee, 1997 —
Member, Church Council
Elder, 1996 —

Past:

Member, Church and Pastor's Council, Various three-year tenures
Chairman, Building and Grounds Committee, 1970-2000
Sunday School Superintendent, 35 years plus
Member, Finance Committee, 1989-1996
Chairman, Master Planning Committee, 1990-92
Member, Church Growth Task Force, 1988-90

General Church

Present:

Member, Lee University Board of Directors, 1982-97; 1998 —
Member, the General Board of Trustees, 1962-68; 1998 —
Member, Lee University Property Acquisition Committee, 1990 —
Member, Barney Creek Property Development Committee, 1991-
Chairman, Construction Oversight Committee, Lee University, 1990 —
Member, Lee University Facilities & Development Committee,   1982-

Chairman, 1986—

Past:

General Director of Publications, Pathway Press, 1997-98
Member, Pentecostal Resource Center Board of Control, 1984-97
Executive, Church of God Publishing House, Cleveland, Tenn., serving as credit and sales promotions manager, sales manager, general sales manager and director of marketing, 1955-74
Chairman, General Architectural Committee of the Church of God, Cleveland, Tenn., 1978-82
Director of Finance and Development, Church of God School of Theology, 1980-82
Member, Lee University President's Council
Member, Surveillance Committee to construct the Pentecostal Resource Center

Business

Present:

General Partner, Starrco (formerly Starrco LLC) Cleveland, Tenn., 1981-
Chairman/CEO, StarrChex LLC, Cleveland, Tenn., 1993—
President, StarrManagement, Inc., Cleveland, Tenn., 1993—
Chief Manager, Columbia KY Plaza LLC, Cleveland, Tenn., 1989-
President, Starr 1, Inc. (formerly Starrco, Inc.) 1982—
Chairman/CEO, StarrChex LA LLC, Cleveland, Tenn., 2000—
Chairman/CEO, StarrChex LARE LLC, Cleveland, Tenn., 2000—
Partner, StarrBelmont LP, Cleveland, Tenn., 1993—
Partner, StarrGraham LP, Cleveland, Tenn., 1993—
Partner, StarrPoint, LP, Cleveland, Tenn., 1993—
Chairman/CEO, StarrChex Holdings LLC, Cleveland, Tenn., 2000—
Partner, StarrProperties LP, Cleveland, Te
Chairman/CEO, StarrWestwind LLC, Cleveland, Tenn., 2000—
Partner, 75 Wade Green Business Center LLC, Kennesaw, Ga.,

1999—
Partner, Dominion One LLC, Kenesaw, Ga., 2000—
Partner, MBSL LLC, Cleveland, Tenn., 1999—
Partner, Holt Partnership, Alpharetta, Ga., 1999—
Partner, Medford & Dixon, Cleveland, Tenn.
Co-organizer, Director and Secretary, First Citizens Bank
of Cleveland, Tenn., 1973—
Director, Secretary and Treasurer, First Citizens Bancorp
of Cleveland, Tenn., 1980—
Chairman, Executive Committee, First Citizens Bank of
Cleveland,Tenn., 1980—
Chairman, Audit Committee, First Citizens Bancorp of
Cleveland, Tenn., 1998—

Past:

Partner, Service Cleaning Center, Cleveland, Tenn.
President, Gateway Investments, Inc., Cleveland, Tenn.,
1992-94
Vice President, Dixon Foods, Inc., Wilson, N.C., 1970-90
Treasurer, Bradley Advertising Agency, Wilson, N.C., 1973-80
President, M.I.T., Inc., Wilson, N.C., 1973-80
Director, Media Central, Chattanooga, Tenn., 1981-84
President (1984-86), Vice President/Secretary and Director,
Jackson Family Television, Inc, Jackson, Miss., 1981-86
President/Director, Knoxville Family Television, Inc.,
Knoxville, Tenn., 1983-1985
General Partner, Cherokee Communications Systems, LP,
Cleveland, Tenn., 1990-92

Hal's business interests, past and present, include
television stations, owner/operator of McDonald's and Checkers
restaurants, partners in shopping centers, office condos,
townhouse development, banking, and real estate. His projects
are varied, located in several southern states, and each presents
its own set of challenges and rewards. Because Hal looks at
problems as opportunities to learn and to grow, he is always
willing to meet the challenge and find a solution.

A Lesson Learned

According to Hal's thinking, ministers fill one of the most important roles in society. After becoming a Christian, he had a desire to become a minister, but as has been mentioned, he never received the call from God. However, through the years and through his life experiences, he learned that even though he wasn't called to preach, any task he was assigned was as important as he chose to make it. This realization had its roots during his stay in North Carolina while developing the McDonald's stores.

Hal had several occasions to observe a particular employee whose task was to keep the grounds and building clean at one of the stores. A part of the man's responsibility was to purchase supplies needed to do his job. There was a set amount in the budget for this purpose. He took great pride in keeping the grounds and building meticulously clean. In fact, his particular store always received superior ratings during inspections. He made wise purchases and took such good care of his supplies and equipment that he consistently stayed under budget.

Even though this employee had what most considered a menial job, he made the job important—to himself and to his employers. He wanted to do his very best. Perhaps the admonition in Colossians 3:17 was his motivation: "And whatever you do in word or deed, do all in the name of the Lord Jesus giving thanks to God the Father through Him."

No, Hal wasn't called to preach, but he entered into his job as superintendent of Sunday school with enthusiasm and diligent attention to the task at hand—making the Sunday school bigger and better. The Wake Forest Church of God Sunday school grew from about 110 to 323 during his tenure as superintendent. This was phenomenal for a church in a small mill village.

Hal held several influential positions in local government agencies that impacted the lives of the people in the community. As a member and chairman of the Bradley County Board of

Education, several of the initiatives put in place during his tenure still impact education in Bradley County today.

As a member of the Bradley County Commission, he served four years as chairman and several years as chairman of the finance committee. This body is responsible for setting the tax rate for the county and for allocating the monies for each agency of the county government. He always tried to look at "the big picture" and do what was best for the county as a whole, not just special interest groups.

Whatever the task, whether a so-called menial job or one that will impact thousands of people, it truly is as important as you are willing to make it.

Vision Foundation

Vision Foundation has been a vital part of Hal's life since 1979. He has been a member of the board of directors and has served the foundation as its treasurer.

Giving Through the Dixon Foundation

Someone asked Hal once about how he chooses the projects to which he gives. His reply was, "It depends on the project itself and who presents it. The timing has to be right."

The Dixon Foundation Mission Statement is to make a difference by demonstrating concern for the well being of the Christian community, the development of qualified leaders to minister to others in a chain reaction process for exponential results and to participate in the creation, development, production, and distribution of life-changing Christian resources that are not readily or ordinarily available.

The criteria to consider: Will it make a difference? Is it life changing? Is it needed? Is it otherwise not available?

All funds expended are intended to reflect God's love as demonstrated through the life and teachings of Jesus Christ.

The first objective is to give to organizations whose purpose is to help struggling persons to overcome a temporary crisis situation.

The second objective is to provide scholarships or grants-in-aid to institutions for education, training or development of those whose lifework will be to make a godly difference in other people's lives, which in turn will make a godly difference in the lives of others.

The third objective is to participate in or to give support to the creation, development, production, and distribution of life-changing Christian resources that make a godly difference and that are not otherwise available. These resources might include books, brochures, videos, audios, curriculum materials, speakers, etc.

Matthew 6:33 has been a reality in this family's life. "Seek ye first the kingdom of God and His righteousness, and all these things shall be added unto you."

H. Bernard Dixon
123 Bentley Park Drive, NW
Cleveland, TN 37312

Telephone
423-478-5238

Fax
423-478-2519

E-mail
hbdixon@bellsouth.net

Jim Hamilton—The Kingdom Investor

Jim Hamilton—The Kingdom Investor

If anyone ever wonders whether or not it pays to be a giver, they need to study Jim Hamilton. In the last few years, this man has given away what he was worth 15 years ago. Yet, now he is worth over twice what he had when he started. Because of His obedience, God has given him an open heaven. He is a humble man. He has humbled himself and God has exalted him.

The Childhood of This Great Giver

Jim Hamilton was born in Lenoir City, Tennessee, on May 26, 1932. He had three sisters and one brother. His father owned a grocery store and worked hard.

The family lived across from the Lenoir City Church of God. It seemed that his mother was always in church. When she went to church, she sought the Lord for hours. Jim recalls her receiving the Baptism of the Holy Spirit when he was 6 years of age. He remembers her speaking in tongues for a long period of time.

The Conversion of Jim Hamilton

Every time the altar call was given, young Jim thought he was supposed to go. Even though he was active in such an outstanding church, Jim had a bad experience. One evangelist, who was hard and harsh, came to the church for a revival. One night he asked a man in the church to come to the altar. The man answered, "Not tonight." The evangelist replied, "Go to hell then." Jim felt the evangelist was rude and crude. However, Bill Hildreth was saved in that same revival.

At about the age of 12 in June 1944, Jim received Christ as His Savior. Evangelist Davis from Chattanooga was in a meeting at their church in Lenoir City. He just had a special way with children. Thus, he catered to the children more than the adults.

About two months later, Jim received the Holy Spirit baptism and joined the church. This happened during a six-week revival when C. M. Newman was pastor. When Jim went to the altar, he began to speak in other tongues as the Spirit gave the utterance. It was an exhilarating moment.

At this time Jim made a promise to God that he has kept through the years. He said, "Lord, I'll do anything you ask me to do." Jim says now, "That may be dangerous when you're dealing with God, because He may ask you to do some things you don't want to do."

About 12 young people were saved and filled with the Spirit during that revival. Out of that came the "Trailer Gang." They met in a trailer to study the deeper things of God. All of these young people have stayed with the church. Some of them have become pastors. Others are outstanding leaders in the church today.

Jim has gone out and helped get other churches started; but he always comes home to the Lenoir City Church of God. He was greatly influenced by Pastor C. M. Newman. Pastor Newman came to Lenoir City in 1941 and left in 1950. The church went from a small group to 300 in attendance. Jim received much teaching from his pastor and church leaders. He realized that one of the keys to his success was receiving the word of the Lord from the anointed vessels God put in his life. Growing up in the church and always being there made a lasting impact on Jim Hamilton.

The Kind of Family This Kind of Man Must Have

Jim met Margaret at the Lenoir City Church of God. In fact, they did their dating at church. They sat together. They walked home after church together. At the age of 14, they were married. Before Jim turned 16, he was a father.

Jim's father built them a four-room frame house. Margaret chose not to work. She stayed home and took care of the family.

The Hamiltons have five children—Linda Gail, Diane, Jim Jr., Regina and Jo—all serving the Lord today. They have 10 grandchildren and one great-grandchild.

Top Leadership in the Church at the Age of 19

At the age of 19, Jim was elected to the church council. He has since served on that council 45 years out of 58 years. Jim was forced to grow up in a hurry. He was young, and the men were all older. Members of this council often had difficult decisions to make. Though he had no training, he just jumped into the work of church administration. Jim Hamilton was always faithful to God and the church. His children today will tell you that the greatest lesson their father taught them was faithfulness—the same kind of faithfulness he demonstrated throughout his life in work and in church.

The Most Difficult Struggle in Deciding to Be a Giver

The most difficult trial concerning giving came to Jim at the age of 24. The pastor got up one Sunday morning and said they needed to build 10 Sunday school rooms. He asked for some people to give $300 each. This would be above his tithes.

The tithe is the basic minimum that God requires. An offering is what we give above and beyond the tithe. Jim wondered how could he give that amount with all the bills he had to pay in order to raise his children? Was this really an opportunity to get an open heaven?

It was a great struggle. Finally, Jim's hand went up in commitment to give $300. It broke the barrier. Miracles are produced through obedience. Suddenly others began giving and pledging to give. The people said, "We were waiting to see if you would give. When you made your decision, we made ours." The church got the money they needed for the building project. This was the beginning of Jim Hamilton taking the lead in giving. In fact, this early struggle with giving prepared him for the blessings God had waiting for him in the years ahead.

Jim kept a teachable spirit. He had been taught that tithing and giving were the way to an open heaven. He wanted to be taught by the Word, by the Holy Spirit, and the ministers of the gospel that God had put in his path. Jim's attitude became, "Show me your ways, oh God."

The Beginning of His Career

Jim worked at a grocery store. He did not wait for his "ship to come in." He went to work and worked hard. Soon he was promoted to the position of manager.

In 1950, Jim's father bought a 250-acre farm. His dad still kept the grocery store, so somebody else had to be on the farm. The elder Hamilton always dealt in livestock and real estate. Gradually Jim got into livestock to help him.

Mr. Hamilton died at the age of 62. Jim was only 31 years old at the time, and his brother was about 19 years old. For a while, Jim took care of the farm. Finally, the family decided that the younger brother would tend the farm.

Launching Into the Business World

It was a family decision, but it was traumatic for Jim. He was now on his own. However, God provided the help he needed. His wife's brother, Bill Hildreth, mortgaged his house for Jim to go into business on his own.

Bill was not only a brother-in-law, he was Jim's friend. They did a lot of things together. They owned some businesses together. Bill believed that what he made happen for Jim, God would make happen for him. Bill Hildreth was blessed many times for showing his love to his brother-in-law. Risk-taking is imperative for success.

Jim took the money Bill gave him and went into the construction business. He built houses, sold them, and did subcontract work on the side.

In the 1960s, things became very tough financially. Jim determined that whatever he did, he would do well. He prayed much and strived for excellence.

A Turn-Around Came for Jim Hamilton

Finances were very tight for the Hamiltons until Jim was about 33 years of age. He had been concerned about supporting his children. The thought of educating all of them was frightening. At about age 32, things got very rough. Doors started closing. But then suddenly God turned things around for him. Jim had no idea of the extent to which God would enlarge his business. He had no way to foresee what great plans God had in store for him. He was simply obedient.

God began to speak to Jim in unusual ways. He would hear the voice of the Lord say, "Don't go this way." Then God would open another door, and it seemed, "This is the way, walk in it." Success always begins inside a person. It begins with a thought. Jim was learning to spend quality time in deep thought.

The only way to achieve your destiny is to take the first step by faith. Then embrace the next step by the Lord's direction. Continue moving faithfully as God leads. This is one of the reasons for the success of Jim Hamilton.

In 20 years, he built 300 houses. He took real estate classes. He built a motel in Lenoir City in the 1970s just to have something to do. He planned to sell it but decided to operate it instead. It became successful, so Jim kept it for years; and Margaret worked for him. Jim bought other motels such as the Inn of Lenoir City, the King's Inn, etc.

The 1970s were a great time of blessing for Jim in real estate. He would buy property for $100,000 and before long it was worth $500,000. He and Margaret lived on some of the money, spent some, and gave some to the Lord's work. His business had become very successful.

God gave Jim the opportunity to buy stock in the First National Bank in Lenoir City. God blessed him, and he became a director. Jim put his money in a place where it would work for him.

Dealing With the Spirit of Fear

Because Jim was a heavy tither and giver, God always blessed his business. There were never any really great crisis times for him.

Problems with fear can grip any successful businessman. In the mid-1970s Jim started worrying about what might happen if things went "bad." He was in debt $3 million. A lot of money was coming in, but also a lot of it was going out. He worried about what would happen if he lost everything. What if? If he lost it all, he would have survived, but the worry was there. The spirit of fear gripped him and tormented him day and night. He became sick and had to be hospitalized for two weeks.

While lying in the hospital bed, God began to deal with Jim's heart. The Word of God began to renew its work in him. He knew he had no control over things. The Lord was in control of it all. Whatever he did was in God's sovereign hands. God began to let Jim see that He was in charge. Jim says today, "God spoke to me, but not in an audible voice." Soon Jim Hamilton was well; knowing that "the steps of a good man are ordered by the Lord." The Word had driven out his fear. God's Word had told him, "Fear not, for I am with you; be not dismayed, for I am your God. I will strengthen you, yes, I will help you, I will uphold you with my righteous right hand" (Isaiah 41:10).

He let go of his fears and moved forward with new vision. "What time I am afraid, I will trust in thee. ... In God I have put my trust; I will not fear. ..." (Psalm 56:3, 4).

God Revealed to Jim How to Give a Million Dollars

Jim Hamilton believes strongly that God wants us to make disciples of all nations. This takes commitment as well as money. We cannot proclaim the gospel without money. He understands that giving is God's nature, and He created us to be like Him. The Bible explains, "Give to those who ask of you." Jim loves giving to meet the needs of the body of Christ. He is a hilarious giver. He loves it.

One night God gave Jim a dream. He dreamed he could give the Lord a million dollars if he lived 20 years. It was as if God were telling him to give $50,000 a year. God had inspired him, so he went to work. But instead of giving a million dollars in 20 years, he did it in seven years.

Jim has a philosophy of giving that works. Buy cheap. Give away big. One piece of property cost him $8,000. He sold it for $85,000. Another tract of land cost him $80,000. He sold it for $180,000. He was able to transfer the profit to a foundation or the church. He gave to Vision Foundation, his local church, the seminary and the denomination.

Jim explains how taxes and giving can work through appreciated assets. He buys land cheap. He holds the property until it becomes valuable, and then He gives it to the work of the Lord. The tax people give him credit for what the land was worth when he gave it away. For instance, if he gave $140,000 for property, he sold it (and gave away) for $500,000. He probably saved $140,000 in taxes.

"God's shovel is bigger than ours," Jim says. "We shovel small amounts, and God gives bigger amounts."

Jim has learned not to bargain with God. On one occasion, Jim was lying in bed praying. Someone had presented a need for $5,000. As he lay there Jim said, "God, I've got this piece of property. If you'll help me sell this and make $10,000, I'll be able to give you the $5,000." God spoke in a still voice, "Haven't I done enough for you? Can't you give to Me without bargaining with Me? You already have enough to do that. I've blessed you that much already." Jim said, "Yes, Lord." He immediately took $5,000 and gave it to prison ministry.

When Jim is asked how he made so much money, he has a simple answer. "I have an open heaven. I'm not smart enough to do what I've done. The Lord just blesses me."

About 1980, God's blessings began coming from offsprings of the businesses. He got into the banking business, real estate, and more construction. He built 300 houses, a motel, some commercial work, and five restaurants—two he built; three he remodeled. He bought General's Barbecue, Carl's A & W Drive-in, Weather Kings Restaurant—all debt free. He bought 15 subdivisions with 58 lots. He obtained 25 acres of commercial property along the highway. He began selling the property an acre at a time. He sold three motel sites, one restaurant site and one doctor's office site.

He Shares His Knowledge With the City and Church

Jim gives himself to civic groups. He served on the Planning Commission for Lenoir City. He further served on the Housing Authority Commission, the Industrial Committee, The Highway Committee and others. He was president of the Jaycees at one time. He served as president of the Rotary Club.

He has served on several administrative boards. God-given ideas seem to always be sitting inside of him. He is a member of the board for the seminary of the Church of God. He served on Men of Action with Bob Pace. He is on the National Prison Commission. He serves on the board for Vision Foundation.

He Goes to Foreign Countries to Use His Skills

Men of Action has always been one of Jim's favorite ministries. He went to Europe on the first Men of Action tour. He was with them when they repaired the building that is now the European Bible School and Church of God Executive Offices for England. The building in England was an old historic building that could have been torn down; but the church was able to obtain it, make repairs and make use of it for the glory of God. The Men of Action went into England, decided what kind of repairs needed to be done on the building, and they soon had it in operating condition. There were 260 rooms. They repaired all of them.

Jim has traveled to many other places with Men of Action. He went to Africa and Haiti and built churches. He went to the Indian reservation and to Alaska and built churches. Men of Action go to these places at their own expense, furnish the materials, and do the work.

He Loves Prison Ministry

Jim loves prison ministry. He at one time went regularly to Brushy Mountain State Prison where they house some of the cruelest of criminals. There were over 900 inmates there. At least 50 men came to the services conducted by Jim and his friends. The roommate of James Earl Ray came regularly to the meetings. One man, serving 238 years in prison, gave his heart to the Lord.

He Lives by Strong Principles

When asked what principles he lives by, Jim quickly tells you, "Seek ye first the kingdom of God and His righteousness." He learned this early in life.

Another principle is, "Use whatever is in your hand." Ezekiel 9:10 says, "Whatsoever thy hand findeth to do, do it with thy might." All too many Christians and businessmen do not use what is in their hands. Jim has stayed in Lenoir City. This is where he found his "acres of diamonds." He has stayed in his place of service and sowed into that city and church; and God has blessed him far beyond what most people who go looking for success ever experience. Many people travel all over the world looking for an opportunity, or a future, and yet there is a great destiny right in their own back yard. Not Jim Hamilton! He has used what was in his hand. God has multiplied it.

Family has always been very important to Jim. He worked hard, but he reserved special times and places for the family to pause and appreciate life and God's blessings together. Further, he has always been there to help his own children in any crises in their lives.

How Jim Hamilton Handles Adversity

Their daughter, Regina, had a crisis when she and her husband, Rickie Moore, received the diagnosis that their daughter, Hannah, had cerebral palsy. Regina was crushed. When she told Jim the news, he took her in his arms. Regina cried, "I wish I was your little girl all over again." Still holding his daughter, he told her she would always be his little girl, but now God had entrusted her with two daughters. He assured her that God knew her situation and had placed her there because she was the best mother for her daughters; and God would help her be all she needed to be.

In 2000, Jim lost his daughter, Diane. That was an upsetting time for the Hamiltons. When Jim is asked, "How did you handle it," his reply is, "I know God is in control." Jim and Margaret remain very close to Diane's husband, Sam Belisle, and their grandchildren. Sam says, "After Diane's death, Jim Hamilton proved even more to be a wonderful father-in-law, confidant, and encourager."

Margaret had a stroke on April 3, 2002. Before that, she had undergone surgery for kidney stones. In 2001, she had broken her hip. This was a traumatic time for the family. Margaret and Jim are still deeply in love. Since he is his own boss, he can plan his schedule to be home when she needs him. They still spend much quality time together and live very happy lives.

No Place to Stop

There is no stopping in Jim Hamilton's life. He says, "As long as I keep going, I can continue supporting the work of God." Jim is still involved in real estate and is on the board of the local bank.

Jim says, "Everything I have, I owe to the Lord. He took nothing and gave me a good life. It's not what I have given Him, but it's what He has given to me. He means everything in my life."

Jim Hamilton
902 Thurmer Circle
Lenoir City, TN 37771

Telephone
865-986-3347

Fax
865-986-9770

Jim Holdman—the Facilitator

Jim Holdman—the Facilitator

Jim was in the sixth grade, his father was in between pastorates in Kansas City, and he was tired of moving. He had to get along in school for his parents' sake. He needed friends and was lonely. Then, the biggest bully he knew came along and picked a fight. Gangs were just starting. The kid had just joined one and was trying to prove himself to his buddies. He beat Jim up for no reason. For days afterwards thoughts ran like a swift stream through Jim's young mind. Why was he here? Why couldn't he live a normal life? Why did his family have to move so often? Why don't people treat pastors better? This one incident alone made a powerful impact on Jim Holdman's life.

Later in life, Jim asked a psychologist for a complete psychological assessment. The doctor said, "Jim, you have a dial on your chest. Whichever way you point it, you get success."

Jim asked, "How did I get here?"

"You got here because when you were in school you knew that you had to make friends with the biggest bully there so you could survive. You have done it through life. You take on the biggest challenges. When you turn the dial, it means success. You succeed at all you do." The psychologist helped him put it all together.

The Facilitator's Childhood

Many things in life affect children. The thing that had the biggest negative impact on Jim Holdman's life was moving. Moving affected the rest of the family in a positive way—but not Jim. Moving always set the boundaries for what Jim could and could not do. It formed what he was able to do in life.

Jim was born in Caruthersville, Missouri. The family moved from there to Knoxville, Iowa; then to Centerville, Iowa; St. Louis, Missouri; Glamorgan, Virginia; Front Royal, Virginia;

back to St Louis again; Festus, Missouri; Flatriver, Missouri; Carthage, Missouri; St. Joseph, Missouri; Tarkio, Missouri; and then to Kansas City, Missouri. They lived in Cleveland, Tennessee, for a short time while Jim's dad was state evangelist for South Carolina and then moved to Erie, Pennsylvania.

Jim had three sisters and a brother—Carmen, Mary Margaret, David, and Joy. They were a very close knit family with a lot of love for each other.

The move to Kansas City was very traumatic. Jim's dad had gotten sick in Carthage, Missouri, with pneumonia. He had started building a church and was not able to complete it because of a fatigued heart. His immune system was run down. There were some disgruntled members who began to rise up against Pastor Holdman as stress increased over the new building program. The overseer decided that Mr. Holdman was a dictator because three families had written letters to him; therefore, he assumed that it was a major problem. The overseer scheduled a meeting with the people. The other families became furious and voted to turn all the troublemakers out who were giving Brother Holdman a rough time.

Jim's dad's health was never the same. The doctor advised him to move away to regain his strength. He moved the family to St. Joseph. Again Jim had to change schools. The pain in the move was excruciating for young Jim.

Once Brother Holdman had regained his health, he was ready to pastor a church again. They moved to Kansas City while Jim was in the sixth grade. Here Mary Margaret and Carmen got jobs with an insurance company in order to support the family. They even moved into an apartment without enough heat to save money. Jim's dad led this congregation through obtaining property and made a couple of moves within Kansas City.

This was a crisis time in Jim's life. He threw a temper tantrum when they moved to Kansas City. The gangs were just beginning. Then the bully turned on Jim and beat him up. He represented the growing street mentality of showing how tough he was. However, this became Jim's greatest strength. That event forced him to be able to take the toughest person and make friends to survive. He became friends with that bully and with the bully's friends. He knew his parents were here to stay. He had nowhere to turn. He had to survive. This would become the hallmark of his ministry. As a result, he loves to go to problem churches and help them get straightened out. He goes into problem situations that need millions of dollars and helps them find donors.

The family was always poor when Jim was a child. Jim still recalls how it made him feel. Once his socks had huge holes in the toes and heels, but they still had the appearance of socks. One of the church members wanted to buy him a new pair of shoes. Jim was so embarrassed about the socks that he literally fought them to keep from taking off his shoes.

The hypocrisy in the church world also bothered Jim. There were several big-name preachers who came through Kansas City. Every time one of them was exposed, it made Jim a little more skeptical.

His Battle for Identity

He always struggled with an identity crisis. Everywhere he went, Jim was somebody's son or somebody's brother. What about him? He longed to have an identity of his own.

Jim went to Lee Academy one year while his dad was state evangelist in South Carolina. He was highly respected and was elected president of the Lee Academy student body for the next year.

However, there was a deep struggle inside of him. He was hurt and bitter. He did not know how to trust God. Even after being elected president of the student body, he felt that he did not fit. He would watch the great moves of God and wonder, "Why doesn't God, or somebody, understand my suffering?"

Because of the deep wounds, he did not accept the Lord until he was 16 years of age at a Sunday evening service at the North Cleveland Church of God.

Feeling that he needed his own identity, he went to Northwest Bible College at age 18. He had planned to go one semester and then return to Lee. The very first official he met at Northwest was Dr. R. B. Thomas, who made a tremendous impact on Jim's life.

Northwest was in the middle of nowhere. The school needed help with promotion. This was his opportunity. Jim had worked at Carroll Printing Company while in Cleveland. So he took an old worn-out printing press that was in the basement of Overseer John Nichols' home and began printing promotional materials for Northwest. He later put a printing department together.

In January 1966, while working on the press, God spoke to him, "I have brought you through all this to bring you here to the center of my will." Someone asked Jim, "Was it an audible voice?" His response, "It was louder than that" (a quote from Billy Graham).

Jim saw Dr. Ray H. Hughes, whom he respected greatly, at a Pennsylvania camp meeting. Dr. Hughes, who was president of Lee College at that time, said, "Jim, I saw your picture on a slide June Becker was carrying around. I had no idea you were at Northwest. But I feel that you are to stay there. You are making an impact."

The Facilitator Meets His Wife

During this time Jim met Linda. Linda had been exposed to hardships Jim never experienced. Her mother was crippled, because she had polio when she was a child. When she got pregnant with Linda, her husband made her drink turpentine in an attempt to kill the baby, because he was afraid she would not be able to pick fruit in order to help with the finances. They finally got a divorce. It left much anger and bitterness in the family, but not in Linda.

Linda had health problems. She had worked for Hanford Engineering, an Atomic Energy Commission Nuclear plant in Richland, Washington, while in high school and was exposed to radiation. (There have been extensive lawsuits about this.)

Noreen and John Nichols respected Linda highly and kept insisting that Jim and Linda get together. They did get together and were married in Pasco, Washington, in the Church of God. Jim borrowed $700 in order to pay for the wedding.

Marriage brought new adjustments. Jim had to learn how to give love. He had always been on the receiving side of love. He came from a family of all love. Linda came from a family where love was not visible much of the time.

The Director of Promotions and Registrar

In 1965, Jim's first year at Northwest, the school had approximately 32 students. His last year as a student, Jim was offered the job as director of promotions and registrar.

All those times Jim moved with his family, inside he was searching for someone to love him. Northwest did. An abundance of favor began to flow to him. It seemed that the Lord was in the business of blessing him. He made friends everywhere.

Working with Dr. Vaught was a wonderful experience because of his excellent managing skills. Dr. Laud O. Vaught was a man of few words with an attorney's mind. Building a Bible college in Minot, North Dakota, for the preparation of ministers and missionaries seemed to be impossible. There was very little Church of God constituency in the area. In a thousand-mile radius there was not one church whose attendance was over 500 people. Dr. Vaught forced his staff to go beyond anything their environment afforded them. He pushed and pushed, and they made it happen.

Jim began making friends everywhere. He was living a life of continual excitement. Mayor Chester "Chet" Reiten became a friend and later became one of the college's biggest supporters.

In this new position, Jim made use of the printing department. He called headquarters and got the mailing addresses for all of the Churches of God. He sent out thousands of letters. With Jim Holdman, Dr. Vaught, and John Nichols all hitting the field, the enrollment grew to 260 students.

Development Director

In 1973, the school had applied for accreditation through the American Association of Bible Colleges. Jim's strength was in public relations. During this time he had meetings lined up with the lieutenant governor of the state, who also became Jim's friend. The Minot Daily News staff became his friends during this study.

The recommendation came back that the school should open a development department. In 1974, Jim was appointed as the development director. The school brought on Consultant Dr. Lamar Rice, an ordained Baptist minister who was getting older, but had been a pioneer in the development area. Jim was young and Lamar was experienced. He was a great mentor to Jim.

Rice had learned through experience how to tap corporate and business gifts and also how to penetrate power structures. His theory was that every community, regardless of the size, is run by a power structure. He taught Jim, "If you want to sell anything to a community, do it one of two ways. Either get the power structure on your side, and they will sell it for you; or you go out and saturate the market place with the message." This became one of the great lessons in Jim's life.

Jim got his facts together, then began to arrange things. If he could get in front of a person, he found that he could make his case. Basically, he could help major donors discover what was important in their giving.

Changes in His Life

Dr. Vaught left Northwest in 1980 to join the Lee College faculty. Dr. Herbert Walker was appointed president of the college. Jim knew he would miss Dr. Vaught, but he was thrilled with the appointment of Dr. Walker to the school. Herb and Lucille Walker had all the expertise and recognition in the church to put the institution on the map. Herb came to the school that summer before the General Assembly. He and Jim spent the summer planning and talking.

Then the bomb fell. Herbert Walker was elected to be the assistant director of World Missions of the Church of God. As a consequence, Jim felt he had lost his energy and zeal.

Other presidents followed. Then, Don Walker became president and his wife, Jackie, became the development director. Jim wrote the proposal to get Jackie hired because he was "burned out." He needed a change. He was offered a contract; but the burden that had been there for 18 years was lifted, and he chose to decline.

New Ventures in Consulting and Fund-raising

Jim went into part-time consulting. He stayed in Minot but took a job with a firm out of Texas in fund-raising for churches.

Before leaving Northwest Bible College, Jim had borrowed money to go into partnership to buy some real estate. The deal turned out unfavorable and left him owing a lot of money. Now he had to make big money.

Leadership in the City

A bond had already been developed between Jim and Mayor Chet Reiten. There had been a flood in 1969. During this time, the mayor had observed how skillful Jim was. After that initial contact, the mayor wanted Jim to be involved in leadership support roles with him.

Jim became the chair of the Public Relations Committee for the Chamber of Commerce in Minot. He increased the chamber membership by 20 percent over a 24-month period. People thought Jim would go up in the chamber chairs, but the mayor wanted him on the city council.

Jim was elected to the city council in 1978 while at Northwest Bible College. He continued to serve on that council until 1986. He had the love of the city. Further, he served on many local and state committees.

Jim Jensen was chairman of the Trinity Medical Center Board. Jim Holdman was appointed to that board. The Trinity Medical Center bought Northwest Bible College. They tore down most of the buildings but retained the Laud O. Vaught Learning Center facility and built a counseling center and an educational center.

The relationship between Jim Holdman and Jim Jensen grew. Jim Jensen was, at that time, one of 13 national vice presidents on the board of realtors with an impeccable reputation for honesty and integrity.

Jensen told Holdman, "I have watched you for many years. I want you to be a partner in a new venture."

Working with Jim Jensen was interesting and provided tremendous experience. After Holdman had been with him for only a year, Jensen slowed down and began restoring classic automobiles in 1986.

Jim Jensen had been on the board of directors for First Western Bank. In 1987, he recommended Jim Holdman to be managing executive of the Investment Center located at First Western Bank and Trust. Jensen said, "It is better to have Jim Holdman part-time than anybody else full-time."

The vice president of First Western Bank and Trust was John Hoeven (who is now governor of North Dakota). John was 26 at the time. Working with him was another learning experience. John was probably the best financial man Holdman had ever dealt with in his entire life. John was appointed president of the Bank of North Dakota at age 33. North Dakota is the only state in the union that has its own bank. John, a brilliant financial strategist, turned the Bank of North Dakota into a very profitable situation. Then John was elected Republican governor in 2000. This experience was great for Jim.

Jim was extremely busy now—running the Investment Center and consulting with Christian ministries and colleges—traveling over 200,000 miles each year.

God helped Jim to know how to network. During this time Jim was beginning to be successful, but he was struggling spiritually. He often felt God was not really interested in what he was interested in. He prayed, "God, I have a few shortcomings. If you will come in and make up on those short comings, I'll have a perfect life."

Personal finances were tight. He had made some unwise deals and owed some personal loans. He learned through these times to trust the Lord completely. This was also preparation for helping others.

His Wife's Career Develops

Linda had gone to Minot State and earned a masters degree in special education and was certified in testing. She already had life membership as a CPS (Certified Professional Secretary).

Jim and Linda's son, Scott, began to have some problems. The teacher said, "This boy is lazy." Linda said, "No. He's not!" She tested Scottie and found out that he had unbelievable intelligence. If you gave him a verbal test, he could tell you all the answers; but he could not write down the answers.

Linda began to speak in seminars in the public school system. The American Disability Act was passed. Linda is an expert in law for Americans with disabilities. While she was lecturing in Minot, North Dakota, at a state conference, Dr. Lynn Chalmers said, "Linda, you do a better job with my material than I do. If you will come to the University of North Dakota and teach part-time, we will help you complete your Ph.D. program in two years. We will give you a full scholarship and a graduate teaching assistantship for two years."

The Move Away From Minot

Jim was trying to decide whether or not to leave Minot. He loved that city. All he had ever searched for and longed for was respect and acceptance for who he was. He found that in Minot. Then Linda got a cancer scare which made the decision much easier. This caused him to agree to sell out and move.

Moving was difficult for Jim emotionally. He and Linda stored their belongings in the basement of on-campus housing. The flood hit Grand Forks in 1997. Most of their material possessions were destroyed. Through this test, God spoke to Jim again. God said, "Simplify your life and get a handle on your debt."

Now in Grand Forks, Linda was the star. She became very successful in her career. Jim had one job—consulting. But through this time the family grew closer together than they had ever been.

Jim was not prepared for the success God was going to give him when he moved to Grand Forks. His respect as a consultant grew. God began to solidify Jim's business. He never dreamed God would bless him as much as he has been blessed. The God who has no limitations directed his path.

A Premiere Development Consultant

Jim Showers, president of a college and seminary foundation says of him, "Jim Holdman has consistently demonstrated the highest professional skills and in-depth knowledge of development. He is one of the premiere development consultants."

Nelson Rumore, former director of Major Gifts of William Jewell College, supports Jim. He says, "If you really want to know how direct mail and face-to-face fund-raising fit together in a seamless and integrated fashion, Jim Holdman is the person you need to call. I have spent quality, private time with one of the best-known names in major gifts fund-raising in the United States and Canada—he's good—Jim Holdman is better."

Jim finds his present work gratifying. He is a private consultant to colleges, seminaries, and ministries. Some of his clients have been with him for a decade. He doesn't have to advertise. He gets clients by word of mouth. He calls his company Integrated Financial Development Systems.

Integrated Financial Development Systems

IFDS is committed to enhancing its client's financial future. Jim Holdman believes it all begins with a commitment to people, not to buildings, money, estates, plans, or programs. He says, "It all begins and ends with people."

He goes into churches, schools, institutions, or ministries and helps them identify their major donors. Every church has mega potential. Regardless of the size, it has major donors who do not give to the church. Jim teaches the church, school, institution, or ministry in a seminar how to market themselves. It is a skill to recognize the mega donor and help him be fulfilled without it wrecking the church.

Dealing With Major Mega Donors

Jim deals with major mega donors. He advises, "Identify what is really important to the donor." He deals with the donor's need to give rather than the institution's need to have. He will go in and strategize an entire development program for schools or ministries. Jim says one of the first principles in securing gifts is to identify the donor's value system and what can make him or her feel fulfilled. The size of the gift has nothing to do with the project but with the donor's resources.

A miracle came to a ministry with which Jim was consulting. A donor gave a check in five figures and indicated, "We give one major gift to Christian organizations."

The leader asked, "Jim, what is she saying?"

Jim thoughtfully responded, "She and her husband have made investments in Christian organizations that didn't spend their gifts wisely. They are spreading their risks. They are looking for fulfillment in their giving. Take the donor to coffee every 30 days and show the donor what her gift is doing." This strategy led to a six figure gift.

Jim had gotten a businessman to give a sizeable contribution to a Bible college. The man called and said, "I want to thank you. I have never given that kind of money. I have been so blessed and so fulfilled since making that commitment."

Because someone taught Jim about power structures, he can walk into the offices of people who own football teams and talk to them about supporting Christian organizations. His job is to find out what it takes to get the community to respond.

Jim has learned to stay positive when people aren't buying what he is selling. While working for a Christian college, he saw God change a hard-hearted banker's heart. Jim walked in and explained that the college wanted to reach into the community, and he was attempting to get a campaign going for them.

The banker said, "Those people don't want to reach into this city. The only way I will make a contribution is if they do business with us!"

"They do business with you!"

"No, they don't!" He called his secretary and asked, "Ann, does this college do business with us?"

In a few minutes on the intercom, she answered, "Yes, sir. They have an account at one of our branches. They have $10.48 in the account." The banker laughed and became one of the biggest supporters in the campaign.

A Spiritual Compass

Jim believes in a spiritual compass. He maintains that leadership is a sense of direction. The spiritual compass is the leadership between the two compasses—spiritual and physical awareness compass. If the spiritual compass is in charge, you will reject any deal not like Christ. The spiritual compass takes the lead. Things that don't fit the model of Christ are rejected.

Refuses to Think Something Can't Be Done

Jim refuses to think something can't be done. He will work on a project until it is done. He says, "Don't accept defeat. Don't try to tell God the outcomes."

His Approach

The approach he sometimes uses is: Go into a town and interview 50 to 100 people. "Look, we have to help this institution succeed. Who comes to your mind as decision makers in this city?" Then he goes to those whose names keep appearing. He feels that his job is to convince the power structure they need to get behind the organization.

Time Management

His clients get 100 percent of Jim's attention. He stays focused. Time management is important to him. He writes down all he does every day and keeps a pocket diary.

Jim writes reflections in a journal nearly every morning. He has learned that when he journals, he learns from past successes and failures. Further, it is easier to discern the voice of God.

What His Clients Say

A president of one seminary said, "Jim Holdman reads people better than anybody I have ever met in my life. He can walk in and read a situation that nobody else can read."

Dave Coleman, vice-president/senior regional field director for Youth for Christ says, "Jim Holdman has done more to help me understand donor development than anyone. Every aspect of the integrated system he teaches works. And when he taught it to a group of us, his down-home illustrations from his experience helped us to understand and apply his principles to our situations. All of this is backed by Jim's passion for development work and his desire to serve his clients."

Ron Brace, administrator for Valley Christian School in St. Croix Falls, Wisconsin, said, "In a nutshell the seminars that were presented were informative, organized and personal. It was fun to see my board members 'drink in' the concepts that were being presented. For some, it was a radical shift in thinking; going from nickel-and-dime fund-raising with much effort to major donor fund-raising that takes time but is enjoyable as they build lasting relationships with people."

Scott Arnold, executive director for Central Ohio YFC, said, "The coaching we received from Jim Holdman helped us triple our annual budget in four years. Jim's grasp of development philosophy combined with a gifted approach with major donors make him a one-of-a-kind in the consulting world."

Jim's work now is to focus on the huge wealth transfer from one generation to the next. His work is to make sure the church is able to get part of that money. Financial services people working under appropriate regulations will be a channel to move money from private sectors into non-profit organizations, including churches and faith-based ministries.

Everything Jim Holdman has been through has made him the man who can help people, ministries, and institutions find their way when there seems to be no way. God has honored him with favor and success, and now he lives to be a blessing to the body of Christ.

Jim Holdman
3627 - 12th Avenue North
Grand Forks, ND 58203-2010

Telephone
800-708-4337

Fax
701-795-6998

Web site
www.ifdsdevelopmentcounsel.com

Don Medlin—The Dreamer

Don Medlin—The Dreamer

"Limitations in your mind will produce limitations in your life." Dreaming will cause the word impossible to be replaced by the word possible. People who have achieved great things are individuals who were dreamers. In fact, the difference between success and failure is the dream. If you can dream it, it can happen.

Don Medlin was and is a dreamer. He has dreams for his own life. He has dreams for his family. He has dreams for his friends. He has dreams for his local church. He has dreams for people in need. He has placed his dreams in the hands of God and has been successful.

Don feels that one of the problems with this present generation is that they don't take time to dream. People want loud music playing. They want activity. They like the busy traffic. He teaches, "If you are going to do anything great with your life, you have got to dream big."

Dreaming in the Field

The rural school in Missouri that Don attended had a break in the early fall. This break was for the students to have time off to help with the harvest and was sometimes referred to as "cotton-picking vacation." However, Don did not think of it in terms of being a vacation. It wasn't fun. It was hard work.

Don's father remembered the hours he had spent in the cotton fields and decided the children should be paid for their work. They were paid $3 per 100 pounds picked, and they had to be quite industrious to be able to pick over 100 pounds a day.

Don began to dream while going up and down those rows of cotton. He dreamed about getting out of that cotton patch. He began to visualize other opportunities for his life's work. People are often lazy and fearful of change, so they don't dream. But not Don Medlin. When dreaming, he sensed that if he remained faithful, God would provide guidance for him.

This time of aloneness on the farm picking cotton was good for Don even though he disliked it. God wants time alone with us so He can build vision into us. Even Jesus sent the multitudes away so He could be alone. During these times Don never shut his ears to the voice of God. He began to see himself successful and blessed of God. He began to visualize great things for his life.

The Dreamer's Childhood

Don was the youngest child born into a Christian farming family of 10 children in Pemiscot County, near Caruthersville, Missouri.

All Don's father had ever done was farm. He grew cotton, corn, soybeans, and wheat. He was not really poor, but certainly not wealthy. However, he knew how to take a little and stretch it a long way.

The entire family had to work. Don often says, "We had one of the first unions that I had ever known. My dad was president of the union, and my mother was vice-president. I always knew what my job was. I knew what I was supposed to do. And I knew if I didn't do my job, I would have to contend with the union boss. And he was very strong."

Mr. Medlin was a strict disciplinarian. When he did not like what the boys were doing, he gave them a thump. Don said, "When we were wrong, we got the thump."

Don's grandfather had been a horse trader and ran a livery stable. When people came to Pemiscot County and wanted to travel, he leased them a horse and buggy and furnished the driver.

However, Don's father enjoyed the cattle and the row crop aspect of farming. The Medlin parents were good parents. Don's father was a Baptist, and his mother was a shouting Methodist. Everybody in town knew Mr. Medlin was an honest man. People today who remember him remember him for his integrity. He never worked on Sunday and had high standards for himself and his family.

Don's mother was a great woman with a head for business. She was more of a business person than her husband. She was a survivor. When Mr. Medlin became discouraged with the farm, she would assure him that everything was going to be okay. Though she was not bossy or outgoing, she was the stabilizer of the business.

The children were allowed to go to church wherever they wished, so the older ones began attending the Church of God. Don, being the youngest, sometimes went with his parents on Sunday night to the Baptist church. However, one Sunday Don went to the Church of God with some of the older brothers and sisters, and that evening he was saved.

Don loved the farm. Today he shares that his time on the farm was one of the greatest blessings he ever received. Don often testifies:

> "I thank the Lord for saving me from tobacco. I want to thank Him for saving me from alcohol. I want to thank Him for saving me from drugs. Now I know that's the popular things if you're going to speak. This has to be one of the criteria. You noticed I said He saved me from them, because He didn't save me out of them; I never was in them. When I was 8 years old, I gave my life to Christ."

Don knew God had instructed the Israelites that the first fruits of all their increase belonged to Him. Being a farm boy, Don could easily understand this principle. Therefore, tithing became a part of Don's life in his youth. When he was paid $3 for picking cotton, he paid 30 cents to the church. Don says to people today, "If you think you will wait until you can afford to tithe, you have already waited too long."

During Don's teen years he did a lot of trading. He would buy a cow and trade it for something he wanted. He would trade a horse for something else. He learned early about hard work. That lesson alone is one of the things that made him the great businessman he is today.

Don relates: "I never had to apply for a job. It was always there. I didn't have to have any interviews or resumes. I just had to get up in the morning, and it was waiting for me."

He was on the farm when people farmed with mules. Tractors came in about 1945.

The Dreamer Goes to College

Don went to Lee College (when it was just a junior college) after he finished high school. At this time, he had no plans to return to the farm.

When he first went to Lee College, he met Carolyn Hollowell and fell in love. He had seen her at the General Assembly of the Church of God in Memphis, Tennessee, but did not officially meet her. While standing in the welcome line at the beginning of the year at Lee, he met her. However, they did not date until after Valentine's Day. They talked at the Western States' banquet held in the dining hall. Then the next night, he asked her out. They went to Arnold School where the Speer Family was singing.

The Dreamer's Career and Marriage

After completing his junior college work, he went to St. Louis. Don got a job as an encyclopedia salesman. It did not take him long to realize this was not his destiny.

His brother, Roger, called and asked him to come back to the farm. Their dad had retired; Roger had bought his farm equipment but needed some help.

Don and Carolyn were married in 1962. This was another marriage made in heaven. Carolyn worked the first year they were married, but chose to stay home after the first child was born and build a strong, Christian family.

The business began expanding. Don rented some land from a farmer who was retiring. The man rented him the land but wanted him to buy his equipment, also. Don did not need his equipment, so he began selling equipment as a side job. He kept doing the same thing—renting land and buying equipment.

Don worked on the principle of supply and demand. There was a greater need for equipment in the South. He began to work auction sales, as well as buying out individual farmers. Don would buy equipment in some of the northern states, such as Illinois and Indiana, and resell it to individual customers and dealers in the southern states. He worked particularly in Arkansas, Mississippi, Louisiana, and Texas.

Don began to expand his selling of equipment. Combines were the volume seller. Much of success is dependent on being consistent and staying focused.

Pressure brings about the best in a dreamer. Things of value are made under pressure. Don Medlin has learned to use the tough times for stepping stones.

In 1987, the stock market took a devastating decline on Black Monday. Times were bad for everyone, including farmers. But on that day Don felt that God proved Himself to be Jehovah Jireh (His provider). There is a large piece of ground across the Mississippi River in Dyer County, Tennessee, that became significant in his life on this day. The name of the community is called "Tigertail." The Prudential Insurance Company had a 6,000-acre tract of land up for auction, and Don bought the land for a considerable savings.

Don began to work the land. He knows how to make a dream become a reality. Dreams will remain dreams until we set goals and go to work. Don set goals, worked hard, and has continually made improvements to that farm. That land is still being farmed today.

The Don Medlin Company is Don's dealership company for agricultural equipment. DDAB Farms is his farming operation growing corn, cotton, rice, soybeans, and wheat.

The Dreamer Keeps an Open Heaven

It has always been evident to Don and Carolyn that giving unto the Lord is the highest form of worship. Tithing is a recognition on their part of the ownership of God. When the Medlins tithe, they acknowledge they are bought with a price and that all they have and all they are, they owe to God. When they give to God, they find themselves in a partnership with God.

Don Medlin knows that according to Malachi 3, tithing gives an open heaven. The Lord says, "Bring ye all the tithes into the storehouse, that there may be meat in mine house, and prove me now herewith, saith the Lord of hosts, if I will not open you the windows of heaven, and pour you out a blessing, that there shall not be room enough to receive it" (v. 10).

Throughout his entire career, Don has paid tithes and given offerings. He realizes that money is sacred. It is a gauge to tell you about your spiritual condition. In a meeting at the Church of God School of Theology, Don explained:

"Everything has to have a gauge. I was driving over here from home yesterday, and I meditated on that thought. The vehicle I was driving had a gauge in it, and it kept getting lower and lower, and then I had to pull over and put some more fuel in it. Everything has to have a gauge to go by. And I really think money is a part of that gauge."

"Money reveals your spiritual level." Don explains, "You have to have money to exist. God wants faithfulness with money. If you are faithful with your money, God can use you. Many people don't have money because they can't be trusted with it. Many people could not handle it, if they were prosperous."

The Dreamer Is a Witness in the Community

The dreamer and his family live in a town of about 7,000 people. Sometimes in a small town, gifted people like the Medlins can wonder why they are there. But their influence is powerful in that town. One man was asked, "Who is your spiritual leader?"

His answer: "Don Medlin."

Don serves his local community in every way possible. He is active in the local church in Caruthersville, supporting his pastor and church. Further, he serves on the Pemiscot County Port Authority Board of Directors.

Carolyn is also active in the local church. She is a pianist, Sunday school teacher, and has served as a leader in Women's Ministries. She also involves herself in community activities, such as community Bible studies.

The Dreamer Serves His Organization

Don Medlin serves not only his local church and community, but he serves the body of Christ at large. He served on the Forward in Faith Board of Directors (1974-1982). He has served on the Lee University Board of Directors from 1982 until the present time. He was a charter member of Vision Foundation and has served on the board of directors ever since its organization. He may live in a small town, but his influence reaches to the nation.

In 1982, he and Carolyn established the Don and Carolyn Medlin Scholarship Fund at Lee University. The first priority of this scholarship is for students from Missouri.

The Dreamer Passes His Dreams on to His Children

Don and Carolyn's four children—Don A. Medlin, Noel Byron Medlin, Cherie A. Medlin Kirby, and J. Clark Medlin—

mean much to them. Don has taught his children the need to dream. He instructs them to be quiet before the Lord and dream. He tells them to dream the impossible dream.

Further, Don and Carolyn are an example of giving to their children and grandchildren. Their children often went to places such as youth camps. Don would always say to them: "I am giving you some extra money. If there is some kid there that doesn't have anything, you make sure they're taken care of." They did it too.

Their daughter completed Lee College and was waiting to be accepted into a program at the University of Alabama. During this time she worked at Bradley Memorial Hospital in Cleveland, Tennessee. One night she called, "Dad, you know you always told me that if someone needed some help to let you know." She continued to tell her dad about a girl who went to school with her. The girl had graduated and was working at Bradley Memorial Hospital. She was also waiting to be accepted in a college in Nashville. Cherie said, "Dad, she's really desperate. Her money did not come through. Her loans didn't come through. She is from a broken home, and her mother is taking in washing just to survive. Dad, she's really hurting." Don responded, "How much do you think I need to send her?" He was shocked but thrilled to hear his daughter's answer, "Well, I gave her $500." Don knew that to adults that may not be a lot of money; but to a girl working at Bradley Memorial Hospital waiting to get into college, it was a lot of money.

Don and Carolyn instilled their philosophy about giving to their children. They taught them that because they tithe faithfully, they can pray and know that God hears them. Tithing and giving gives them a right to go to God and ask Him to supply their needs, whatever they are. Because they have obeyed the Lord, it strengthens their faith.

The Medlin children have watched their father and mother sow in good ground. Don is as much concerned about God's money being in a place where it will return good dividends, as he is in his own business investments. Lee University has been one of the places where Don and Carolyn have sowed much of their finance. They love Lee University and believe the lives of young people are "good ground."

Don's greatest dream is that the Lord be glorified in his life. One of his other dreams is that you begin to dream. Get out of the slow lane and do something about your dream. Go to work. Know that you can do all things through Christ who strengthens you. Dream big!

Don Medlin
1169 State Highway D
Caruthersville, MO 63830

Telephone
573-333-0669

Fax
573-333-5268

Roger Medlin—The Sower

Roger Medlin—The Sower

God has extra blessings for good men who walk uprightly before Him. Being a successful farmer, Roger Medlin understands the principles of sowing and reaping. Much can be learned from this man of God.

Roger Medlin was born in a large family of 10 children. He was the ninth child. His brother Don was the tenth. His older brothers and sisters had great influence upon his life.

The Farm and the Sower

The Medlins are lifetime farmers. Their grandfather was a farmer. Their father was a farmer. Farm life was much harder when Roger and his brothers were at home. The farm was much smaller then. They did not have the modern, sophisticated equipment which makes farming so much easier. Their dad grew corn, cotton, and soybeans.

Roger became a Christian at the age of 10. When he was a teenager he felt a definite call to be involved in missions. Missions became a driving force in his life. However, he began to realize his call was a supportive call rather than a call to go live in a foreign country.

God Prepares the Sower a Wife

While God was preparing Roger on a farm in Missouri, he was preparing Roger's wife at the same time. Kay was born in Pemiscot County, Missouri. When growing up, she lived in several different towns in southeast Missouri.

Kay grew up in a home where God was always honored, and she accepted the Lord at the age of 12. Her parents taught her to love God and the grace of giving. This includes not only money, but also everything about us—our time, our talents, our families, ourselves. Grace is something that we receive that we do not deserve. Giving is to put into possession or keeping of another. She was taught that the grace of giving as a Christian is giving to God everything that we have to His possession or keeping. It belongs to Him. Kay was taught that a sense of destiny should be ours because God has placed us where we are for a purpose.

When she was 8 years of age, she read a booklet about Reverend and Mrs. C. E. French. They pastored the church where her parents attended when Kay was a baby. The Frenches were planning to go to India as missionaries. In this book the family members shared why they wanted to go to India. It made such a profound impression on Kay that she wanted the Lord to call her to be a missionary. But He didn't.

George Alford came to conduct a revival in the little church where Kay's family were attending. He preached a message about missions. This made a lasting impression on Kay's life and thinking. Also, Missionary Pearl Stark came to the same church for a meeting and told her life story.

Kay wanted to be a nurse on the foreign mission field. After she graduated from high school, she wanted to go to college and become a registered nurse. Her parents were financially unable to send her to college, so she settled for a job as a secretary, stayed at home, worked in her local church, and put her dreams on hold.

Kay and Roger began dating on February 6, 1959. While they were dating, they found that they shared the same desire about missions. They were married on January 3, 1960. This union was blessed with six beautiful daughters, including one set of twins.

Just a few weeks after they were married, they pledged to give some money to build a church in the Philippines. This was the beginning of a life-long lifestyle of giving.

The Sower's Career

Roger did not go to college, but stayed home to help his dad on the farm. In 1958, his dad retired. Roger bought the equipment and started farming on his own. He took over his dad's business and kept the family business going. At the time of this writing, he has farmed for 45 years.

To pay tithes or not to pay tithes on what he earned was never a question. Roger and Kay were always faithful to God.

Tragedy struck in 1970 when they had been married for ten years. They had four children and had made a commitment to build a church in Japan. They had gone to Georgia to visit family members and had come back through Cleveland, Tennessee, to visit Roger's sister. On February 15, they were in church at North Cleveland. Pastor T. L. Lowery gave them word that they were needed at Roger's sister's house. They received word that their house had burned. The Medlins had lost everything, except what they had with them.

It seemed that the practical thing to do was declare bankruptcy. What were they going to do? The insurance on the house went into the family estate. They were living in Roger's uncle's home. They received only $2,000, which was from insurance on their household items. Roger desperately needed to find another source of income in addition to the farm. He was encouraged to run for political office, so he took the $2,000 and filed to run for collector of revenue of the county. He won the election and served in this position for12 years. They paid their missions pledge to build a church in Japan and were enabled to give even more. What the enemy meant for harm, God turned into good.

They learned to rejoice in the midst of the pain. One of their favorite verses in the Bible is Habakkuk 3:17-18: "Although the fig tree shall not blossom, neither shall fruit be in the vines; the labour of the olive shall fail, and the fields shall yield no meat; the flock shall be cut off from the fold, and there shall be no herd in the stalls. Yet I will rejoice in the Lord, I will joy in the God of my salvation."

The decade of the 1980s were very difficult. But God had promised the Medlins through His Word that "He would keep the devourer away from their door." God worked miracle after miracle for them on that farm.

Roger and Kay had given $12,000 to help build a medical clinic in China, not realizing God would give it back to them. Roger farmed 400 acres of soybeans along the Mississippi River, which were subject to flooding. He was in the process of moving his tractors and equipment to this farm to apply the chemicals and plant the soybeans, but had an unexpected delay. It prevented him from getting the soybeans planted. In the meantime, the river started to rise and flooded the farm.

As Roger was driving along in his truck thinking about the situation, counting what he would have spent if he had gotten the crop planted, he realized it would have been about $12,000. Immediately the Holy Spirit spoke to him and said, "I gave it back to you—the money you gave to China." This was a confirmation that they had done the right thing in giving to the work of God in China.

The Sower's Wife Goes Back to School

In 1980, Kay and Roger had been married 20 years. Kay was 40 and had always enjoyed staying home with Roger and her daughters. However, something happened. Two colleges had been started in the boot heel area where they lived. Her old dream of being a registered nurse began to live again.

Kay began seeking the Lord for direction. She prayed and asked God what to do with her life. He gave her Jeremiah 33:3: "Call unto me and I will answer thee and show thee great and mighty things which thou knowest not." She felt that this was the call of God to her to go back to school.

Since graduating from college in 1984, she has worked part-time in the local hospital and taught as a clinical instructor at Dyersburg State Community College in Dyersburg,

Tennessee, and Mississippi County Community College in
Blytheville, Arkansas.

A Crisis Time for the Sower

Roger had been out of the collector's office for several
years when another crisis time came. Kay and two of their
daughters were in college. The farm was not doing well.
Farmers everywhere were having a difficult time. Again, God
came on the scene for them.

Without Kay and Roger knowing it, the state auditors
audited the books at the courthouse. When they did, they
discovered the county owed $35,000 to Roger because he had
not collected enough commission from the county while serving
as Collector of Revenue.

Roger and Kay had no idea the money was owed to
them. But God knew, and it came at just the right time. It was
the exact amount of money they owed.

The Sower Is Healed

Roger was scheduled to give his testimony at a Vision
conference at the School of Theology in Cleveland, Tennessee.
While he was working in his office, he lost his eyesight for about
15 minutes. It was like looking through an ice cube. The next
afternoon about the same time, it happened again. He went to
the local optometrist. After several extensive tests, the doctor
told him he had lost all his peripheral vision. The doctor said
that was an indication of a tumor on the optical nerve, or an
aneurysm, and he recommended that he see a specialist. He
made an appointment with a neurologist in Memphis,
Tennessee. He needed to have an MRI and an MRA. All that
Roger could do was cancel his testimony at the conference.
When he called Al Taylor to tell him his sad news, Al responded
by saying that he would contact the Prayerborne team to pray
for him.

When the neurologist talked to Roger before the tests, he confirmed the diagnosis of the other doctor—that it was either a tumor or an aneurysm. But after the doctor saw the results of the MRI and the MRA, he gave Roger the good news—no tumor, no aneurysm. In that Vision conference, Roger did not get to give his testimony, but what a testimony of answered prayer he had!

The Sower Sows Into Foreign Countries

In 1975 and again in 1976, Roger and Kay made a trip to Haiti, which was the beginning of their travels to mission fields. Through the years, Roger and Kay have contributed to many projects, including native workers, building churches, and giving to various ministers and workers. They have never kept a complete record of everything because they know God is the One who is keeping the record.

In 1986, Dr. Stonie Abercrombie started Volunteers in Medical Missions. Kay read about it in the Evangel and immediately joined. Here was her opportunity to become the missionary that she had always dreamed of being. This is why she went to nursing school. This was the longing of her heart. She has since traveled over the world from China to Africa to South America and Central America. God gave her all the things she had dreamed of as a little girl, but He did it in His own time and in His own way.

In 1997, Roger and Kay appealed to the local people in Caruthersville, Missouri, and raised over $35,000 to build a medical clinic in Honduras, Central America. This clinic sees an average of 60 patients per day, and 10 percent of those who come give their lives to Christ.

Another time they raised money to fill a shipping container to be sent to Romania. This container contained an 85 HP Tractor, blankets, food, medicine, and bicycles. At the present time they are working to secure a container to send to Honduras with medical equipment, soybeans, rice, and other supplies.

Volunteers in Medical Missions is an interdenominational Christian organization with headquarters in Seneca, South Carolina. The medical team consists of doctors, nurses, pharmacists, dentists, other allied health field specialists, and also non-medical persons. They also do evangelization as well as medical work. The Medlins have made many trips with this organization.

In 1995, Roger and Kay went to mainland China. They flew into the city of Kunming and traveled from there to a village called Luquan. From Luquan they traveled each day to various places to hold clinics. One day they traveled high into the mountains to a village close to the Burma border. The people were so happy to see them. They cooked for the Medlins with charcoal, giving them the best they had. It was so primitive, like stepping back in time. Kay says she will never be the same again after this experience.

One of their most exciting trips was in 1996 when they went to Iquitos, Peru, to take medicine to the Indians in the Rain Forest. They traveled down the Amazon River in small boats and then walked through the Rain Forest to where they were to stay. They stayed in an old school building built by the government. There was no electricity or running water. They slept on a concrete floor. But in spite of all the inconveniences, this was a most rewarding trip.

One man came into the clinic who had cut his hand with a machete. He had cut the ligaments to his fingers, and they were dangling. Two of the doctors on the team worked on the man's hand for about three hours. They carefully sewed all those ligaments back together. Kay started giving him antibiotics through the IV. The man had to return to the clinic every day for an injection of antibiotics to prevent infection. It was a thrill after six days to see him able to move his fingers. Kay wept, "Had we not been there, he would have died. We were there by divine appointment." They prayed with him and led him to a salvation experience for the first time in his life.

In 1997, the Medlins went with VIMM to Tanzania, Africa. They traveled inland from Arusha to a town called Singida and worked out of there. The village where their clinic was set up was called Yullansoni. Here they treated many traditional Africans. Many were wearing gold and brass rings around their necks and arms. Their clothes were handmade from leather. They carried their babies on their backs in homemade slings.

One man who came to the clinic had a growth on his neck. Dr. Abercrombie thought it was a goiter, but soon realized that it was a cyst. In a tiny grass hut with red dust blowing everywhere, Dr. Abercrombie performed surgery on him. The surgery was successful, and the man came back every day for antibiotics. By the end of the week, he was in great condition.

In 1991, 1998, 2000, 2001, and 2002, the Medlins went to Honduras. They are presently making plans to travel to Ecuador.

Sowing Is a Part of Obedience

Giving is a vital part of the Medlins' lives. It has not always been easy to give; but when there seemed to be no way, God provided a way.

Kay says, "Obedience is the key to blessing. We're valuable to Christ's kingdom because of our obedience." She continues, "You and I are responsible for two kinds of obedience—obedience to general commands and obedience to personalized commands. God's requirements, as taught in His Word, are for everyone, and we're responsible to obey them. If it is in God's Word, we need no further guidance. Tithing falls in this category. It is a matter of obedience for everyone. Some of God's requirements, however, are very personal. They are God's personal guidance to you, and we should obey quickly and gladly and faithfully."

The Medlins have been faithful over the years to God's general commands and His personalized commands. God has always been there for them in the good times and the bad times.

Roger's Elected Positions

1987-72   *R-3 School District Board Member*
1971-83   *Pemiscot County Collector of Revenue*
8 years   *University of Missouri Extension Council*
1991-94   *Presiding Commissioner of Pemiscot County, Mo.*
35 years *Church Clerk—Caruthersville Church of God*
6 years   *Volunteers in Medical Missions Board Member*

Roger's Appointed Positions

10 years *West Coast Christian College Board of Directors*
4 years   *Church of God General Study Commission*
6 years   *World Evangelism Commission Steering Committee*
4 years   *Missouri State World Missions Board*
23 years *Vision Foundation Board of Directors Charter Member*
7 years   *Local Church World Missions Representative*

Kay's Appointed Positions

1997—present   *Leader,Explorer's Bible Study, Caruthersville, Mo.*
2000—present   *Volunteers in Medical Missions Board Member*
2002—present   *Vice President, Habitat for Humanity,*
                       Caruthersville, Mo.

The Sower and His Wife Have a Philosophy

The philosophy of Roger and Kay can be summed up in her words at the School of Theology during a Vision conference. She said, "Does it bother me that most of the world goes to bed hungry at night when I have a pantry, refrigerator, and freezer full of food? Does it bother me that most of the world have only the clothes on their backs and nothing extra when I have a closet full? Does it bother me that most of the world goes to bed at night not knowing what may happen to them by morning or worse have no bed to sleep on while I lay down at night in peace and sleep well? It should and it does bother me. And I just pray that God will give me the grace to do what I can in the years that I have left, to continue to help my neighbors and those around the world that are hungry and naked and afraid. At the end of my life I will not be judged by whether I was a great scholar, if I had great influence or if I have great wealth or a great social background, but I will be judged by 'I was hungry and you gave me to eat. I was naked and you clothed me. I was homeless and you took me in.' It is usually ordinary people like me that Jesus calls, and Jesus needs ordinary people who will give themselves. He can do anything with people like that. ... We have so much to do and so little time to do it. ... Life is not an hour too long. Every moment of time allotted to us is necessary in realizing the divine plan that God has for our lives."

Roger Medlin
649 State Highway D
Caruthersville, MO 63830

Telephone
573-333-0379

E-mail
rogkmedlin@semo.net

Tony Metler—Visions From the Valley

Tony Metler—Visions From the Valley

Tony Metler was born in Knoxville, Tennessee, in a community called Lincoln Park. He had a hard-working family. His father was a contractor and a bridge builder. He started the trucking business in 1933. He was a tough, hard individual. Because of his work, he was gone a lot; but he had strong values which he passed down to his children.

Tony's mother was a kind and loving person. She chose not to work so that the children could always have her full attention. In every sense of the word, she was a homemaker.

Tony had two sisters, Jackie and Jane. They attended a very conservative school with good teachers who were also strong disciplinarians.

A Mighty Conversion

The Metler family always attended church and was involved in the Nazarene denomination until Tony was 11 years of age.

One of their neighbors was a church bus driver for Eighth Avenue Church of God. In 1950, there was a Thea Jones tent revival being held in Knoxville. This neighbor was gathering people to attend the revival. He invited Tony and his sisters to ride the bus with them.

The healing line at the end of the service impressed Tony and his sister Jackie. One night after the healing line was finished, Thea Jones gave an invitation for those who needed salvation to come forward. Tony and his sister could not get there fast enough. This became a life-changing experience for Tony. The lady who led him to the Lord that night was from the Nazarene church, but Tony felt a drawing to the Church of God at this time. Shortly afterwards, he and his sister, Jackie, started attending the Eighth Avenue Church of God. The Eighth Avenue Church had a lot of young people, and this was an added blessing for Tony and his sister. Soon his mother and other sister came. From this point on, church became Tony's life.

The Army Brought Discipline

Two weeks after graduation from high school, Tony volunteered for military service in the U. S. Army. This transition came as a shock to him. He loved his family and his home. However, the Army gave a lot of discipline to his life. Now it wasn't just mother and dad's standards, but the standards of the U. S. Army!

College Life

After the military time was served, Tony went home and attended college at Tennessee Tech in Cookeville, Tennessee. He knew he needed college in order to be successful working with his father in the trucking business.

Starting Into Business

After two and a half years, Tony chose to go home and work with his father. His father needed his help and felt that the business knowledge would be of more importance to him than the college education. Tony conceded to his father because he was tired of studying and wanted to make money.

Tony was 20 years of age by now. In 1960, he started out working in the maintenance, dispatch, and operations area of the company. From time to time, he filled in as a truck driver. From there, after two years his father gradually moved him into a management position. He accepted more and more responsibility and began saving for his own trucks.

He Rededicates His Life to the Lord and Finds a Wife

Tony had not been really involved in church while in the military or college. Getting home, he rededicated his life to the Lord.

At this time, he also met his wife, Billie. She is a giant among Christians. When they met, Tony was engrossed in trying to be successful in the business. Billie attended church every service. She prayed for Tony every day and stressed the importance of putting God first.

Soon after marriage they had two sons. Anthony was diagnosed as a diabetic when he was 16 months old. Paul was also diagnosed as a diabetic when he was 8 years old. Billie had attended Saint Mary's Hospital Nursing School. Therefore, she was prepared to be both nurse and mother. Several times they thought they would lose Anthony because he became so very sick. God always came through, and the Master Physician still cares for both sons!

Working in a family business can be challenging and difficult. In 1973 (only 13 years in the business), Tony's father made him president of the company, but his dad remained in charge. He set the salaries and had the final word. It was a big promotion for such a young man.

Cancer struck Mr. Metler, Tony's father, in 1978. Within a year, he went to be with the Lord. This was a tough time. There was pain at the reading of the will. Tony was hurt and bitter. He had thought he would be in total charge, but things changed while his father was on his deathbed. Tony says, "I was hurt. My response was to create hurt, and I did." He was soon convicted of that attitude. Immediately, he went to his sisters and his brothers-in-law and apologized. He publicly apologized before the church. It was at this difficult time Tony received the Holy Ghost, and a new Comforter touched his life.

However, the pain remained. There were many long nights when Tony just wanted to be with his sisters; but they weren't there. He had his mother. He had Billie's mother, sister, and dad for support, but he didn't have his sisters. He says, "It took me 15 years and a million dollars to restore the relationships with my relatives." The days of resolving family issues were difficult. However, this time of suffering caused

Tony to grow closer to God and his family. After much prayer, God restored the family as one family again.

God Blesses the Business

After their father's death, the sisters took the construction business, and Tony took the trucking transport business.

God's blessings came to Tony's business. There were difficult times, but God was always there. Driver demand is a part of this business. Further, his business was a highly specialized business, so he had to have excellent drivers. Finding these drivers was sometimes challenging.

Tony's philosophy was to do what you do better than everybody else does it. He knew you had to add value to whatever you do and do better than your competing carrier. He came up with a unique idea. The A. J. Metler Hauling and Rigging, Inc., transported flat glass from the factory to the manufacturers and the distributing centers. This added value. They devised systems to transport without crates. This saved the shipper the expense of buying a crate; then the consumer did not have to destroy the crate.

The company grew until they were operating in the United States, Canada, and Mexico. They had 600 employees.

Many things affected the business. The ups and downs in the housing industry affected them. When the housing projects were booming, they would be busy.

When the business was strong, Tony blessed people in ministry. T. L. Lowery needed a prefabricated building brought from Alabama to Washington, D. C., when he was building his new church. Metler Hauling and Rigging, Inc., transported the building for him. Tony also transported shrubbery for the church. Further, he gathered clothes and food in Knoxville and hauled it to Terry Gooden on the Indian Reservation in New Mexico.

T. L. Lowery had them haul the huge tent he used for revivals almost everywhere he went. The Metlers even stored his tent in some of their trailers. When churches needed help in transportation, if they could fit it into their schedule on their way to some city, they did it. Tony's father had been a very giving person. That made an impact on Tony and all of his employees.

Open Door Policy

Once you walked inside the office building of Metler Hauling and Rigging, Inc., you saw only open offices with modular furniture. Tony wanted employees and customers to know he was always available. One of the guiding principles was "be accessible."

Tony attempted to hire people with high morals and leadership skills. He let Christ shine through him to his employees, as he ran the business with high standards. He required high integrity from all employees. Alcohol was never permitted. Inappropriate language was not allowed.

Tony shared the budget of the company with the employees. They always knew his plans and goals. They knew if the business was successful or failing. Further, they knew when they needed to put their best foot forward for the company. He always reinvested in the company, knowing God would bless him for his openness.

Seeing the Needs in Foreign Countries

Another change came in 1985 when Tony went to Germany to buy some trailers. When he arrived in Germany the plant was closed. The owner lived next door; so Tony knocked on the door, and the owner's wife appeared. No English. No German. They had a hard time trying to communicate. She knew he was an American and wanted to look at trailers. Finally, she found someone to show him the trailers. The Metlers and this couple are friends to this day.

In 1988 Tony was invited to go to China. This opened Tony's eyes to the needs of the world. He asked, "What can I do in China? I am just one person." Since then, he has made four trips to China. On one occasion in 1995, Tony worked there for eight weeks.

Later, Tony went to Vietnam to meet with the underground church. It took him five weeks to get to the underground church, which he was determined to reach. He was there when this group became members of the Church of God. God was dealing with Tony Metler about the great harvest around the world.

God Heals Their Son

Tony's son, Anthony, was in business with him, and his diabetes was getting worse. In 1998, Anthony was in the intensive care unit of the hospital. He had the flu and became dehydrated. His blood sugar elevated tremendously. Anthony and his family were frightened when a nurse could not find a pulse in Anthony's foot. The doctors thought they might have to amputate. The foot was snow white and felt like ice. They X-rayed his leg and found no circulation from the knee down. They could not identify arteries. Billie and Tony and all the family, church families, employees, and Max Morris' World Wide Prayer Partners prayed. In a few days, Anthony was up playing golf, living a normal life. God gave Anthony a testimony to use for His glory.

God Leads Them to Sell the Business

In 1998, there was strong competition in the business. They either had to make major investments in their technology or sell. Tony and Billie prayed much. Schneider National was the number one company in the United States. They heard Tony might be willing to sell, so they purchased the company assets. The family had the assurance this was God's will; that He had answered prayer.

Tony was left with property that provides a good income. He owns the truck terminal. He takes care of the property and leases space out to the company that bought him out. He also leases space to a hospital, and a health care provider leases one office. Tony's concern is just to keep the buildings occupied. He has become a landlord of Metler properties in three states.

God Closes One Door and Opens Another

After God directed the Metlers out of the business, He led them to missions work. Tony has done much work in Ecuador. He also works on various projects with the Indians in New Mexico.

Tony saw 1,500 people saved in one crusade in Ecuador. He loves the Church of God superintendent of Ecuador. Tony saw the man's heart was consumed by God's work. They did not have churches ready for the new converts. They did not have ministers ready to take care of the people. Metler learned that a training center could be built for $75,000. It appeared it would take them three years to get the building built.

Tony's mother had just died and left him some money. He and Billie did not need the money for anything. Tony told the people to go ahead and build. He said, "Take my mother's money and build it today so that God can train men and women tomorrow and not have to wait three years." They got the building completed in nine months. Then inflation hit the country. If Tony had waited to give the money for the training center, it would have cost $200,000. He said, "What Mom did for me, I just passed it right on to the work of the Lord."

Tony and Billie are consumed by the work of God. They work through the Church of God World Missions Department and Visions From the Valley, their own 501C-3 corporation. This way, Tony can work through the church or his own non-profit organization. Further, he can get help from major corporations.

Tony is always getting containers ready to send to the field. He gets people to donate items such as computers, hospital equipment, desks, clothes, wedding gowns, etc. He finds people are willing to give to the cause of Christ, if they are asked.

Tony has worked with numerous projects in Ecuador. On one occasion he supplied money so that the ministers could buy guinea pigs to start a business. He also provided motorcycles for ministers.

One of Tony's special projects was funding a Christian corporation in Ecuador to provide day-care facilities for 18 locations. They feed 800 children from birth to age 6. They feed them two meals a day and two snacks. They have preschool activities. This is conducted in some churches and other locations.

Metler basically furnishes the seed money. When the facility is operating, the government will give support.

The success in Ecuador and other countries of the world is unbelievable. Tony says, "The biggest challenge we have is to build facilities and then follow up on them."

Tony is sometimes asked, "What is your title?" He has a standard answer, "Layman!" He does not need a title. When he sees a need, he fills it. When he sees a hurt, he heals it. When he goes to Ecuador and sees the people camped out in tents just to be in a crusade, he is rewarded for all he does. A good crusade there will attract 7,000 people. He often provides food for the people and straw mats for them to sleep on.

There are many needs and many hurting people, but Ecuador is Tony's project. It is the place that makes his heart beat faster. He loves the people and the country.

Billie prays for the Ecuadorian people daily. She also spends many hours on the computer praying with people on-line all over the world. She prays mostly in the evenings. However, throughout the day she stops, gets prayer requests off the computer, and then prays.

Tony and Billie are faithful to the Church of God. Tony has been a member of the Church of God for 50 years, and Billie is a third generation member. Both sons and their families are actively involved in teaching ministries in their home churches.

Memberships and Offices Held

- *Chairman and Board member, Specialized Carriers and Riggers Association*
- *Board of Directors, First Tennessee Bank*
- *Chairman, Business Development Committee*
- *Board of Directors, Church of God Theological Seminary*
- *Chancellor's Associate, University of Tennessee*
- *Vision Foundation, Board of Directors*

Special Awards

- *Church of God Layman's Hall of Fame*
- *Pinnacle Award, Transportation*
- *Golden Achievement Award, Transportation*

Tony and Billie have one purpose in life—get the gospel to as many people as possible and bless everybody they meet.

Tony Metler
6507 South Northshore
Knoxville, TN 37919

Telephone
865-558-9901

His e-mail
AaMetler@juno.com

Her e-mail
BBMetler@aol.com

Carl Richardson—The Imaginator

Carl Richardson—The Imaginator

It had been prophesied to Carl Richardson, "I will use you in a larger place." How could this happen? He had already preached to masses around the world. He had held large crusades throughout the nation. He had been the director of Forward in Faith, had been on radio and television all over the nation. Then he finds himself standing on a platform in an open field situated between four mountains and a huge valley in Petersburg, South Africa. It was the most awesome sight he had ever seen. The people looked like ants moving in the distance from every direction, coming toward the crowd. South African army and police officials estimated the crowd to be more than 3 million people.

Two hundred trains and 2,000 buses were chartered to bring the South Africans to the meeting from all over the country. The African National Congress, a militant guerilla group, had claimed the credit for dynamiting a train the night before, killing 15 people and sending over 50 to the hospital.

The Johannesburg Sun's morning paper read, "The African National Congress plans to turn that valley into a sea of blood. If anyone is foolish enough to come hear the American evangelist, they will choke on their own blood."

Carl preached, "Never give up!" After he had finished this powerful sermon, he asked the people to kneel before the living God. Tears flooded Carl's eyes as he saw all 3 million kneel and ask God to become Lord of their lives and heal their land. He then led them in a simple prayer for salvation.

The 900 pastors who sponsored the meeting lined the riverbanks. Carl shouted, "All of you who prayed that prayer for the first time in your life, please make your way to the riverbank. There will be a pastor there to baptize you in water." Nine hundred pastors baptized at lest 200 new converts each.

Carl and his team also traveled on a top-secret mission to record other footage in the revolutionary capital of Jamba, located deep in the jungles of Angola. Their military helicopter flew at tree-top level to keep stinger missiles, manned by the Angolan Communist military, from shooting them out of the sky. Carl and his team were moved by the abject poverty of the people.

The TV special was aired Labor Day weekend, 1989, on more than 100 stations. The next day it was said that the U. S. Capitol switchboard lighted up like a Christmas tree. People were calling in, asking the U. S. government to drop the sanctions against South Africa because it was hurting the people the sanctions were intended to help.

The Making of an Imaginator

What qualified Carl Richardson, who had been born in a coal camp in Harlan, Kentucky, to be trusted with such a weighty responsibility? There was always turmoil in the Richardson home when Carl was a child. His father was an alcoholic, bringing much suffering to the family. But he dropped an idea in Carl's mind early. At Christmas, when Carl was about 5 years old, his father bought him a special Christmas gift—a microphone. Paul Richardson helped his son hook the microphone up to the family's table-top radio to amplify his voice through the radio speaker. Carl wore the microphone out, practicing every day to be a radio announcer and a preacher.

Carl accepted the Lord at the age of 9. He was called to preach at age 14. His first sermon was a disaster. Cora Watson, mother of Missionary Bill Watson, invited the young preacher for a weekend youth revival for her in Centerburg, Ohio, about 40 miles from his hometown of Columbus. He knew he had to prepare three sermons—one for Saturday night and two for Sunday. He started fantasizing that perhaps they would invite him back the following weekend, so he prepared six sermons, all designed for a duration which Carl reckoned to be about 20 minutes each.

On opening night, he stood up to preach. Within only seven minutes he had finished preaching—all six sermons. He said later he secretly wished that a trap door would have opened up and swallowed him.

Many years later, Carl shared that story of what he had surmised to be total failure in a camp meeting service at the Canton, Ohio, Memorial Auditorium with several thousand present. After the service when he was moving through the crowd, someone grabbed him by the elbow and turned him around. A couple and two ladies stood there smiling. The man spoke: "I am Silvo Stewart. This is my wife Dorothy and her two sisters. I want you to know all four of us were present in that service when you preached your first sermon. And we don't remember your first sermon as a failure. We had never been to that kind of church before that night. In fact, we were so touched by your sincerity that night that Dorothy and I were the first couple to walk forward and accept the Lord. We did not know how to pray, but you instructed us word for word in the sinner's prayer. We've been serving the Lord ever since. I've been a Sunday school superintendent for 24 years. My wife has been an officer in the church. That was the greatest night of our lives."

His big thinking really developed when he attended the Ohio State University. He took all the courses in radio and television the school offered at that time. He requested to take even the graduate courses. The dean agreed—if he maintained a 3.5 grade average (B+).

During this time he gained practical experience. He began working with the college-owned television station. He worked with both sides of the camera. He did commercials, standups, news, sports, and weather.

The Evangelist Imaginator

In the summer of 1954, the 15-year-old Carl Richardson boarded a Greyhound bus headed for Toledo for his first revival after Centerburg. Soon talk began about the Richardson boy who blew the trumpet and had such a passion for souls. Carl had posters printed with his picture on them with the words: Teenage Evangelist. His revivals became very successful.

At this early age, Carl had the conviction that if you were going to see revival, then you had to pray. He prayed every day during his meetings. He often called all night prayer vigils on Friday night.

The Beginning of a Worldwide Ministry

It became obvious that the hand of God rested heavily upon this young evangelist. But God had bigger plans—a worldwide ministry. Pastor Odine Wolfe invited him to come to Nassau, Bahamas, where he had started a new church called Faith Temple out of the old Fowler Street New Testament Church of God. Odine had a beautiful building, but his attendance was small. Carl went. This was the greatest revival he had ever held up to this time. The building was packed every night for three weeks. The altars were filled with hungry people seeking God. The church had averaged about 60 in attendance before the revival and never dipped under 400 after the revival.

While conducting a revival in Canton, Ohio, he met the young lady who became his partner throughout his ministry around the world. She sang the last night of his revival. Carl liked her immediately. As soon as church was over, he went down to the front, right at the altar where she was standing and formally introduced himself. A year and a half later he married Bev at the same altar where he met her. Memorable places and events hold meaning to Carl.

By the time Carl was 21 years old, he was preaching camp meetings. H. B. Ramsey had first invited him to be the night speaker for the Georgia camp meeting. Then while Carl was still only 21, D. A. Biggs, who became a father figure to Carl, invited him to be the night speaker in South Carolina.

Things changed! Their first son, Paul David, was born to this evangelistic couple. Traveling and staying in homes with pastors was very difficult on Bev. There are always seasons for every ministry.

Carl and Bev went for a revival campaign with W. C. and Tannis Byrd in Lakeland, Florida. Somebody was saved or filled with the Holy Ghost every night. Over 50 people received the Holy Ghost in the meeting and joined the church. Many were baptized in water. Carl and W. C. would get up every day at 5 a.m. and head for the church to pray for at least two hours. Men on their way to work would come by and join them in prayer. This began a relationship which lasted through the years.

The Imaginator Learns to Be a Shepherd

The church in Ashland, Ohio, needed a pastor and Carl and Bev were appointed. Ashland was a small conservative town. God blessed their ministry while here and let them learn some of the joys of shepherding. Their second child, Juanelle, was born while they were here.

New Adventures for Anointed Imagination

The phone rang one day with new direction for the couple. The Executive Committee of the Church of God asked Carl to move to Chicago to plant new churches. He and Bev decided to do it as a new adventure of faith. In only six months they had planted three new churches—all of which are still thriving today. His strategy here was a relational-driven ministry. During their ministry in Chicago, a little girl named Christi was born into the Richardson family.

Very shortly after Christi's birth, there was a call for another new assignment. Dr. James A. Cross, the overseer of Florida called saying that the Lake Wire Church of God in Lakeland had voted 100 percent for him to come be their pastor.

The second Sunday Carl and Bev were at the Lake Wire church, Overseer James Cross came to dedicate their new baby and to ordain Carl and Bev into the ministry. At that time you

had to be 25 years old to be ordained. Here they spent three of
the happiest years of their lives.

Imagination as a State Leader

Then an unexpected call came to be evangelism director
of Florida. Overseer D.A. Biggs said, "I want you to build the
best evangelism program in the country. You do the evangelism,
and I will do the conflict resolution."

Once again Carl turned his creativity loose. He built a
team of about 15 powerful evangelists whose pay was
subsidized from their state. He created news releases for them,
business cards, posters, hand-out invitation cards, etc. When the
evangelists had cancellations, Carl helped get them booked. He
and Tommy Morse started Surfside Challenge, a ministry to the
street people and drug addicted youth. This was a happy four
years for the Richardsons. During this time Carl was invited to
be camp meeting speaker for about 12 states and conducted yet
another revival campaign at Lee College.   Carl's reputation was
spreading.

The Call for Imagination for Radio and Television

Next came one of the greatest fulfillments of his calling to
the ministry. In May 1972, at age 32, Carl received a call from
General Overseer Ray H. Hughes, Sr. "Carl, I'm calling to
inform you that you have been elected to be the new Forward in
Faith radio speaker. I feel, along with the Council, that this is an
opportunity for an expanded ministry for you and for the
denomination. You will assume your duties on June 1."   Carl
and Bev knew this was a call of destiny.

Divine appointments have always been significant to
Carl. In 1970, Carl met Al Taylor at an altar where they had
randomly prayed together during a General Assembly. He
learned that Al was a regional manager for Encyclopedia
Britannica and was a very successful businessman with whom
Bev attended Lee College.

One year later, while serving as evangelism director in Florida, he went to Cleveland for an evangelism and home missions rally. He walked into the Lee College auditorium while Al Taylor, a layman, was speaking. Carl was captivated by Al's voice. It was perfectly modulated. At that time Carl thought, "That guy would make a great radio announcer." He never forgot Al; nor Al's voice.

Only days after beginning his duties with *Forward in Faith*, Carl was preaching a long-scheduled camp meeting in Jackson, Mississippi. That night he lay awake thinking, dreaming, and praying about his new assignment. He knew he had to have the right staff. Suddenly it hit him. Al Taylor! I wonder where he lives? He made a mental note to have his secretary get Al's phone number the next day.

Then the most unusual thing happened. At 7:30 a.m. he heard a knock at his motel door. There stood Al Taylor. He was there that day for the layman's luncheon and was in the room next door to Carl. "Hi, Brother Carl! I have heard about your new appointment and wanted to say congratulations and let's have breakfast." This was destiny.

As they shared over breakfast, Al talked about some of the people he had won to Christ. He led as many of his salesmen to Christ as possible. He felt it was good business because once they found Christ they made better workers. He shared his vision of getting laymen turned on to witnessing. He witnessed to people everywhere he could get a listening ear.

Then Carl asked Al if he believed in signs, dreams, and visions. He shared with Al what had just happened. Carl told Al, "I want to invite you, if you will come with me, and we will put together a communications ministry like this denomination has never seen before."

Then Carl asked respectfully, "How much do you make in your annual pay?" The pay by the church for an administrative assistant was a meager $10,000 per year. Al was earning many times that amount. He argued with Carl, "The Executive

Committee will never appoint a layman to that position anyway. There are too many preachers wanting it." They both agreed to pray about it.

Carl sent the recommendation for Al Taylor to be his administrative assistant to the Executive Committee. He knew it was revolutionary to think a layman would be appointed to such a position, but he felt they might possibly go along with it.

He received word back: "Sorry, we cannot approve Al Taylor, a layman, to serve as administrative assistant for *Forward in Faith*. Send us another name."

Carl's response to them was, "I have no other name. Will you please reconsider?" They turned him down the second time.

On Friday night of the 54th General Assembly, August 18, 1972, Carl preached to more than 10,000 people. His assigned subject was "It is time to seek the Lord." Even the compliments about Carl's powerful message did not stop the ache in his heart. He wanted Al Taylor to come with him to Forward in Faith.

The next morning Al was scheduled to speak at the Layman's Breakfast. Carl's mentor, W. C. Byrd, was now serving on the Executive Committee. Carl went to find W. C.

"Brother Byrd, I have a ticket to the layman's breakfast in the morning. I would like for you to be my guest. I need to talk with you."

"Sure, Carl. I was proud of you tonight."

Carl and Brother Byrd sat together at breakfast. Al was at his best as he spoke to the laymen that morning. Carl began to share with W. C. Byrd the events that had happened and how he felt God was leading the two of them together. Carl then said to W. C. Byrd, "I would appreciate your not asking how I found out about the vote, but I understand the vote was three to two. I also learned that you voted no. If you will change your vote, I can have the man I feel God wants for *Forward in Faith.* Will you consider changing your vote?"

Byrd replied, "You know this is unprecedented in church history to appoint a layman to such a position, but if it means that much to you, you have my vote. I'll tell the other committee members that I have changed my mind." Carl and Al were now coworkers for *Forward in Faith.*

It was as if Carl had been born for this hour in the history of *Forward in Faith.* Writer Hoyt Stone describes his radio style: "Carl spoke in a rapid, staccato voice, consuming paragraphs like a news commentator. He was fond of alliterations, each line building on the previous one, with his words, flooding faster and higher to a climax." Much time had to be spent in research and sermon preparation, about 20 hours per sermon.

The moments the new coworkers had together were precious indeed. Hoyt Stone writes in his book, The Fire Within: "Listen to this Al," Carl would say. "A letter from Illinois. The penitentiary. Fellow writes he heard us last week right in his prison cell. Fell on his knees there and accepted Christ as Lord. That's what is great about radio. It gets in behind the closed doors where other preachers can't go. It catches people in their cars, when they least expect it. Oh, man, I tell you, Al, this has to be the most exciting ministry in the world." Letters began to flood the office.

In 1974, Jerry Noble, a long-time minister friend from Ohio, was added to the staff as media coordinator; also in answer to prayer and hard work behind the scenes. Jerry proved adept at organizing and coordinating the burgeoning ministry opportunities.

It became immediately obvious that they had to get more radio stations and more money. Al knew how to get money— sales. The team began to produce tapes and books for additional income to the ministry. After his regular office hours, Carl recorded an interpretative reading of the entire New Testament, the Psalms and the Proverbs.

They were "in business" for *Forward in Faith.* Professional voice-actor Greg Oliver from Atlanta did the interpretative reading of the "Words of Jesus." He read 582 pages of script in one day and later testified that it was the hardest day's work in his life but also by far the most enjoyable.

Within a year after Carl became radio speaker and director of *Forward in Faith,* he made plans for a nationwide TV special to be called "New World Coming." Subsequently it was to be aired on 187 network television stations on a pre-emptible basis mainly on the Tuesday night before Thanksgiving in November 1974. Before it could be aired, a budget of $300,000 had to be raised. Carl, Jerry, and Al traveled throughout the United States with promotional rallies. Miraculously, the budget was raised after an exhausting schedule of one-night events in local churches.

Carl knew that network affiliated television stations would not accept just another church service, especially during prime evening viewing hours of 8:00 to 10:30.

Carl planned the program for the unsaved. It was aimed at those who had lost hope. However, it also brought hope to discouraged believers. He intended for this to be a program of network-quality excellence. Tom Ivy, a professional producer from Hollywood and Ted Dienert, son-in-law and producer for Billy Graham, came in to help. Carl, Al, and Jerry set up special toll-free phone lines.

Within seconds after the program went off the air in 187 network affiliated stations, the lines lit up. Over 600 people were saved. They recorded some of the phone calls. Al and Jerry stayed with Carl until 5 o'clock in the next morning answering the phones and leading people to Christ until the calls slowed. Then the cleaning lady led over 11 people to the Lord. The next morning when the headquarters building opened, the phones started ringing again. The Holy Spirit had touched people from all over the nation.

Over 20,000 letters flooded the *Forward in Faith* office the following week. Many of the letters were telling of experiences of salvation. Others were letters from Christians congratulating the team for the professional cutting-edge approach. There were also critics. Some thought it had too much Hollywood glitz and expressed that they had rather have seen a good robed church choir sing followed by Carl preaching a traditional style sermon.

Further, Carl was called in to see the Executive Council. He thought they were going to congratulate his team for a job well done. But instead, the general overseer told him his office had been bombarded with complaints.

Stunned, Carl responded cautiously at first, "What are you being bombarded with: B-52's? Two B-52's, a thousand F-105 jet fighters? What kind of bombardment?" Reluctantly, they admitted to Carl that the "bombardment" came from only five preachers and two state overseers.

Carl's answer was, "I have 20,000 letters in my office of appreciation. There were 5,300 letters that arrived just today. Would you mind just briefly, brethren, listening to this tape that we recorded of what really happened?" Then Carl played the tape of people being saved recorded spontaneously on the telephone. From across the room, men began to weep.

At this time, Carl began to understand that you often recognize a pioneer by the arrows in his back. He and his team encouraged themselves in the Lord and went forward in faith.

His next television production was the week of April 4-10, 1976. This was the most costly production he ever did. The production cost was over $100,000, and he and his team had to raise the money for it themselves. It was staged in a jam-packed Constitution Hall in Washington, D.C., on Friday evening, April 9, 1976. The next morning, Saturday, April 10, almost 5,000 people went to their knees with Carl and his team in a prayer for the nation during the bicentennial prayer gathering.

People from all over the nation had responded to Carl's invitation to be with him for this historic production. He had advertised heavily using the scripture: "If my people, which are called by my name, shall humble themselves and pray, and seek my face, and turn from their wicked ways; then will I hear from heaven, and will forgive their sin and will heal their land" (2 Chronicles 7:14). Steve Brock sang the new song written by Bennie Triplett, "Jesus, Heal the People." The Lee College Singers sang a medley of songs, including "Praise the Lord" and "Give Thanks America." The Churchmen Trio from Cullman, Alabama, sang "The Cross: My Statue of Liberty." The thousands who were present from across the nation felt they were a part of history, and they were.

When "Freedom Celebration" was aired, on Saturday night, July 3, 1976, there were over 18 million people watching the only Christian program broadcast nationally during America's 200th celebration. The people of the Church of God felt justifiable pride in the daring and scope of this outreach.

"Twentieth Century Day of Pentecost" was the next nationwide TV special aired in 1978. Previous to this viewing, Carl had become a friend of J. F. Rowlands from South Africa. In 1975 Carl had been the featured speaker in the South African Bethesda Ministry's 25th anniversary. More than 25,000 assembled at the Royal Showgrounds in Pietermaritzburg; at the time a record numerical gathering for the denomination.

In early 1978, Carl conducted a series of crusades for Rowlands, ending on Pentecost Sunday. There were 37,000 people present with over a thousand people receiving the Holy Spirit. It seemed natural that South Africa would play a part in the TV special "Twentieth Century Day of Pentecost." Many felt that this was the best production.

By this time Carl had a mailing list of 50,000 people. About 8,000 of these were regular supporters. A weekly program called "Power Unlimited" was begun in 1983. This was exhausting work—scheduling special guests, making travel arrangements, rehearsals, and raising the budget. Over 1,800 cable systems were airing this program, including TBN, CBN, PTL, NCN, and some 80 other regular television stations.

From 1972 until 1984 the staff grew to about 57 full-time employees and over 100 during TV specials. Fred Mercer and Henry "Bud" Robinson headed up other administrative duties and marketing. This executive staff, including Al, Jerry, and Carl became a band of Christian brothers, a tightly knit group of abiding friends.

He Imagines Vision Foundation

Carl always surrounded himself with people who could help birth his vision. He envisioned a foundation of business persons owned by the laymen themselves, which had the capacity to sponsor projects such as Forward in Faith and other ministries.

Carl understood there were times when businessmen and women wanted to give to ministry, but their local churches often wanted to control their giving. The businessmen and women often had dreams and visions much bigger than their local church could handle. Further, when they gave heavily, they often felt ostracized from other members of their church. There was a need for men and women who could give, and there was a need for relationship among leading business persons. God helped Carl put together a good group of men and women who could have their own foundation and put their money where they felt impressed of the Lord to do so.

Thus, Vision Foundation was officially formed on May 10, 1977, in Cleveland, Tennessee. It was and yet remains a corporation "not for profit" to be operated exclusively for religious, educational, and charitable purposes. Three men signed the articles of incorporation: Carl H. Richardson, successful businessman Hugh Statum, and Attorney John B. White. Hoyt Stone reports in the history of Vision Foundation: "From the very beginning Vision Foundation recognized *Forward in Faith* ministries as a primary but not an exclusive avenue of ministry."

On September 23, 1977, there was a meeting of the Vision Foundation members at the Sheraton Inn in Gatlinburg, Tennessee. Carl Richardson and John White were made ex officio nonvoting members of the board. The elected board of directors were Hugh Statum, Bill Higginbotham, Don Medlin, Bill Hildreth, Art Hodge, Ron Free, Roger Gupton, Francis Duncan, Dan Winters, Autry Dawsey, Arlis Roberts and Wilburn Powell.

In their first year of existence, the Vision Foundation team was responsible for almost $2 million, which was channeled into Holy Spirit directed ministries.

At a Vision banquet at a subsequent General Assembly, Carl mentioned that *Forward in Faith* needed television equipment. Someone asked the cost. A man wrote a check for $38,000 right there on the spot. It broke open the floodgates. Over $100,000 was raised at that banquet, which enabled the purchase of cameras, other needed equipment and began the actual planning for a regular weekly television program which soon followed.

Missionary L. E. Heil had returned from Japan to Cleveland because of his wife's health. L. E. was an outstanding builder. He had built a commercial building on property located just off 25th Street on Guthrie Drive. This contemporary building was called the Pan Southern Building and was ideal for office space. The property was difficult to lease. Al Taylor approached Heil about making the building a charitable contribution. Vision Foundation would accept it, pay off all creditors, and then give it to the Church of God for a ministry building.

When Carl returned from a trip to Africa, Al told him that while he was away, Vision had obtained a building which could be used by *Forward in Faith*. Astonished to a state of uncharacteristic silence, Carl could hardly believe it. Their chronic office space problem had been miraculously solved. Carl, Al, Jerry, and Hugh Statum celebrated God's faithfulness.

In December 1978, ownership of the building was transferred to the Church of God, and it was named the Forward in Faith Center. From this building flowed ministry, including cassettetapes, books, supplies and letters recognizing donor gifts from around the world. In 1980, the Forward in Faith team built and dedicated new state-of-the-art studio facilities for recording just behind the *Forward in Faith* Center, on land purchased by Vision Foundation and given for that purpose.

One of the ongoing highlights of the General Assembly was the Vision Awards Banquet. Staff and board members from *Forward in Faith* would listen to radio and television programs submitted by pastors. Numerous "Golden Mike" awards were given away at this banquet. Carl's philosophy was that any organization reproduces what it rewards. In the summer of 1980, the general overseer phoned Carl while he and Bev were traveling near Tuscon, Arizona, to give him the "good news" and the "bad news" that Al Taylor had been selected to head up a newly formed stewardship ministry in the denomination. Carl knew the loss to himself, personally, and to the ministries of *Forward in Faith* would be severe, but he reasoned that Al had more than deserved to be the first layman ever selected as an executive department head. He and Carl have remained steadfast friends over the years. Al's connection with the men and women of Vision Foundation would be vital in the years to come.

The months and the years seemed to fly by. The ministry growth and expansion seemed nonstop. Carl and his staff continued working 12-16 hours a day. They were being blessed, but were tired; bone tired. The staff went to major cities every weekend to conduct television rallies. They sold tapes and Bibles and got monthly pledges.

Sunday mornings the team split up and conducted four services in four different churches, then four more churches on Sunday night. Hoyt Stone reports: "In 1972 when Carl took office, the department's annual budget was $159,000 with 90 percent of the money coming from church tithe appropriation; but by 1984, the department's annual budget had expanded to approximately $2 million, with only about 10 percent of that money coming from the tithe fund. Sales, services, and freewill contributions were generating the rest of the ministry's budget."

Over the months of late 1983 and early 1984, Carl became spiritually restless. One day while thumbing through his Bible during one of those restless seasons, he read the words again: "Enlarge the place of thy tent, and let them stretch forth the curtains of thine habitations; spare not, lengthen thy cords, and strengthen thy stakes; for thou shalt break forth on the right hand and on the left" (Isaiah 54:2-3).

Of course, he and Beverly processed the change occurring, and he even opened the subject of a radical change of direction in ministry with Jerry Noble en route to their weekly series of TV rallies in Columbus, Ohio.

There were rumblings of a dramatic change in the financial priorities of the church. Carl had called for such a rethinking of the denominational financial priorities for several years in public forums and in private meetings. He had fervently hoped for media to become a major financial priority of the church.

Months later at a regularly scheduled lunch, he talked to his good friends Bob Fisher and Lamar Vest. "Who knows? Maybe I could do more for the Lord as just Carl Richardson than director of radio and television." Carl really expected his friends to try and talk him out of it; but they didn't.

While there, he received an urgent message from the Executive Council Finance Committee to be there in 10 minutes with copies of his annual budget. Who knows? Carl thought to himself as he drove toward the headquarters building from his working lunch with Bob Fisher and Lamar Vest. They may, at last, be willing to include radio and television as a major priority by providing more money to help impact the global harvest.

That day the Council was working urgently on the entire budget. Within a minute of when Carl walked into their meeting with copies of his budget in hand, one of the members spoke up: "Carl, the reason we have asked you to come is because we want to know if your department can handle it if we take the $145,000 we give your ministry and give it all to education? Our education centers are in desperate need."

Carl responded earnestly (and surprisingly to the committee members), "Yes, of course. If education is the top priority of the church, by all means take it and give it to education."

When he left the room, he knew he was going to be an international evangelist. The denominational leaders did not even suspect what had been happening in Carl's heart for months. And now, verification, and reverse affirmation, of what he had earnestly hoped would happen. On the way home, he seemed to hear the Lord say (with a smile in His voice), "What else do I have to do to convince you, Carl? Now do you believe I want you to leave *Forward in Faith*? I am calling you to a new direction."

How could he have been so blind? Carl began to laugh uproariously. Then his laughter turned to weeping. He went home, told Beverly, and together they decided, "Our future is changing. We are going to be bridge builders to the whole body of Christ. We're going to see what God will do."

Bev asked Carl when he was going to resign. Carl replied, "Next week after the council has left." Jerry Noble and Fred Mercer also felt led to resign at the same time after talking with their wives with Carl and Bev.

On April 10, 1984, Carl and his coworkers submitted their resignations. They did not mean for it to be made immediately public, but the editor of the *Cleveland Daily Banner* got the word quickly and had it on the afternoon's front page. Phone calls, letters, cards, telegrams, and cablegrams started pouring in from all over the world. Carl and Bev felt loved and appreciated.

On May 14, 1984, Carl met with the Executive Council to discuss the state of the ministry. After about 50 minutes, Carl closed his notebook and left the room. As he exited, the Council gave him a standing ovation. He went outside the Council chambers into a nearby empty room and wept profusely.

At a farewell gathering of 120 employees of the Church of God, Carl and Bev delivered a message on "What Makes a Good Goodbye?" They quoted author Ellen Goodman who said, "I believe there's a trick to the graceful exit. It begins with the vision to recognize when a job, a life stage, a relationship is over—and to let go. It means leaving what's over without denying its validity or its past importance in our lives. It involves a sense of future, a belief that with every exit line is an entry, that we are moving on, rather than out." Carl and Bev felt that this was for their best and the best for God's work.

The Imaginator Expands His Borders

At this time the Richardsons felt led of the Lord to move to Brandon, Florida, in suburban Tampa. Understandably, they also consulted their youngest son, Jonathan, a senior in high school. He said earnestly, "Go wherever the Lord leads you. No problem with me." That typified the spirit of the other children who were by now also young adults.

Bev's brother had found a large house that required no money down. It was a well-built, repossessed house with five bedrooms, five baths, and a recreation room, which they immediately turned into offices. There was another area in the back, a hobby room that they turned into temporary recording studios.

It was a new day for the Richardsons. With no salary, no underwriting, and no official position in the church, they leaned even more heavily on the Lord than ever before.

Carl and Bev are both visionaries. They know that vision is the key to success. You must be able to see it; to preplay it in your mind. Vision is a spiritual principle. It is the ability to see what almost no one else can see and the ability to do what almost nobody else believes can be done. Autry Dawsey can look at a piece of property or land and can know if it has potential and what to do with it to make a success. Carl has that same ability with the harvest. He can look at a city or even an entire nation and instinctively know what needs to be done to reap a mighty harvest.

Miracles in the Philippines Surpassed His Imagination

The Philippines were always a love of Carl's. In 1988, he took what he called a Healing Team to the Philippines. The team set up a Daytime School of Ministry. There were over 300 in attendance. Carl Richardson Ministries paid everybody's tuition, fed them for five days, gave them a salary and humanitarian assistance. The school went from 8:30 a.m. until 4 p.m. each day. They came hungry for the Word, ready to be taught, and eager to learn that they might teach others.

Each night Carl ministered in the historic Rizal Theater auditorium, which was packed. Every night hundreds responded to receive Christ. In one night more than 200 received the Holy Spirit baptism. Hundreds were miraculously healed. One lady who had a huge goiter came forward. As Carl and the team prayed, it instantly dissolved. The next night she returned to show the people the loose skin where her goiter had been until it had instantly disappeared the previous evening.

There were many other miracles. A 12-year-old deaf girl was healed. Twisted arms and legs were healed and bodies that had been bent over for years straightened.

Another miracle happened during a previous trip. Cornelio L. Villareal Jr. was governor of the Capiz Province in the Philippines. He had money, success, and power. But he was an alcoholic and a compulsive gambler. His wife was in the process of getting a divorce. Carl Richardson was to speak at an Easter sunrise breakfast at 6 o'clock in 1978 in the grand ballroom of the elegant Intercontinental Hotel in Manila.

Someone invited the governor. More than a hundred souls were saved that morning. After the prayer breakfast the governor made his way to Carl. He said, "I was bewildered this morning as you spoke. It was as if the entire place became supercharged with some sort of static electricity. The hairs on the back of my neck and on my hands and arms stood up. What's the explanation for this electricity in the atmosphere?"

Carl explained that this is the way many people respond to the anointing and presence of God. With eyes wide with excitement, the governor stated that he had never felt the presence of the Lord before and asked if his wife and seven children might be able to feel this presence of the Lord later that morning in the final service of the crusade.

When the final service of Carl's crusade began later on that Easter Sunday morning, Governor Cornelio L. Villareal, his wife, and seven children filled the second row of the sanctuary of the Pasay City Church of God. Again the governor felt the electricity of the presence of the Lord. His wife felt it, too. When Carl gave an invitation for people to be saved, the governor and his entire family came to the altar and stood beside the Filipino peasants. He was delivered of his addictions and began a prayer meeting in the governor's mansion. During a later crusade, the governor dedicated his life to full-time ministry. From that moment, Carl affectionately called Cornelio Villareal "Brother Governor."

Imagination for the Communist World

Carl and Bev became burdened for the Communist world around 1989. They were watching a TV news report about an underground revival. The Berlin Wall was still standing. Gorbachev was still in charge. The Richardsons knew that the Communist countries were off limits for preaching the gospel.

Choking back tears, Carl said, "Bev, God is speaking to me about these people." Within days, Carl met with denominational world missions leader, Dr. Robert White, to get the names of some underground leaders in Communist nations.

Immediately after receiving the names of some of these great underground leaders, Carl planned to go on a fact-finding tour of Russia, Bulgaria, Poland, and Romania. However, his car was broadsided by another car, injuring his back and making it difficult for him to walk. Feeling that they had to go forward in faith, the Richardsons made a decision that Bev and the boys would go without him, along with Dr. Robert White, David Lanier and his wife, Betty, and two pastors.

Upon their safe return two weeks later, they began the painstaking process of putting together a powerful video project titled "An Open Door," which was shown to an enthusiastic audience at the General Assembly that August in San Antonio. This video presentation was a portent of many spectacular video presentations at the General Assembly every year from 1990.

At the 1990 General Assembly Carl personally met the two presiding bishops of the Russian underground church, Ivan Fedotov and Victor Belykh, who invited him to come to Russia. Carl made the decision to conduct a crusade in Moscow, a city of about 10 million people.

By the third night of the crusade, 2,000 people packed into the building. Again almost the entire congregation stood to receive Christ. Though Pastor Sergei Ryavhovsky of a small underground church in Moscow made a request that seems strange by our standards; namely, that the Christians stay at home so that there would be room for the unsaved, the attendance continued to exponentially build with the crowds overflowing into the massive lobby of the Lenin Auditorium.

The fourth night there were miraculous results everywhere. Carl preached an anointed 20-minute message. Then, as he had done on the previous three nights he asked for those who had never prayed, but wanted to accept Christ, to stand to their feet.

The closing night of one of the crusades was aired for three hours into millions of homes in Moscow, Minsk, St. Petersburg, and Kiev.

A daring School of Ministry was envisioned sponsored by Carl Richardson Ministries and followed a similar format as previous Schools of Ministry since 1984; namely, the participant's travel and living expenses of their families (back home) would be paid in full, their hotel and meals would be fully paid, free learning materials including Bibles would be provided to them free, and a generous box of groceries would be provided after the School of Ministry ended.

Astonishingly, 1,022 delegates registered for this first-ever School of Ministry conducted in Russia and the other nations of the then, Soviet Union since communism had taken control in the bloody revolution of 1917.

G. W. (Bill) Wilson, a man who had already planted nearly 100 churches in his ministry and who then lived in Tampa, was invited by Carl to coordinate the selection of a team of about 30 teachers to participate in this historic Moscow School of Ministry.

The teachers were select pastors and business persons, including Al Taylor, whose presentation on tithing was eagerly embraced by leaders of Russia's underground church and helped revolutionize their ministries. Al's son, Todd, had only days earlier graduated from Lee College and came on this trip to Moscow as a graduation gift.

As an impromptu part of that School of Ministry, Carl arranged a meeting on Red Square and did a quick Freedom Celebration. The Lee College Singers were there. Hundreds of people from the underground church were there. They all went to their knees for prayer similar to the way it was done in Washington, D. C., on the U.S. Capitol steps back in 1976.

Now Carl was leading hundreds of Russians in the same exercise of faith. Vladimir (Walter) Bagrin, Carl's interpreter, was concerned they might be arrested by the KGB. Carl preached anyway (with Bagrin faithfully providing the Russian translation), the Lee College Singers sang, the people worshiped and went to their knees in prayer in the shadow of Lenin's tomb. After prayer, they clapped their hands and shouted.

Then, 50 of those underground Christians boarded chartered buses to revisit the Moscow prisons where many of them had spent time for the so-called "crime" of preaching the gospel. The people laid their hands on the walls and tearfully asked God to forgive their captors.

That night, back at the auditorium, would prove to be a historic meeting. Carl was exhausted. He prayed, "Lord, if anything good happens here tonight, it will be all You." At times he could hardly stand, but he preached on "New Beginnings."

With images still fresh in his mind of the stirring scenes he had personally witnessed early in the day at the Moscow area prison, during his message Carl asked, "How many of you served time in prison?" Many stood up.

Carl was touched and continued, "We honor you. You kept the faith. You are my heroes."

"How many of you would go through it again?" Everybody stood again.

"How many of you would go through it for the first time if you had to?" Everybody stood.

Carl was moved to tears. He put his head down on the podium and began to weep. Soon weeping broke out all over that huge auditorium. Al Taylor glanced at his watch when this "Divine intervention" began. For 16 minutes Carl did not utter a word as he and the people wept profusely.

Spontaneously, the hundreds of Russians began going to each other from the two major "schisms" of the unregistered church, asking for forgiveness for their distrust and mistreatment of each other in the past. It was a "God moment."

The always resourceful Bill Wilson quickly got a golden goblet for Communion. The two bishops drank from a common cup with Carl Richardson. Then the crowd took Communion. After midnight, the people were still worshiping. The two groups in the underground church led by the two different bishops decided to amalgamate, which was not unlike the Church of God and the Assemblies of God—two different denominations amalgamating.

A year later, Carl Richardson, a church-planting team led by Bill Wilson, Dave Lanier, and about 20 others from America, returned to Moscow to plant a new Church of God in Moscow.

It was exciting when the first new church was planted. On that Sunday morning, people got off buses and subways and literally ran to the church. Carl announced during the first few nights of the crusade at the theater that everybody in attendance on Sunday morning would receive a Bible. The leaders started the service an hour ahead of time because the auditorium was full and the people were standing outside in the snow. They had church for 1,000 people; then for the next 1,000; then the third 1,000. That day over 5,000 Bibles were given away. They had not planned for that many people to be there, so it took their entire inventory of Bibles.

John D. Nichols, at the time assistant general overseer of the Church of God, visited the crusade and was invited by Carl to preach on that Sunday morning. Nichols still refers to that Sunday as the most exciting single day of his ministry with several hundred praying the sinner's prayer in each service.

Tanya Korschunova was a university student in Moscow and was hired by Bill Wilson, head of what came to be known as the Ministry Strike Force. She became the chief interpreter of a team of Russian young men and women she helped assemble to translate for the team. Her father was an officer in the Communist Party and her sister was a translator for Russian President Mikhail Gorbachev, who was still in power at that time.

Tanya helped make arrangements for the big crusade in a large theater where the first church was to be planted at the conclusion of the crusade. On Friday morning of that crusade, Carl told her that in prayer the Holy Spirit had impressed him to ask her to interpret for him on Friday night. Sheer terror went through her. She told Carl, "Oh! I can't do that. The thought of standing up and translating in front of all those people terrifies me. Besides, I am not even a believer."

Carl assured Tanya that she was not required to do translation for his message on that Friday night, but that he would wait until 5 p.m. for an answer. He also told her that all she had to do was translate into Russian exactly what he said in English to the audience. By 3 p.m., she had agreed.

Just before 7 p.m. Tanya stood next to Carl and the team on stage holding a Bible in her hand marked to the location of "their" sermon. Thirty minutes later she was trembling and her hands were clammy when she stepped onto center stage next to Carl to translate the sermon into Russian.

As Carl began to speak that night to the overflow crowd, Tanya started to relax. Then as she and Carl continued, their words flowed as one person. She felt a mysterious kind of electricity. Not unlike the governor in Manila, she did not realize that it was the anointing of the Holy Spirit.

The message was not long, but she knew it impacted the people throughout the packed auditorium. Almost everyone in the building had responded to the invitation to accept Christ. Sentence by sentence she interpreted the sinner's prayer as led by Carl, and the people followed.

Suddenly it became the single most momentous night of her life. Almost everyone wept as they prayed. She was weeping too. Jesus was coming into her life. She was, for the first time in her 18-year life, believing upon Jesus. Her life was changing forever.

But when the team loaded onto the chartered bus, Tanya was missing. Carl went back inside the theater auditorium looking for her. When he found her backstage, she was crumpled up on the floor in a corner weeping.

As Carl quietly knelt beside her, she sobbed, "I can't believe it. It happened to me! As I was leading the people to pray the sinner's prayer, Jesus came into my heart and I feel like a new person! Jesus is so real!"

From this very first church plant in Moscow, Carl has been involved either directly or through sponsorship at some level. An impressive number (more than 650) new lifegiving churches have been planted throughout Russia and the 15 nations which comprised the former Soviet Union. Carl's goal is to help plant 1,000 new churches in that part of the world.

In 1998, when Carl and his team were on their way to Belarus, he was abruptly notified that his crusade in the soccer stadium had been canceled. When he arrived into Minsk, he soon understood why. The hammer and sickle red flag of communism was back and was flying again over the city center and the other government buildings.

With the help of David Lanier, Carl arranged with the bishop of the Belarus Pentecostal Union, a fellowship which numbered about 300 churches, for the meeting location to be changed to the largest church (800 members) located at the end of the Minsk City Bus Line on the outskirts of the city. The church had never been part of a crusade since Carl and Bill had preached together there in 1993, and they did not know what to do. But they agreed that Carl should come in view of the Communist government's cancellation of the rental of the soccer stadium in Minsk.

Richardson launched an aggressive advertising campaign over the local TV station, inviting people to the revival. The officers of the government's "Religious Freedom" who had stopped the crusade in the stadium were now working to stop the crusade even in the large local church.

Carl responded, "Let's go to Communist headquarters and see those who are trying to stop this meeting. We must do something bold and decisive so the gospel can be preached here." Carl and his team, along with a crew from the Canadian Broadcasting Network who were in town and met his plane, went to the headquarters.

Fear gripped some of the church leaders. They knew the people they were going to see could have all of them killed or arrested. Amazingly as the bus got close to the Communist headquarters, the Pentecostal bishop saw a man walking up the sidewalk. It was the director of the Office of Religious Freedom. It was as if God had brought the man right to them.

Carl and the crew got out of their chartered bus with the CBC cameras rolling. The man smiled. He appeared nervous.

Courteously, Carl asked what could be done to keep the meetings going. This was something new to have his decisions challenged. Knowing that cameras from the United States and Canada were on him, the director agreed to let the meeting continue at the church. Writer Doyle Daugherty said, "Richardson's bold and forceful leadership at that important moment in their history may have helped preserve religious freedom in this tiny country of the former Soviet Union."

Over 1,000 souls were gloriously converted in a week which saw the local churches' number more than double. Many of these people had never prayed before. The bishop of the church asked his church members to remain outside so that unbelievers would be able to get a seat and be saved.

The new people did not know how to respond in church. But they watched the leaders. When staff members raised their hands, everybody else raised theirs. They were wide open to the gospel.

But even before that, the year 1993 was a glorious time for harvest, especially in Moscow. Teams of church-planting pastors from America were brought in by Carl and Bill Wilson to help reap the ripened harvest. It was a gigantic task with almost 100 church planters and support teams coming to help from America, South Africa, and Australia. God helped the team win over 12,600 souls to Christ in one week in 16 simultaneous soulwinning, church-planting crusades. It was a historic event of unprecedented significance.

On Sunday, May 16, 1993, 16 new churches were planted in one day. New converts were immediately taught about tithing and giving. The lease of all 16 buildings and the 16 pastors' salaries were underwritten for six months by Carl Richardson Ministries.

Hundreds of thousands pounds of food, clothing, and medicine were all shipped into Russia and stored in a giant rented warehouse and distributed by the ministry teams and leaders of the cooperating underground churches. Also, they were given New Testaments, Gospels of John, children's picture Bibles and family Bibles all, of course, printed in the Russian language.

Vision Foundation Helps

At the General Assembly in New Orleans in 1992 Carl gave a report to the Vision Foundation members concerning Russia and China. Hoyt Stone records in the history of Vision: "He testified concerning the many churches that were established and now going strong. The Muldova Bible College had already graduated 401 people, new works and new units in Macedonia were in operation, ministers' training centers had been set up and food and clothing were being distributed ... with 50 million people in Russia and 70 million in China, is it any wonder we should do all we can to promote this ministry of the gospel in these areas?"

The Imaginator Turns His Attention to Mainland China

In 1994, Carl also turned his attention to China, a country of 1.3 billion souls. He began working through some of the underground "Wilderness Churches" which has by some estimates as many as 10 million members.

For a while he took mandatory government-sponsored translators into the country. But at night he and his team would meet with the underground church leaders at undisclosed places where the leaders were treated to dinner.

It was during these secret strategy sessions that massive Chinese study Bibles distribution was arranged. Carl readily testifies that he and those who have accompanied him have been blest in far greater measure than they were able to bless the heroes of China's underground church.

A discipleship training course is being regularly updated and is being shared throughout mainland China through high-tech electronic media and print.

Imagination for a Million Souls

Like many ministers, Carl and Bev have always wanted to win at least a million souls over the lifespan of their ministry. In 1996, Carl and Bev decided to begin a grand effort to win a million souls to Jesus by no later than December 31, 1999.

However, according to their personal ministry statistical summations, they were far from their goal. Therefore, they decided that they needed to form ministry networks in Russia, China, South Africa, India, Central and South America, and places where they had held crusades and Schools of Ministry over the years.

These "key" ministries would report their spiritual results to Carl Richardson Ministries, and in return the ministry would send them financial aid and soulwinning strategies and materials.

By 1999, over a million souls had been won. Because the soul-winning network was already in place, they decided to do it all over again.

God helped them achieve that goal within 12 months.

Now, their ongoing goals are simple: "To help win and train a multitude of new converts globally. And, to help plant 1,000 new life-giving churches in Russia and the former Soviet Union, and inside mainland China and India."

The Oasis Broadcast

Carl is still the ever-imaginative broadcaster. Five days every week since 1990, Carl's voice continues to be heard around the world on a five-minute daily radio broadcast called Oasis.

Oasis is defined as "a fertile, life-giving spot in an otherwise barren dry wasteland." He produces this program only in English at the present time. There are 2.4 billion people in the world who speak English.

Carl Richardson's plans are to continue moving forward in faith as long as he lives. Those who know him best, believe that he will always be full of imagination and vision with which to bless the body of Christ.

Imagining a Bold New Direction

Over the years, Carl and Bev have worked within the parameters of the principle that whatever you help make happen for others, God will make happen for you.

In that spirit, Carl served for 30 consecutive years as an elected member of the Board of Directors of the National Religious Broadcasters and was a featured speaker at many of their conventions.

He currently serves as chairman of several important ministries which he also has helped create:

- *Chair, Operation Compassion, Inc.*
- *Chair, Children of the World Foundation, Inc.*
- *Chair, World-Class Cities International, Inc.*

• *Chair, Center for Spiritual Renewal, Inc.*

His ministry web site addresses include:

www.CarlRichardson.com
www.BeyondBorders.com
www.CarlRichardson.org

The most important ingredient in success is vision with creative daring. Many people dream big dreams but don't implement daring faith. Carl Richardson just steps out and does it.

Carl H. Richardson
P. O. Box 1000
Brandon, FL 33509-1000

Telephone
813-684-3300

E-mail
crmint@aol.com

Al Taylor—The Helper

Al Taylor—The Helper

Al Taylor is a devout man of God. He is tall, walks with
a purpose, and stands out in a crowd. He is loved everywhere
he goes. His voice is captivating. If you were asked what his
differentiating distinctive is, you might say leader, man with a
clear vision, gentle authority figure, man of the hour, faithful
family man, radio announcer, author, facilitator, or some other
complementary title. But Al Taylor sees himself as one called
along side to help. He prefers the title—Helper. He sees
himself as a helper to other people. He helps his family, he
helps his church, he helps his friends, he helped Carl Richardson
with Forward in Faith, he has helped thousands of pastors in
their stewardship programs, he helps his staff become all they
can become, and he helps the men and women of Vision
Foundation do what they feel God has called them to do.

Called Along Side to Help His Parents and Church as a Child

Al's parents, P. F. and Helen Taylor, were in ministry all of
his life. His father planted eight churches, served as an overseer
in the United States and on the mission field, served on school
boards, state councils, and was chairman of the Benevolence
Board. He felt obligated wherever he was pastoring to plant
another church in a nearby city. He had done some entertaining
before entering the ministry and, therefore, had many gifts. He
would put up a tent in the city, sing and preach there on Sunday
afternoons and during the week.

Al's mother, a great woman of God, was from a Primitive
Baptist background. The county she lived in was successful in
keeping the Pentecostal message out. But a young girl at school
invited 13-year-old Helen to go home with her so she could go
to a revival meeting with her at the Church of God of Prophecy.

The first time she went to the revival, Helen was born
again. Further, God gave her a 30-minute tour of heaven. That
night she was out in the Spirit for over a half-hour. When Helen
saw heaven, she did not want to come back. God said, "You

must go back; but you will be returning." Suddenly she began to hear singing that sounded like it was a thousand miles away. It was the singing at the revival. As she was becoming conscious, the singing got louder and louder. Since that day, Helen has always wanted to go back to heaven. There has never been any fear concerning death since that experience.

Helen Taylor could have been a great businesswoman, but she gave all her talents to the church. She would go to stores and ask them to make contributions of clothing to her rummage sales. She often had new clothes in her sales. Therefore, she had the best sales in town. Her husband, P. F. Taylor, was asked to speak in the Virginia Camp Meeting on one occasion. He went to her sale and found a beautiful, white linen suit just delivered from Leggetts Department store. She let him have it, but made him pay the asking price for it. He preached in it and looked great.

Al's First Experience With Stewardship

Al's first exposure with stewardship was when he was 5 years old. The church his dad had recently started was planning to build. Money was tight. It was during World War II when everything was rationed. The task of raising money was expansive. His family had taken him to Charlottesville, Virginia, to have his tonsils extracted. He took with him some of the little booklet folders with slots for dimes. Every time a doctor or nurse came into the room, he solicited them for money for the new church. They filled up his dime collector. When he completed one booklet, he put it aside and started another one.

When Al was 7, the ladies of the church turned him loose on the streets of Waynesboro, Virginia. At that time it was safe. The Willing Worker Band (what the ladies of the church were called at that time) made candy to sell in order to help the church. He sold everything they made. When the candy ran out, he got out his booklet folders with dime slots and hit the streets again.

Al soon learned that the beer drinkers were great givers. He spent much of his time in the beer joints. Nobody bothered the sassy little preacher's kid. They always tolerated him. He was never asked to leave. He would approach every drinker in the bar. He would fill his coin folder, go outside and put the money in his pocket, and then return with the empty coin folder. He could raise $10 a day, which was a lot of money in those days.

In St. Charles, Virginia, the ladies decided to sell fried pies. They baked apple, apricot, and peach pies. The boys in the church would sell the pies on the streets for 15 cents each. They also made iced snowballs. Al's older brother would scrape a 50-pound block of ice, making snowballs to raise money for the church.

In the Taylor family, tithing became easy because they had learned that when you take care of God's business, God takes care of you. The pastor of the Waynesboro, Virginia, Church of God has records to this day of Al's few pennies of tithes when he was 5 years old.

Al made a strong commitment to the Lord when he was about 10 years of age. His mother said, "Son, you may as well live right. We're not going to let you live wrong." He accepted Jesus as the Lord of his life.

Al was 15 years of age when his family moved to the mission field in Jamaica. They did not know that Jamaica had a great system of education and therefore left him at Lee Academy in 1954. It was a very challenging experience to be separated from his parents.

Needing to make some money for college, Al took off for Alaska with Roger Gupton when he was 17. The boys spent two weeks looking for work. Because Roger was three years older than Al, he was given job opportunities. Some suggested to Al that he get a paper route. But he had not driven 6,000 miles to deliver papers.

When Roger and Al left Anchorage to go to Fairbanks, Al decided to tell people he was 22 years old. He first got a chauffeur's license and took a job driving a taxicab. "Real life" was a shocking experience for Al, but he made $63 a night.

Al and Roger then applied for a job with Distance Early Warning Radar Network at Point Barrow, which is located as far away as you can go on the North American continent. The boys took the typing tests and filled out their applications. The director asked, "Mr. Taylor, when would you like to leave?" Al responded, "Ready to go any minute." Then the director said, "We'll fly you out. Be here Monday morning." Then he turned to Roger and said, "Mr. Gupton, you are not 21 yet. We cannot take you. Come back in September when you turn 21, and we will take you."

After Al was on the job for two months, he was next in line to be paymaster, handling a $2 million payroll. His pay would have been $25,000—a great salary for that day.

Al was flattered that Mr. Stokes would offer him such a great job, but he wanted to go back to school. Mr. Stokes had to approve his leaving or Al would have to pay his own way out. The superintendent agreed to pay his way back to Fairbanks. When he arrived back at Lee, though, he was backslidden and cynical. Al completed junior college in three semesters and then went back to Alaska to work as a forest fire fighter.

Later when back in Virginia, Al received a telegram from Roger asking, "If you want to make more money than we made in Alaska, call me tonight at 11 o'clock." When Al called that night, he asked Roger, "Have you joined the Mafia?"

"Better than that!" was Roger's reply. I am selling encyclopedias. You work four hours a night. I made $140 last night."

Al said that he would need to turn in a notice to his foreman. Roger responded, "Get on up here. Catch a plane. I'll wire you the money. You'll never go back to that job so no need to turn in a notice."

The next day Al was on his way. That night he went out with Roger and watched him make $134 in just a few hours. Roger gave Al sheets to memorize to help him with the sales. Al could only learn two pages, then he began to ad lib. He made $420 the first week selling Americana Encyclopedias. They were based in Akron, Ohio, and went all over the area.

Al and Roger went back to college for the summer session of 1958. They were not the most cooperative students. They played tennis all week then went into the library on Thursday night and spent all night studying and getting the week's work caught up.

Al then moved to Canton to sell encyclopedias. His pastor was J. H. Hughes. T. L. Lowery came to town for a revival. Al gave his heart back to the Lord on August 2, 1959.

In the meantime, his parents had moved from Kingston, Jamaica, to Lemmon, South Dakota, so Al went home to be with his family again.

In January 1960, Al took a job selling Britannica in North Carolina. Roger had been given a job as branch manager and had sent for him. With Americana they had to canvass leads cold on the telephone. But with Britannica, they already had the leads from advertising. All they had to do was sell.

Al was in the Wilson, North Carolina, area doing well with Britannica in the daytime and showing T.L. Osborne films on weekends. Osborne was the biggest contributor to World Missions at that time. He went to the Wilson, North Carolina, Church of God to speak one Sunday morning, and there he met Brenda Owen.

While sitting in a Sunday school class, he asked himself the question, Where are the pretty girls? A church this size surely has some pretty girls. About that time Brenda turned her face toward the teacher. He got a view of her profile. That was it. He knew this was his girl.

That morning after the service, Brenda's mother invited Al to go home with them for lunch. Brenda's father asked, "Are your parents missionaries?" Al responded, "Yes!" Brenda's mother and father had letters from Al's parents because of offerings they had sent them.

Brenda's background was similar to his. Her father and mother were great Christians. Her dad was a lumbergrader. He moved lumber eight to 10 hours a day. He had an eight-hour workout every day. Not only was he strong physically, he was strong spiritually.

Mr. Owen witnessed to everybody he saw. His boss said, "He bugged us all so much that I would have fired him, but I would have fired the best worker I had." After Mr. Owen retired, this boss found him to tell him that he had accepted Christ. The boss sent Mr. Owen a bonus every year. When Mr. Owen's son-in-law built a church in the area, this man gave him land and lumber to build.

Brenda had a boyfriend, and she was a very loyal person. It was a tough decision for her. Al remained in the area. He would find a way to be at her home when she got home in the afternoon. Her mother loved shaved ice, so he would bring her shaved ice and a carton of Pepsi every day just to get to be there when Brenda got home.

He hired Brenda to make phone calls for him. He had a phone installed beside her bed so he could call her. When they were talking late, he would say, "Don't you hang up. If you do, I'll call back and it will wake up your father."

Al poured out his love to Brenda in many creative ways. He gave her gifts from a tailor-made suit to albums of her favorite music. He sang romantic songs to her with his deep bass voice.

He knew how to make people feel wonderful. He was always doing something special for Brenda's family. He took them out for meals in a restaurant (something special for the family in 1960). He entertained them with funny stories and shared insights from God's Word.

Al proposed marriage to Brenda two weeks after they met. She was not able, at first, to break away from her other boyfriend. This did not stop Al from seeing her. He came to her house every day. He insisted on teaching her how to drive. He found ways to stay in her life.

Finally, Brenda broke up with her boyfriend and fell in love with Al. She turned all that loyalty to him. It was time for Al to go back to school. He told Brenda that he would be back to marry her in a year.

Called Along Side to Help a Wife

On June 4, 1961, Al and Brenda were married. He was 22 and she was 17. They moved 200 miles away from her family.

Al worked day and night selling Britannica. His days were spent in the office as branch manager of Encyclopedia Britannica, and his nights were spent selling the books door to door. He was very conscious of his role as provider.

Brenda wanted to be the perfect wife for Al. She chose never to work. All she was interested in was serving God and her family. She began studying the Word of God very seriously.

Called Along Side to Help Laymen

While working in Nebraska, Al taught a Sunday school class. The pastor had asked him to become a Sunday school superintendent. He agreed to do so if the teachers would get together every Friday night to study the lesson together. They had a great time.

In 1971, Al received an invitation to speak at a leadership conference in Cleveland, Tennessee. Art Hodge was scheduled to speak, but at the last minute he could not make it. Gene Rice, overseer of Nebraska, called Al one morning about 7 o'clock, and said, "Al, the speaker cancelled. I told them you would do it. They want a layman. You will be preaching to the preachers."

In that Cleveland conference, Al shared the story of a preacher who came to Nebraska to start a church. Brother Rice asked Al to give the man a job. Al sent the preacher out with one of his Christian salesmen. That day the salesman sold two sets of encyclopedias and led one of the couples to the Lord.

The preacher was excited. "You mean, you made $150 and led a couple to the Lord? I can build my church and get rich, too!"

Al continued, "Many of you have preached for years in the place where there are no prospects. This man took the preacher to where the prospects are. You are telling us to go witness, but you don't do it. We have laid down a tradition that people get saved in church. If you win them in their homes, then they will go to church."

When Al finished he thought, They will never invite me back. He received a standing ovation.

It was at this meeting that Carl Richardson thought, "That guy would make a great radio announcer." Little did Al or Carl know they would end up working together at Forward in Faith.

The Helper Called Along Side of Carl Richardson

Carl Richardson was the night speaker for the 1972 Mississippi Camp Meeting. Al felt led of the Lord to knock on his door and congratulate him on being appointed the speaker for Forward in Faith. When he did, Carl was very happy to see him. They went to breakfast together and shared the burdens of their hearts. When Carl mentioned to Al the thought of being the announcer for *Forward in Faith*, Al hesitated. He said, "Carl, you have the wrong man in mind. I have no experience with radio or television. I have no interest in it. I am interested in seeing the laymen of the Church of God mobilized to witness."

Carl responded, "You can reach more laymen through Forward in Faith than you can through Britannica. You can win souls and mobilize laymen."

Al went back to Omaha and told Brenda about it. They put it before the Lord. After Carl had gotten approval from the Executive Committee, Al and Brenda moved to Cleveland, Tennessee.

When Al left Britannica, he had built the largest district Britannica had. He had also been offered a promotion. Had he taken it, he could have earned a very large income. He abandoned the financial opportunity for the work of God.

The lifestyle in Cleveland was drastically different for Al and Brenda and their children. Al had been accustomed to making a lot of money. About 1974 they ran out of their savings. When Brenda told Al that she was drawing the last of their savings out of the bank, he said, "Go ahead. It's the Lord's responsibility to take care of us."

And take care of them, God did! A man called from North Carolina and asked, "Al, if you will give me two hours a week, I'll send a plane to get you and pay you $100 an hour." Jehovah Jireh always takes care of God's workers.

When Carl first approached Al about working with him, Al was concerned because sales had been his life's career. Little did he know that there was a great need for sales in Forward in Faith. They could not do what had to be done without sales.

One of Al's assignments was to get *Forward in Faith* on as many stations as possible. He did a series of brochures. The first one read: "You could have something in common with these

50,000 watt stations WCKY, WHAS, WOAI, WBT. You could carry the fastest growing religious broadcast in America. You can have the program free of charge. You must give us a regular broadcast time. You keep the tape. We will advertise the program in your market."

Another one read, "You could be the number one station in your market, and you already know how to make it happen. All you have to do is read the trends in your market and serve those trends. They will make you number one. Notice the trends toward Evangelical broadcasting. We have the biggest segment of your market. The fastest growing program is *Forward in Faith*. We have Carl Richardson. We have Steve Brock. We send you the tape, and you don't have to send it back."

The responses poured in. The first time 270 stations responded. The next time more than 100 were added.

Audiocassettes were new at this time. Many people did not have cassette players. Al went to Chattanooga and negotiated with Curle Electronics to purchase large quantities of cassette recorder/players. The Forward in Faith team was building their road so they could run on it. In addition, they recorded Carl reading the New Testament on cassette ape. This became a great seller.

One day Al got an idea about the ministers tape service. He thought, Pastors do not have study time. They run from one hospital to another, from one member to another. They want to study; but do not have time. He told Carl, "If we could send them a preached message on tape, it would be great. The tape stops when the preacher stops, and starts when he starts." He further had the idea of introducing it by saying, "Thank you for what you have done for Forward in Faith. This is your ministry. Preachers voted to have a radio and TV ministry. Preachers give through their monthly report to support this ministry. Thank you. Here is a gift. Two of your colleagues in ministry are preaching. Now sit back and let someone minister to you. You may get sermon ideas. By the way, if you include us in your monthly report for as much as $5 a month, you will automatically get two sermons every month. Give yourself a chance to be ministered to and inspired."

The contributions from ministers went from $300 a month to $100,000 a year.

When *Forward in Faith* was getting ready for the big TV specials, they hired Walter Bennett, who also produced and directed the Billy Graham programs. Several cities refused to air the new *Forward in Faith* telecast. Carl decided to send Al to those who had said no to Mr. Bennett.

Al visited those cities. He walked into the TV station and said to the manager. "I've come to spend some money with you. I want to buy prime time. Our production was made in Hollywood. I have the production proof sets with me. We have good singing and good preaching." All of the cities Al visited agreed to air the program.

In Wichita, Kansas, the station manager saw the program and was elated. He asked, "How would you like to be on six stations?" Al said, "I came to spend money, but I don't know about spending that much." The man replied, "Wichita is the anchor. We'll air it for you on all six stations for the cost of just Wichita."

Called Along Side to Help Vision Foundation

While working with *Forward in Faith*, Vision Foundation had been organized. Al was not a board member; but he worked diligently for them because of his position with Forward in Faith, which Vision supported financially.

Al wrote their statement of purpose as well as their brochures.

Because the Lord Jesus Christ issued an assignment to take the gospel to every person, and because now that task is larger than ever before, and increasing in size daily, and because the fulfillment of prophecy shows us that time is very short, we therefore purpose to maximize our efforts and hereby covenant with God to do the following:

1. I purpose to use the expertise and experience which God has given to me for creative planning and problem solving in response to the Lord's Great Commission.
2. I purpose to inspire and enlarge the vision of Christian ministers and laymen in the use of the electronic media as the God-given tools for reaching the greatest number of people in the shortest amount of time at the lowest cost.
3. I purpose to accept the personal responsibility for my shareof the spiritual harvest field as God helps me to recognize my opportunities.
4. I purpose to work as a man or woman of Vision to implement each idea and plan which God gives to this team for reaching our nation and our world.
5. I purpose to pray to the Lord of the harvest that He will direct and inspire the members of Vision Foundation to create accomplishments for His glory and honor.

Al was hired to be the interim director of Vision in 1979, then he was hired to be Director of Vision when Roger Gupton resigned in 1980. He was given $500-a-month honorarium.

Called Along Side to Help the
Stewardship Department of the Church of God

In the summer of 1980, Al received a call from General Overseer Ray H. Hughes, Sr. Brother Hughes reported to him that the Executive Committee wanted him to become the director of Stewardship for the Church of God.

Al questioned, "You mean a real director with a director's salary?" The general overseer assured him that it was a real director's position and salary.

Al began to realize how much he would miss *Forward in Faith*. He loved working with Carl Richardson. It was a tough decision. *Forward in Faith* was on the air on 520 radio stations.

There were only 161 when he came. Further, they were selling over a million dollars in cassettes and materials.

When Al told Brenda what was unfolding, she was not surprised. She said, "The Lord told me six months ago that we were going to make a change." The Lord began to show Al how to disentangle himself from all that he was doing.

The Stewardship Department consisted of Al and one secretary. One of the first things Al did was to hire a consultant, Dr. Walter Thomas, from Denver. He paid him a thousand dollars for three days-a-month, plus travel expenses, and worked him 12 hours a day. Al watched Walter interview people about estate planning. While Thomas worked, Al learned. They traveled all over the United States together. They went to Fresno, Dallas, and Missouri.

Very early in the new department, Al realized that it took too long to get money for the church through wills and estate planning. He recognized that if stewardship lasted, it must show immediate giving. He started touring the country, speaking about tithing. Since that time the department has run on two tracks—current giving (tithes and offerings) and future giving (trusts and estate planning).

Many pastors don't like to preach on tithing for fear of being accused of being too interested in money. However, Al found that people are hungry to learn what God tells them about their money.

Called Along Side to Help Pastors

The Stewardship Department entered into capital campaigns in 1993. This service is for a church that needs to build, move, or pay off heavy debt. The work of the campaign is to prepare for more of the presence of God. The trust factor is taught. People are brought to the place of trusting God enough to ask, "God, what do you want me to give?" Al maintains, "Money is not a problem. Trust is the problem."

Called Along Side to Help Staff Members

When Louis Cross left West Coast Bible College as business manager, Al asked the Executive Committee to let him hire Cross for the Stewardship Department. Al believed that God was bringing them together. Al laid out the simple plan. He said, "It's our job to sell the church back to the people." He and Louis prayed together and worked together like champions.

God began to use Cross, just as Al had anticipated. When Louis Cross went to a church in Tallahassee, Florida, he found Robert Angerer, a lawyer who was praying for God to use his talents.

Further, as Cross began working the field, new things began to happen. They had never put testimonies in wills before. But a little old lady asked Brother Cross if she could include her testimony in her will. He asked Attorney Angerer, and since then many people have done that. It leaves a legacy for the family. As Cross researched, he learned that the wills of many famous people contained their testimonies. In fact, Teddy Roosevelt left his testimony in his will.

This addition of personnel was good for the Stewardship Department. Al said, "I'd like to have had a dozen like Louis Cross."

In 1985 Gerald Redman joined the staff. Gerald wrote wills and preached on stewardship. He had much useful material to bless the people about stewardship. When Gerald left the department, he was greatly missed.

Steve Holder came into the department in 1993. Then, Todd Taylor was added in 1994. Todd brought a different perspective to the department because he is from a different generation.

Todd teaches from the Great Commandment, "Thou shalt love the Lord thy God with all thy heart, mind, soul, and strength. And love not the world neither the things that are in the world." He draws a chart of love, purpose, and manifestation. He teaches, "Love God, love self, love neighbor, and don't love money. If you love God more than money, you can follow God's instructions about using money. If you love money more than God, you will use God to try to get more money. If you love man more than money, you will minister to man. If you love money more than man, you will exploit man. If you love self more than money, you will do that which is best for you and money will be a tool and God your Master. If you love God, you will be free to use money. If you don't love God, money will be your master and wipe you out spiritually because you are trying to get more and more of your god."

Todd further teaches, "Cain loved money. Abel loved God. Abel gave the first fruits of his flock. Cain restrained and gave a nice offering, but not the first fruits offering. Because Abel loved God, he sacrificed his sheep. Cain loved money and sacrificed his brother."

In 1995, Hoyt Stone was leaving the office of the general overseer, where he had served as the general overseer's aide. Al asked Hoyt to come into the Stewardship Department. They had been roommates years ago when Hoyt was in college and Al was in high school. Al knew Hoyt and loved him.

Hoyt is a prolific writer. He took the materials in the Stewardship Department and updated them. During that time he wrote the history of Vision Foundation and made a great contribution to the department. Hoyt remained with the Stewardship Department until 2000, at which time he retired.

Called Along Side to Help the Church of God

In 1990, the Executive Committee needed to cut budgets. Al did not feel that the budget for Stewardship could be cut. Before he went to the committee to discuss the budget with them, he received a check for $200,000 from a client. This was timely. Al went in to share with the committee. He reviewed his assignment—to teach stewardship to the Church of God. He reminded them that they had commitments of more than $50 million through wills and the tithe fund had increased every year.

The committee gave him permission to present his case to the Executive Council. Al went before them in the same spirit. He told the Council, "It's like a hand pump that you have to prime. You may be thirsty. But you have to remember that you have to pour water into the primer so that the pump can produce lots of fresh water. There is no need for me to keep pumping if you are going to drink the primer water now. Give me money to operate. I can't pump the pump if you drink the primer water."

He then asked Orville Hagan if Tennessee had been helped after the stewardship campaigns in his state. Hagan answered, "We broke all tithe records." Raymond Culpepper spoke up and said, "Al came to my church and taught on tithing. I had a great increase. In fact, the increase in the tithe of tithes from my church is more than the proposed cut to his budget. Let the department keep the money and let him do his work." The Executive Council withdrew the proposed cut.

Called Along Side to Mentor

Al felt for a long period of time that he needed to bring a man whom he could mentor into the Stewardship Department. He wants someone to be prepared to follow in his steps when the time comes for him to move to another level of ministry. He chose Ken Davis. Ken is a lawyer and a preacher. He is a great communicator. He is a witness everywhere he goes. When he goes into a restaurant, he begins a slow process of winning the waiters and waitresses to the Lord. Further, he is a man of prayer. He has already done a strategic study of the department and its ministries. He also is unafraid of work and works many long hours.

Called Along Side to Help the Prayer Movement

Brenda had become a powerful intercessor. Al and Brenda had gone to Alabama to speak in a church pastored by

Mary Graves. Sunday morning Mary Graves received a phone call from a lady needing directions to the church. She also wanted to confirm that this was where the Al Taylor advertised in the newspaper would be speaking.

After the morning service, Brenda overheard the lady say she had been called to be an intercessor. God gave her names of people she didn't know, and she interceded for them in the Spirit. Sometimes God gave her the face with the name. She had been interceding for an Al Taylor. She had come to see if this was the man whose name and face God had shown her; he was.

Brenda became grieved when she realized that God raised up somebody her husband didn't even know to intercede for him. When she returned home, she sought the Lord diligently. Before long she was able to pray in the Spirit for Al and for others, too. She began spending at least an hour a day interceding for Al and his work. This became a dramatic changing point in their lives. Both Brenda and Al moved into a new dimension of prayer.

When Raymond Crowley was the first assistant general overseer in 1986, he wanted to begin a Prayer Commission. He appointed Al to be the chairman. Al asked, "Brother Crowley, have you prayed about this? I feel very feeble in this area. There are some mighty prayer warriors in our church."

Crowley insisted, "I have appointed you." This became one of the most thrilling assignments Al has ever had. And God has always given him great people of prayer to work with him.

One of the things the commission did first was to emphasize Praying People—Spend Time With the Father. Further, they sent one of General Overseer Raymond Crowley's message tapes on prayer to every pastor in the Church of God. The reports started coming in from churches everywhere, telling about their taking prayer seriously and God sending revival to their churches.

The Prayer Commission's current prayer emphasis is "Lift Him Up."

Called Along Side to Help NAE Stewardship Commission

In 1983, Al was given the assignment as chairman of the NAE Stewardship Commission. One of the greatest delights of this work was getting to know people doing the same thing he does.

One of the select speakers NAE brought in was Jim Jackson, author of Christonomics. Getting to know him was a special blessing. When God saved Jim, He asked him to give away all his assets except his home and car. He was worth $6 million. He obeyed, and God has used him powerfully around the world. Today, God allows him to give away $15 million to $20 million a year. Jackson says he is the happiest man in the world.

Al also was able to meet Stanley Tam. Stanley Tam is a dedicated, Christian businessman from Lima, Ohio. God spoke to Stanley and instructed him to give the full ownership of his business to God. Stanley reacted, "Well, God, I have already given you half of my business. I don't know anyone else who has done that much. My wife owns 25 percent, and I own 25 percent. Do you want her share, too?" God responded that He wanted it all.

Stanley shared with his wife what God was speaking to him. When Stanley asked his wife how she felt about giving God all of her shares in their company, she responded, "If God wants it, give it to Him."

When Stanley explained to his attorney what God had instructed him to do, the attorney thought he had lost his mind. The transfer was eventually completed. God owned all the stock, and He would receive all the profits. Stanley would serve as president and receive a salary like all the other employees of the company.

It didn't take long for the company to become the largest company of its kind in America, perhaps the largest in the world. Its president now readily admits that the new owner is unbelievably smart. He knows the solution to every problem. That company has now given millions of dollars for the work of the church.

Further, there is another dimension to Stanley's story. He asked God to give him one soul a day. At the end of the year, he had led 365 people to the Lord. Then he asked God for two souls a day. Now he is winning three people to the Lord every day.

These are the kind of people God began to bring across Al's path.

Al met Norm Edwards, who had raised millions of dollars for Wheaton College. He was president of the Christian Stewardship Council. One day he said, "Al, it's time for us to talk about merging NAE Stewardship Commission and the Christian Stewardship Council." They met in Chattanooga and proceeded to plan the merger that would create Christian Stewardship Association of NAE. They were able to successfully marry the two organizations.

The Christian Stewardship Association conducts a premier stewardship training conference each year. Previously they had averaged about 250 delegates each year. At the time of this writing, they average over 1,000 in attendance. On one occasion they gave Al the Best of the Best Faculty Award, and in 2000 they honored him with the Outstanding Stewardship Professional Award.

Called Along Side to Help Pathway Credit Union

Al has been with Pathway Credit Union for 18 years. He was on the board for a year, then became president. The credit union has gone from $300,000 to $3 million. They have over a thousand members. This is a help to pastors and laymen of the Church of God.

Called Along Side to Help as an Author

Pathway Press published Al's book, Proving God, in 1991. This book is one of the most helpful on the market today in knowing how to receive blessings through tithing. Every minister and layman should read it. Al says, "Faithfulness in tithing and giving will bring prosperity, and the world will see proof of God's power and goodness." He addresses the subject of tithing through faith in God's Word. He gives the reader proof positive that tithing is Biblical and still works today.

Being a Helper to Other Organizations

Doors outside of the denomination began opening to Al. The Church of God of Prophecy invited him to speak on stewardship at their General Assembly in 1991. This was history making because nobody outside their church had been allowed to speak in the plenary sessions. Al was given three sessions for three consecutive days. Over 1,250 copies of Proving God sold in that one meeting alone. They invited him to speak again in 1996 for two sessions.

Not being a credentialed minister has given Al access to a lot of invitations and open doors that would not have otherwise been opened to him. The Freewill Baptist Church invited him to speak for two sessions in their Leadership Conference in Nashville in 1997.

When He Lost His Helper

When Brenda and Al moved to Cleveland, Brenda wrapped her life up in the church, soulwinning, and prayer. She became involved in home Bible studies. Also, she taught a couples class at North Cleveland Church of God. But eventually God called her to the east side of Cleveland to Crowder Chapel to again witness to and teach the poor.

Brenda discovered it was easy to win them, but difficult to get them to church. She went before the Lord with the problem. The Lord spoke to her that they were too weak to come to church. He instructed her to go back and teach them in their homes until they were stronger. She visited on Tuesday nights, then went back on Wednesday nights to teach them. It seems that this is an interesting insight that is missing on the radar screen of the church.

People all over the world knew about Brenda's powerful prayer life. She prayed by the hours. Intercession was her real call.

In 1993, she detected a spot on her breast. Al pleaded with her to see the doctor. He finally convinced her to go for a mammogram. The doctor told her that the spot looked like cancer and she needed to have an operation. She did not feel comfortable with medical care. She leaned on the Lord to be her healer.

In August 1994, Al and Brenda left Cleveland, Tennessee, to go to the General Assembly in San Antonio, Texas. Brenda shared with Al that God had told her she was to make a speech at the General Assembly. He reminded her that the program had been finalized a long time ago. She understood that; but God had spoken.

On Thursday of the Assembly she fasted and prayed all day, seeking God for the message. God revealed to her that she would deliver a message of identification repentance for the laity of the church. He also told her that He would tell her when to go into the auditorium to speak.

Friday afternoon God sent her into the General Assembly business session. During that session the proposals to give laymen more ministry opportunities were being rejected. That was the mood when she stepped to the microphone. The general overseer recognized her and asked what she wanted to address. He then instructed her to come to the platform and discuss it with an Executive Committee member. Then, if possible, they would accommodate her request.

Brenda shared with Ray Hughes the content of her message. He recommended to Lamar Vest that she be allowed to speak. Then a little later Brother Vest said, "Brenda Taylor asked for permission to make a statement of privilege, and we are going to hear her now."

As she spoke, the anointing was so heavy that people began to weep all over the auditorium. Here is the Statement of Privilege Brenda delivered:

> To me the things that have been said during this General Assembly are an indication of a need for healing and reconciliation between the laity and the leaders and/or clergy. I see forgiveness as the first step for breaking down barriers. If we are going to cooperate and operate as one and work together to bring the lost and dying world to Jesus Christ, I believe all barriers need to be brought down. The Lord has put on my heart to represent the laity in asking the leaders and clergy for forgiveness in some specific areas for our fathers, forefathers, and ourselves. This does not represent everyone, but it will represent someone somewhere at some time. Many of these represent feelings that I have had in my heart at one time or another over the years. I would like to ask this body to forgive me and any of the laymen who have ever had:
>
> • Lack of respect for our leaders and clergy.
> • Attitude of vengeance, such as withholding of tithes, offerings, talents or gifts because we disagree with the way things are done.
> • For having higher expectations of you than you could fulfill.
> • Lack of faith in the almighty God who lives in you and is conforming you to the image of Christ.
> • For the times that we have quenched the Spirit, not being bold to respond honestly for fear of having all communications cut off between us or being misunderstood.

- For the lack of submission; for the many times we have not trusted God to use you as the instruments and help mold our lives.
- For every time we have deceived you and other people around us, pretending to be where we are not in our spiritual walk, trying to please you instead of God.
- For envying you for your gifts, your blessings and your abilities; for every time we have coveted and had jealousy—jealous of the attention and credit you have received.
- For any resentment we have held against you, especially over any decisions that we feel you have made that affected our lives in an adverse way.
- For every time we have spread rumors instead of telling God about the needs and interceding in the Spirit concerning them.
- For competing with you instead of completing you by focusing on fulfilling the specific call God has placed on our lives.
- For criticism of the things you did and said instead of looking beyond your faults and seeing that you have needs just like the rest of us do and then taking time to intercede for you until your needs are met.
- For every time we have been guilty of accusing and judging and condemning you as you carry out your responsibilities so faithfully.
- For not extending to you the same love, acceptance and forgiveness that we so desire from you, and for leaning to our own understanding and going our own way instead of God's way.

I want to express appreciation to you for being patient with us as laity and for being willing to take the responsibilities that many of us would not be able to carry. I pray that God will bless you and lift you up this day.

   When she finished, the men gave her a standing ovation. When the ovation was over, the Holy Spirit spoke through tongues and interpretation.

Interpretation: For I tell you today to repent of bitterness and unforgiveness and see the healing flow of my Holy Spirit as I reconcile the body of believers. As a light in this dark world, give yourselves to one another in love and see the mighty hand of God at work in your midst.

This message was delivered at a time of physical crisis for Brenda. This was the last General Assembly she ever attended. She came home and continued the battle against cancer.

In 1996, Brenda agreed to go to Mexico to a hospital where they used natural medicine. This was not a good experience for Al or Brenda. The nurses worked on 12-hour shifts. If their replacement did not come, they had to work that shift and then their own—sometimes working 36 hours at a time. Brenda was only able to take very small doses of the prescribed medicine. This frustrated the doctors.

Further, they placed her in the nurses' break room instead of a real hospital room. The Taylors could not rest. Finally, Al became irritated with the doctors. When they saw his frustration, they got a room for Brenda. However, the doctor said that there was no chance for her to survive. Al went into a state of grieving.

They came back to Cleveland. The doctor said, "If we can operate, she may have a 50/50 chance." Brenda again chose to trust the Lord. She said, "If God wants to heal me, I'll be healed. If not, I'll go to heaven."

Being an intercessor, Brenda believed that her affliction was comparable to what the body of Christ suffered. She said, "I believe the Lord has said to me that the affliction of the body is located in that part of the body that nurtures the children." Rickie Moore visited with her once. He reported, "I found nothing that felt like death, but rather I encountered an experience that felt like life."

Brenda went to heaven on June 17, 1996. Thousands who loved her and have been blessed by her life and ministry have missed her. But we will see her again.

The Helper Finds a Wife Again

Al continued working harder than ever. He missed Brenda. But after his time of grieving, he began to occasionally date. Then one day Charlene McCullough called and asked him if he had thought of dating Norma, his next-door neighbor.

Norma Pierce had lived alone for 11 years after her husband had left. Al called her and asked her to go to dinner with him. She responded, "I don't know. I have been dating two guys, and they are driving me crazy." But he kept calling. Sometimes he would call just to pray with her.

Finally, one evening he called and said, "Norma, I have just traded cars. Let me pick you up and take you for a ride." She agreed. Al came by, got her in the car, and they took off. They had a great time talking and singing. From that time on, it was love.

They were married in 1997. Norma is just what Al needs. She is a beautiful lady inside and out. She sells books in his meetings. She is the gracious, loving one who cares for people. It they stay in a pastor's home, she takes a gift bag. She is a great housekeeper, loves the family, and is interested in keeping the two families all connected.

Called Along Side Vision in This Hour

Vision Foundation is a real love of Al's life and ministry. It was a thrill to him when the Foundation gave $50,000 to the general overseer to fund 50 prayer centers connected on the Internet. Vision members are "stubborn givers." Al says, "Stubborn giving is good because it shows Christian maturity. The giver is going to give regardless of the circumstances."

Future Plans to Be a Helper

Al feels that the future is bright for stewardship of the Church of God. Our people respond to the Word of God— which commands us to be tithers. He feels that the two areas of his ministry—stewardship and prayer—are keys to revival. No revival will come without prayer. And revival will not come if people are robbing God.

God continues to use Al Taylor. He prays that his life will bless everybody he touches.

Al Taylor
3817 Cambridge Lane, NW
Cleveland, TN 37312

Telephone
423-478-7179

Dan Winters—God's Man of Action

Dan Winters—God's Man of Action

Dan Winters—God's Man of Action

There he stood in front of the School of Ministry in Moldova, Russia, at the age of 64. Near him stood two bishops of the underground church. Tears of joy were in his eyes. This was the greatest investment of his life. The building was breathtaking in its size and quality. It was built like a fortress with marble floors and marble staircases, a stainless steel commercial kitchen, nicely furnished classrooms, and impressive dormitory rooms for the Bible students. Impressive was the quality not only of the new, multistory masonry building, but also the quality of the student body and faculty. This was one of the greatest moments of Dan Winters' life.

Dan had seen a divine opportunity, seized a divine moment, and helped bring to reality the practical training of ministers and other workers for the ripened harvest in what had been the USSR.

He had learned early in life the value of seeing an opportunity and acting upon it. He recalled seized opportunities as a young man.

Seizing Opportunities as a Young Man

Dan Winters, at the age of 18, was successfully selling vacuum cleaners to people in the mountain areas near Hazard, Kentucky, and Logan, West Virginia. He has always been able to see an opportunity and move with it.

Dan's prior experiences had prepared him for this job. His first sales job was selling and delivering newspapers at the age of 6 to the dozen or so homes up the rail tracks and around the hillside at Peck's Mill. He sold Ferry Garden Seeds to the neighbors. At age 11 he was selling home-baked bread and pastries to the neighbors in the housing development where his family lived in Huntington, West Virginia, where at the age of 12 he also sold farm produce from his grandparents' farm. He mowed small yards for a dime, and by the age of 14 he worked in the grocery store for his uncle. He then started business for himself, including a newspaper route with a large number of customers. He plowed gardens on the hillside and bottomland for his father and neighbors on Crooked Creek. At age 16 he cut trees from the mountainside and sold short timbers to the coal mines. He didn't realize he was too young to engage in business enterprises. He just did it. His uncle taught him much about marketing and allowed him to be the assistant manager of his hardware store by the time he was 17.

The Childhood Life of God's Man of Action

Dan was born the third child of six in the Appalachian Mountains in Logan, West Virginia. His father and grandfather worked for the railroad and lived in Logan. The railroad hauled coal out of the mountains of southern West Virginia into New York and other industrialized cities. Dan's father earned about $3.50 a day. But the day came that he had a back injury and was unable to work for months at a time.

Dan says of his childhood, "We were never poor; we just did not have what other people had."

Dan and his brothers sometimes took their lunch to school wrapped in a newspaper with a string tied around it. The days were better when they could carry their lunch in a brown bag. They were all in the same classroom since grades one through six all shared the same teacher in a one-room school house. He took a glass jelly jar from home to use at school. He dipped the glass into the two-gallon open metal bucket for drinking water. When the bucket was empty the oldest boys in the class would go to the mountain spring and refill the bucket. The girls had one outdoor toilet and the boys used a different one.

If the glass window got broken out of the old family car, sometimes the family put cardboard in its place to keep the wind from blowing in on them. When the car would not start the children assisted his mother in pushing the car so the engine would crank. Sometimes Dan had holes in his shoes. Dan remembers when he was 6 years old that his mother put a piece of cardboard inside the bottom of his shoes before he went to school.

He started to school in September when he was 5. Dan and his two older brothers walked a mile and crossed a long bridge. There was not a walk space so they had to stand on the curb and hug the metal side rail as the large coal trucks and numerous cars passed them on the bridge. Childhood memories of family were delightful. His mother showered her children with love and made each one of them feel special.

The family was very involved in church and serving God. The children joined their parents in working in the garden, maintaining the yard, and doing family chores. Work was a family activity. His father had nine siblings and his mother had eight siblings; therefore Dan had lots of cousins in the large extended family living in Logan County. Family gatherings and attending the Aracoma Church of God with his family and grandparents are among his fondest memories.

His grandparents and his uncle, Bill Winters, lived next door. Bill soon left the hills of West Virginia and went to Bible Training School in Sevierville, Tennessee. There he met a lovely lady named Frieda and married her. The children thought it was appalling that some strange woman had unexpectedly become a part of their family. But soon they loved her too. Bill spent his lifetime pastoring in towns such as Rhodell and Mullens, West Virginia, and later in the cities of Columbus and Findley, Ohio.

Bill's older brother, Eugene, also spent his life as a Church of God pastor in West Virginia, Ohio, and Michigan, in such cities as Wyandotte and Pontiac. Eugene had two sons, Ernest Eugene, Jr., and James, who were also Church of God ministers. Dan's mother also preached in the Church of God. However, she did not hold a license. So Dan has a rich heritage in the Church of God.

Shortly afterwards, Lovell Cary and his new bride, Virginia Glass, began to evangelize in West Virginia. The family was attending the Mill Creek Church of God at this time where Lovell had a great revival. Later Lovell decided to begin a revival campaign in the Crooked Creek neighborhood. The Winters family helped him get permission to use the local school building for the meeting. This newly married couple lived during this time in the Winters home. Those were exciting and memorable days for the Winters family, including six children plus Lovell and Ginny. A relationship was born that has lasted a lifetime.

It was a glorious revival, lasting six weeks with over 100 people getting saved. The schoolhouse was full every night. There was no advertisement. The message was carried by word of mouth. This meeting impacted Dan Winters' life. Once you taste such a move of God as this, you can never be satisfied with a mediocre Christian experience.

The Conversion of Dan Winters

One Sunday night, Reverend Messer preached in Dan's home church at Mill Creek, West Virginia. The boys had gone outside at the end of the service; but something was happening on the inside. Dan's sister, Nancy, accepted Jesus as the Lord of her life. When Dan saw what was happening to his sister, he purposed in his heart to be saved the next night. The next time he got to church was Tuesday evening.

As soon as Reverend Messer gave the altar call, Dan headed for the altar. He did not want to miss out on anything that life changing. In those days in West Virginia when people got saved, they prayed through, wept and repented and had a real experience. On January 17, 1949, at the age of 15, Dan's priorities were set. He would walk with God as long as he lived.

A few days later he was baptized in ice cold mountain creek water.

The Man of Action Goes to College

It was a belief in the Winters home that when you graduated from high school, you should go to college. However, very few of the children could afford to go. It seemed everybody attending the Logan Church thought that while attending Lee College you would get called to preach, get married, and know your direction in life. Dan decided to try it. He graduated from high school in 1950 and headed for Lee College at the age of 17. He had saved a little money from working. His grandfather gave him $10, someone else gave him another $10; so he was off to Cleveland, Tennessee.

But God never called him to preach. Dan did not meet his wife. He even bought a mandolin, hoping he could have a music ministry. Professor Jim Humbertson tried to teach him to play the mandolin, but the flow did not go to his brain. He tried voice lessons from Professor Andrew Yates, but he gave up on Dan. He traveled for a short time with A. T. Humphries and the campus choir, but decided God had given the ear for music to someone else. Dan did not like not having money. He decided to do something about it. He went looking for an opportunity. He walked down the street in Cleveland, Tennessee, to Calloway's Grocery Store and asked if they had any work he could do. They asked him what he wanted to do. The answer was "Whatever you want me to do."

"How much pay do you have to have?"

"Whatever you pay." Dan worked for 50 cents an hour bagging groceries, stocking shelves, and cutting meat. He walked to work every Saturday morning. Then walked back to Lee College for lunch and returned to the grocery store to work the remainder of the day. He missed out on some campus activities, but he generated income to pay his school bills.

Funds were not adequate for college expenses, so after a semester Dan had to leave Lee College and return home, where he worked with the dry cleaners and later sold Electrolux Vacuum Cleaners. His father's health was very poor because of the pinched nerves in his back. The doctor prescribed that he

move to a warmer climate and suggested either Florida or
Arizona.

God Guides Dan's Steps

Lovell and Ginny Cary had moved to her hometown in
Florida, where Lovell served as an associate pastor at the Eloise
Church of God in Winter Haven. Because of Mr. Winters' health,
the family decided to join Lovell and Ginny in Winter Haven.
So Dan gave up his vacuum cleaner job. His dad sold their farm,
the animals, the house, and their furniture. Dan's un-air-
conditioned car was loaded with four of the family members
plus their clothing and household goods. In January 1952, they
were off to Florida for a new life for all of them. This was the
first time any of them had been to Florida. They arrived without
any idea of where any of them would live or work. Because of
such a deep friendship with the Carys, they spent the first few
days with Lovell Cary's in-laws. Some members of the Winters
family slept on the floor, but they felt welcome and happy to be
with their friends. Other church members accepted them as
friends immediately. The warm sunshine of Florida felt good
compared to the cold winter air of West Virginia.

At first Dan got a job picking fruit. He picked fruit from
daylight until dark. He only made $4.10 a day with this job.
Feeling responsible for helping to support his family, Dan
decided to find a job with better pay. He got in his car and
started looking for another job. He made plans, expecting God
to direct him.

Dan's faith was fixed. He knew that faith was a major
ingredient in obtaining the blessings of God. He knew his faith
was vital if he was going to break out of the bonds of
insufficiency. Dan drove until he saw an aluminum sign that
had the name of an irrigation company on it. He walked in and
said, "Hi! My name is Dan Winters. I am looking for a job."
The foreman liked Dan's driving personality. They hired him on
the spot. This was a "God thing." This job came from the Lord.
Dan knew that he had the favor of the Lord. God was in
business with him; and God was in the business of blessing Dan.

Dan worked in the office, then in the plant. He worked as a bookkeeper and a timekeeper. He also worked overtime on Saturdays, unloading pipes or boxes from railroad cars onto trucks. Dan only weighed about 125 pounds so this was tough work, but this opportunist would work with the older guys doing hard labor to make money.

After being with the company only a few months, Dan was bonded and given the legal responsibility of being custodian of the inventory during the vacation period. During this vacation period, the company also placed him in charge of the entire assembly plant, which had dozens of older employees. Unbelievably, everything ran smoothly with this 19-year-old in charge. Looking back, he doesn't know how he avoided conflict with guys who had worked there 15 or 20 years and obviously knew far more than he did.

Dan had always paid tithes on his earnings, even when in high school. Now he continued that practice. It was simple. If you earned a dollar, you paid a dime back to the Lord's work.

In May 1953, he was drafted into the Army. This was an upsetting trial at first. It seemed unfair. He was helping support his parents with a good income for himself. He had fallen in love with Mary Nell King from the Eloise church. He had enrolled in a local business school and was excelling in his night studies.

Further, Dan's two older brothers were already in the Army. Dan desired to be stationed at Ft. Eustis, Virginia, with his brothers. He knew it would be unusual for the Army to allow three brothers to be stationed at the same base. But he knew that God is a great giver and gives liberally to His children. His two brothers were already assigned to the railroad transportation division. He was not trained in transportation.

However, Dan did visit with the chaplain and the company officers explaining his desire to be stationed with his brothers in Virginia. He planned ahead of time what he would say. After some negotiation, Dan was miraculously sent to Ft.

Eustis where his brothers were stationed. Being with his two brothers gave him a great sense of security.

The Army officials found that Dan had a higher I.Q. than most of the other men in his group; therefore, he qualified for helicopter training in Oklahoma. He declined the invitation to attend officers training because it required a one-year extension of time in the Army.

Talk about frustration! Dan had gotten accustomed to making good money. Now he was making only $68 a month in the Army. He had a $56 monthly payment on the car he left in Florida for his parents to use. He had to have money to get his hair cut and to purchase shoe polish and other incidentals. Further, he wanted to have money to make trips home to see his 16-year-old fiancée. Was he supposed to pay $6.80 tithes out of the $12 he had remaining or not? Impossible! He went to talk it over with his brother Tom. "Tom, am I supposed to pay tithes on so little money?" Tom had an expeditious response. "I cannot tell you what to do. But if you obey God and do what He says, He is obligated to take care of you. Disobedience does not work well."

That was all Dan needed. It became clear to him that if he did not tithe, he was stealing from God and the windows of financial blessing would be shut. Ten percent would come out of his check before anything else, because he wanted God's protection. Dan learned early that in God's economy, the tithe and the offering always prosper you beyond where you were when you gave the gift in the first place.

The girl Dan loved was in Florida, and he wanted her with him. It seemed preposterous that they could be together. Dan did not accept the words: "It can't be done." Those words never fit well with him. That's what makes him tick. He does not take the standard answer.

It was obvious that he needed more income; therefore, a job was the best solution. Since he was a tither, he knew the windows of heaven were open. He believed God would supply all of his needs according to His riches in glory. He borrowed his brother's car, drove all over the area near the Army base and stopped at every place of business. "Hello! My name is Dan Winters. I need a job. I am in the Army, but I have Saturday and Sunday off. The Army is first; but I will work all available time." Three businesses turned him down, but the next one told him about a grocery store about 12 miles away that stayed open until midnight every night. Rich's Supermarket in New Port News, Virginia, hired him for one dollar an hour.

Work enough hours and I'll have $100," he reasoned. Since the store was 12 miles from the Army base, Dan had to walk and/or hitchhike to and from work. Many Saturdays he worked from 8 a.m. to 12 midnight then would catch a ride to the barracks. Difficult? Yes, but not impossible.

Within one year he had earned and saved enough money to get married. Many of the other soldiers in his company were spending all of their income, and some were writing their parents for financial help. Dan was living a different lifestyle. He was willing to pray, work, and resist temptation to spend in order to accomplish his goal.

Because of Dan's typing skills, he was assigned to a responsible administrative position in the personnel office. This was before the days of computers, and there were many reports to be done. Soldiers with typing skills were scarce. He made a quality decision that obeying orders was his duty every day.

He realized he could not support a wife on $68 a month. He had to get promoted. He was E-1. Then he moved to E-2 and got raised to $79 a month. He set a goal to hit E-4 in that year so he could get married and have enough money to support a wife. That was three promotions in a year. Impossible? Army regulations required that you spend a certain number of months in one rank before being eligible for promotion to the next higher rank. Dan did not have enough time to wait the required time. He and Mary Nell did a lot of praying. He worked hard, obeyed orders, and made his superiors look good. Twice in succession, his commanding officer waived the required time and allowed him to be promoted. He was elated when he was promoted to E-4 just a few weeks before the wedding date—June 6, 1954. That meant his wife would get $137.50 a month, and he would get $91 monthly. He felt they could live on that income provided he continued working at the supermarket. He knew how Jacob must have felt working for Rachel.

During the meantime, Dan learned once again that God has divine connections for him—the right friends and the right associations. He had learned to seek God for direction and to push on the door of opportunity to see if you can open it. One day the company chaplain was in his office and said he was looking for a soldier to be the chaplain's assistant. Dan pondered if he should volunteer.

This was once again a miracle for Dan Winters. It was as if God had come to Dan and placed a crown of favor upon his head because he was a faithful tither and giver. He became the chaplain's assistant. He received the same amount of money that he had been getting, because in the armed service they were paid by their rank. As chaplain's assistant he was exempt from most duties of the ordinary soldiers and was responsible for operations at the chapel. He was also given a priority position for a mobile home space on post, which was very limited with a waiting list. There the rent and utilities were only $14 per month. If he had not been assigned to the position of chaplain's assistant, he would not have qualified for this priority space. To live in a trailer park off-post, the rent would have been over $50, and the newlyweds were unable to afford to pay $50.

After this first year in the Army, Dan purchased a small used mobile home from his brother, Donald, and made a trip to Florida to marry the love of his life. After one week of honeymoon, they returned to Virginia to live in their 8 by 14 foot mobile home on the military base. Dan also was able to purchase a new Oldsmobile automobile for their wedding gift. Few people understood how Dan was obtaining the desires of his heart. He felt it was God.

Knowing God requires the first fruit, every month when Dan got his paycheck, he mailed his tithes back to his home church in Eloise, Florida.

Mary Nell would have worked, but she was too young. Jobs were available on the military base, but at that time you had to be 18 years of age to apply for a job. So she stayed home while she and Dan built a strong marriage. They both took a typing course at night, and Dan took a night course in Economics 101 at the college of William & Mary at nearby Williamsburg, Virginia. Mary Nell would often go during the daytime to the chapel where Dan worked and rehearse her music and practice her piano playing.

After a few weeks, the head chaplain moved to another military base for a six-month training class. Dan became the person in charge of the chapel. He had favor with the Lord. In this office there was very little to do except refer any visitors to the main chapel where a chaplain was on duty. All he had to do was answer the phone, keep the songbooks out, and prepare the weekly bulletin. This gave him plenty of spare time. He chose to use this time to take correspondence courses in accounting from the University of Florida. Seldom was anyone else in the chapel on weekdays, so it provided opportunity for Mary Nell to spend as much time as she desired at the chapel with Dan.

Most weekends Dan worked at the grocery store to help balance the family budget. One year after Dan and Mary Nell were married, he was discharged from the Army. It was an exciting day when they moved back to Winter Haven, Florida, on May 25, 1955.

Dan immediately got a job with an appliance store. He was the bookkeeper, but was also allowed to go out into the display area and sell whenever all the hired sales people were busy with other customers.

Again Dan made use of the door of opportunity. He became a natural at selling. He became aware that the person who moves ahead is going to be the person who does more than is required. When the store had sales contests, he sometimes sold more than the full-time sales people. On one occasion he hit the top with sales and earned a trip for two to Cuba. He had sold more television sets than any of the others. He did not take his job lightly. He was not required to attend the sales meetings; however, if there was a sales meeting, he was there. He worked overtime and learned all he could learn about sales and the products that were sold in the store. This training has proven to be very valuable during his lifetime.

The Opportunity for Home Building

Dan was always looking for opportunities to better his life. God sends you blessings in disguised packages. He will raise up individuals to be your divine connection to His next level for you. They will have the word of the Lord for you. One day he was visiting with Mr. Thompson, a member of the church.

"Dan," Mr. Thompson said, "If you will buy a lot, I'll build a house and we will split the profit."

"How much is the profit?"

"About $1,000 each."

Mr. Thompson gave the young opportunist a goal. Dan found a lot, took his life savings up to that time and purchased it for $600. Elijah Thompson built the house, and they split the profit. This divine connection gave Dan Winters a new life. He was quickly getting an education in homebuilding.

In 1958, at the age of 25, Dan Winters, the builder, was now on his way. He bought land, built houses and sold them for profit. He became the general contractor. He kept his bookkeeping job even though his heart was now in building. His philosophy was, "Hold on to the sure thing until you have proved something better." He worked about 10 hours a day at the office. He figured with 24 hours in a day, he still had 14 more hours to do what he wanted to do.

Dan subcontracted the work out to licensed people who knew how to do the different jobs. He purchased the materials after working hours at the office and also sold the houses. He soon was making more money building houses than the appliance store was earning. He admired his bosses and thought they were fine people. He decided to offer to merge the building business with the appliance store business with the expectation they would all be more successful. The businesses did merge; thus, Dan became a stockholder and had ownership with them.

After a few months, it became evident Dan had made a bad decision. He was working more hours than the other owner, yet the profits were being shared equally. He felt he was unequally yoked. People of action can learn and grow from bad business decisions. His heart was in home development, so he gave his partners at the store a 30-day written notice of his intended resignation. He thought the owners would give him back what he had put into their company, and they would keep the store. He did not anticipate a problem with his decision.

The other owners of the company did not want Dan to leave. He was a valuable sales person. One man said, "We do not want you to leave; therefore, we will not give you any money for your stock, and we want to keep all of the houses that are sold and under construction. The car you drive belongs to the company. If you leave, we'll send you home walking." It looked as if this was going to be a major crisis for Dan.

Mary Nell and Dan went to earnest prayer. After an hour of heart-broken prayer, Dan returned to the meeting. The storeowners had changed their minds about the car. They decided to allow him to keep the car and the one 20-acre piece of nearly worthless land about 20 miles from Winter Haven. His partners kept the store and all of the valuable real estate. Dan would have to start over.

Dan was very disappointed; however, he was relieved to be free. He rejoiced that God had intervened on his behalf, and he had enough to start over again in the building business. That was the last time Dan worked in joint ownership with anyone else unless he owned the controlling interest. From that time on, he became independent in business.

The man of action knew that he had to find a way to make this 20-acre piece of land profitable. Driving down the highway one day soon afterward, he saw a sign advertising land being sold for a small down payment with monthly payments. The idea hit Dan, Why can't I do the same thing?

Dan has always had to be careful of his thoughts because they tend to break into action. He took his 20 acres of worthless land, split it into 143 small lots. There was no road, no water, and no electricity; just raw land.

The brain of this man of action started working. He went to the sign company and bargained, "I'll give you two lots if you put me up a highway sign advertising my lots for sale." They agreed. He went to the radio station and said, "I'll give you two lots in exchange for advertisement." He also bartered with the local office supply store for office furniture in exchange for two lots. He began selling lots for $195 each. Five dollars down and five dollars a month. He quickly found out that the time payment plan worked best. "More people will buy," Dan says, "if you make it affordable to them." Anyone qualified. No credit check was required. It was understood that if a buyer defaulted on the payments, Dan would simply resell the lot to a new buyer at the original price.

Dan further learned that there was value in interest. If you charge 8 percent interest and it takes four years to pay for the land, you get 32 percent more money than you would otherwise get. Dan was excited. With the five dollars a month plan, people were now buying land they were otherwise unable to afford. Soon a clay road and electricity came into the area. Some people started buying lots and pulling in small mobile homes.

Dan's obedience brought his success. Every time he received any money from the sale of a lot, he gave the tithe to the Lord.

He developed that land and then went to other larger pieces of land. The man of action soon noticed that most people were installing mobile homes on their land. He got the idea that if he could provide a mobile home and land together, he would increase the number of sales. It would be easier for the buyer. He went to a mobile home company and bargained with them, "If you will put your mobile home on my land, on consignment, I'll sell the mobile home, and you will get the money. I'll get money out of the land." The company he contacted said, "We can't do it."

Dan hated the word *can't*. He found a mobile home manufacturer willing to sell mobile homes wholesale, and Dan would resell them at a profit. He immediately expanded his business by selling and making a profit on both the land and mobile homes as a packaged deal.

Dan purchased a tract of land and the owner promised to connect any new homes to an existing well the man owned. After the man broke his promise several times to install a water system, Dan and Mary Nell began to pray hard about the situation. If the water lines did not get installed to provide water for the two new homes Dan was constructing, it could cause Dan extreme financial difficulties. After praying, Dan approached the man again and ended up purchasing the well at a good price and developing the water system himself. He felt God delivered him out of a near impossible situation. Now he owned the water company providing water to his trailer lots and home sites. He started selling land, mobile homes and water. He also continued the new home construction.

Each time he made a sale he would telephone Pathway Insurance and buy an insurance policy for the new homeowner. He then made the decision to form his own company and provide insurance coverage for his new home owners. The company was known as Southern Insurance Services, Inc.

Dan increased his buying of mobile homes from the manufacturer and soon became one of their 10 top-selling dealers in the nation. Dan eventually became a manufacturer and built his own mobile homes. Now he was getting income from manufacturing mobile homes, selling land, selling water, retailing mobile homes, selling insurance—five areas of profit.

To better market his manufactured homes, he built a mobile home display center in downtown Winter Haven. The center was known as the Dan Winters Mobile Home Display Center. In 1963, Dan founded the Dan Winters Corporation. He is still the president. One breakthrough led to another. He began financing mobile homes and formed a company known as Southern Guaranty Corporation.

In addition to working with the banks, he later obtained approval and became a VA approved lender and a FHA approved mobile home lender. He then became a Government National Mortgage Association (GNMA) mobile home lender at the age of 45. He obtained authority to issue GNMA securities and sell them to major investors on Wall Street. He expanded so quickly that within a few short years he had eight offices in five states with over 300 employees servicing loans in 40 different states. His company was now competing with large national companies such as General Electric Credit Corporation, United States Steel, Barclay Financial, Greentree Acceptance, and others. His company that started with one mobile home loan in 1971 grew in 15 years to become the third largest in the nation in mobile home lending and was servicing over 30,000 loans.

Two of the most important aspects of Dan's business were hiring the right people and providing a high level of customer service. Dan developed a keen insight into people. He was able to spot the real workers. He shared with them his faith and the necessity for strong moral and ethical values.

Dan often prayed earnestly asking God for wisdom according to James 5: "If any man lack wisdom let him ask of God who gives to all men liberally." Dan knew he did not know how to do many of these things, but he knew God would provide the wisdom if he would seek Him and do the very best he knew how.

The Opportunity of Being a Member of Vision Foundation

When Carl Richardson founded Vision Foundation in 1977, Dan and Mary Nell became charter members. Being a member of the board of Vision Foundation has had a great effect on Dan's life. Vision provided Christian friends, fellowship and a vehicle to utilize his talent and resources for the kingdom of God. He desired a place through which he could channel his contributions without being so visible. He knew the money God had blessed him with could help to pave the way for sinners to hear the gospel message. Giving brought joy to his heart, and he wanted to sow into good ground.

Vision provided a niche for businessmen to minister without being spotlighted by their local brethren. Members of Vision have become some of the most important friends in his life. Dan held the office of president of Vision Foundation from 1979 to1983. He has served as chairman since that time.

The Opportunities to Witness for Jesus Christ

While a member of the local Home Builders Association, the members always made a big event out of the social hour at the monthly meetings. When Dan was nominated for the office of president, he refused to serve as long as they continued to serve alcoholic beverages at their dinners or parties. In order to get him to serve as president, the association suspended alcoholic beverages from their meetings during his term in office. He was elected president of the Home Builders Association of greater Winter Haven in his late 20s.

Southern Guaranty Corporation was a large lender approved by the Veterans Administration. As president and owner of the company, he was invited to provide a testimony at a hearing held by U.S. Senator Stone in Miami. Dan's testimony helped to get VA mobile home lending regulations changed for veterans.

He has served on numerous boards: the local real estate board of the National Association of Realtors, president of

Home Builders Association of Winter Haven, and president of National Manufacturing Housing Finance Association. He appeared as a witness in another U.S. Senate hearing held in Washington, D. C., by the Veterans Administration. He has served on church boards and has held a variety of offices at his local church.

Dan tried to always acknowledge God's leadership and provisions in his business as well as in his personal life. When he built a new four-story brick corporate office for his mortgage business on the lakefront in Winter Haven, he invited the mayor and other community leaders to the dedication. The Reverend Lewis J. Willis, president of the Church of God Theological Seminary, and the Reverend Karl Strader, pastor of Carpenters Home Church in Lakeland, participated in the program and offered public prayer of dedication of the new building and giving thanks to God.

The Man of Action Is Involved With Educational Institutions

In 1983, Dan learned that the Church of God Theological Seminary did not have a computer system. Dan gave the seminary their first two computers, which greatly helped with their financial operation.

Further, he established a $10,000 permanent loan fund, known as the Dan Winters Emergency Loan Fund for the seminary students. At the same time he established the Dan Winters Revolving Loan Fund at Lee University.

In 1984, Dan also provided Lee University with their first computer system. When Dan heard of these needs, he took action.

How a Man of Action Faces Sickness

Dan had always been healthy. Doctors had told him several times he could expect to live to be 100 years old. But one day in 1986 at the age of 53, he felt a slight twitching in his left upper arm. He went to the doctor and was diagnosed as having ischemic heart disease. His mother had died of the same disease at the age of 50. The doctor told him the coronary heart disease is hereditary.

Within a three-month period he had three angioplasty procedures followed by open-heart surgery—a five-artery bypass during a 10-hour procedure. At this time, things drastically changed in Dan's life. Three days after the surgery he developed arterial fibrillation with two chambers of his heart beating twice as fast as the other two chambers. To Dan it felt like the room was moving about three inches with each heartbeat. He began reflecting upon how his mother had died 24 hours after her first heart attack. She was three years younger than he now was when she died. Also, he had read that with arterial fibrillation some patients die within a few minutes.

Dan wondered if he was dying. The thought of dying did not create fear within him. He allowed the prefect love of God to cast out any fear. He was determined to trust God and not allow Satan to bring fear into his heart. He knew fear would undermine his faith if he allowed it. He thought of the scripture, "It is appointed unto man once to die and after that the judgment," and purposed he would not die until God's appointed time.

Dan felt as if God revealed His presence to him at this time of crisis. With no one in the room except Dan and the Holy Spirit, he felt God revealed Himself through the flowers and cards he had received. Dan also felt as if God revealed His love through the gospel music he was listening to. He continued listening to gospel music on his radio headset. As God revealed His presence, Dan rejoiced in the Lord.

As Dan continued to meditate, the joy of the Lord overflowed in his spirit. It was 3 a.m., and Dan was so excited he wanted to proclaim to someone, "GOD IS LOVE." He got out of bed and went out into the hall to share that love with somebody else. Was this an emotional experience? Was this a side effect of the medication? It sure felt good and was a tremendous encouragement at a time when he thought death might be occurring.

Dan began thinking about what death would bring if and when it did happen. If this is God's appointed time what will happen as I die. I will have millions of years in heaven. There will be a river of life. I will see Jesus, and I will talk to Jesus. He pondered, What will we talk about? When I see Jesus and look into His eyes, what will Jesus be interested in discussing with me?

He knew people here on earth are interested in hearing about things people have accomplished, such as building a successful business, or building hundreds of homes, or having a beautiful four-story brick lakefront office building, or how much money you have. But when it comes my time to visit with Jesus face-to-face, what will He really want to talk about? Will anything I have done really be worthy of discussion with Jesus?

In continued meditation, Dan began to evaluate his life. Have I lived my life in the way that really pleases my Lord Jesus Christ? Yes, I have served Him and participated in church practically all my life. Yes, I have taught Sunday school. I have been the Sunday school superintendent. I have been church clerk, and I have held other positions in the church. But, will the Lord be pleased and say, "Well done?" Have I fulfilled His will or are there things lacking in my life? Have I followed His written instructions or have I chosen a path of my own?

He began to reflect on how when he hired employees he wrote them a job description. He acknowledged God also wrote him and all Christians a job description in the Bible. As he recalled the scriptures, the answer seemed to be: he who wins souls is wise. Go into all the world and teach all people, making disciples of them. Heal the sick, save the lost, set the captive free, and bind up the broken hearted. Give a cup of water in the name of Jesus. Give a piece of bread to the hungry in the name of Jesus. Provide clothing to the poor. Visit those in jails and hospitals. He resolved to strive harder to do the will of the Lord all the remaining days of his life.

During that same night as he continued to meditate, Dan also received revelation or understanding of the fruit of the spirit versus the works of the flesh.

Dan received a renewed understanding that same night of how faith will destroy fear. God gives us faith as we read and believe His Word. Satan twists and changes the Scripture and tries to deceive us and cause us to doubt.

Healing and deliverance come as we exercise our faith in what God promised in His Word. Applying a Bible scripture in faith will remove the worry or fear.

To increase his faith, Dan soon began writing scriptures about healing on five by seven inch cards. He found that believing these scriptures produced faith.

After getting out of the hospital, Dan was somewhat confused by all of the medical advice from the doctors and the books he was reading as to diet, stress, genes, and his disease. He was seeking God for the answer to so many questions. "What about stress? What should I do about my diet? What should I do about my business? It is not easy to change your personality from a Type 'A.' However, if God would only speak, I would adjust my life in any way He says."

One night Dan had a dream or a vision. The drapes on the window began to blow. They looked like angels' wings. It seemed that God sat down on the side of his bed, stretched out His hand, and waved as if to a child being sent out to play. Then Dan heard the Lord say, "Go out and have fun!" The dream was over. He woke up instantly. He knew in his spirit that fun is living a life in total harmony with the plan of God. God has all of life in control and will take care of everything. No need for Dan to worry or fret. Those five words, "Go out and have fun," will always be remembered by Dan.

The year 1986 became a turning point in Dan's life. Before this he felt young, strong, and did not plan to die any time soon. But he realized that medically he could die any time. The doctors told him they had only performed a bypass, and they could not cure his heart disease. They warned him to expect future heart problems.

He spent considerable time at home recuperating, reading his Bible and meditating upon the plan of God. He began a long journey of liquidating the various business endeavors to reduce the stress in his life. If he should die he did not want to leave so much responsibility on his young wife, Mary Nell. He became serious about estate planning and spent time considering how to leave instructions for other people on how to finish whatever he started.

Dan repeatedly felt that he had a story to tell of what God had done for him, but He was very reluctant to talk about himself. He felt that everybody appeared too busy to listen. There did not appear to be a platform for his message. He had an image as an outstanding businessman, but he now had a message that he did not have before. What should he do with all of those feelings?

The Opportunity for Winning Souls

One Sunday morning his pastor preached, "Win souls! Win souls!" He continued, "You do not have to have a platform. Go to the street corners. Go to the hospitals. Go to the jails. No excuses for not sharing the gospel."

Dan immediately obeyed the voice of the Lord. He went to the Polk County Jail in Bartow, Florida, and applied for permission to hold an evangelistic meeting once each week. Dan had never been in jail so this was a new experience for him. There were no musical instruments so Dan purchased a tape recorder and some music on cassettetapes. He used his computer and printed out the words of the songs so the prisoners could sing along with the tape. Dan and the prisoners sang and worshiped Jesus together. He was amazed at the spiritual hunger and thirst of the prisoners. He was more amazed that they would respond and pray for salvation as he shared a simple gospel message with them. Later he invited another man, Joe Aplin, from the Village Church of God, to assist him in the jail meetings. Every time Dan or his friend brought a short message, some of the prisoners accepted Jesus as their Lord and Savior. Dan and Joe faithfully wrote down all the names of the new converts until the list held over 1,500 names. He felt that "winning souls" was the will of the Lord according to the Holy Bible. To him it was also having fun. It was a real joy to hear the redeemed prisoners testify week after week of how God was working in their lives.

During 1986 and 1987 Dan and Mary Nell sold most of their businesses so they could have more time together for ministry. Dan was happy spending time with the love of his life. He and Mary Nell had spent many happy years together. They had worked together and shared most of their time except during the three years he worked in the appliance store. Their office was in their home for several years and afterwards Mary Nell always had her own desk in the office adjoining his. She played an active role in their business and was an officer of the companies.

In June 1989, their daughter, Teri, was scheduled to direct the praise and worship during a crusade with Carl Richardson in South Africa. Dan and Mary Nell were to accompany them and teach a class. Mary Nell was not feeling well, so she cancelled; however, she insisted that Dan and Teri go on and minister.

While Dan and Teri were in South Africa with Carl, the doctor gave Mary Nell the initial report that she had ovarian cancer. She was shocked. Dan immediately flew back home. Within a few days his wife had major surgery and began chemotherapy treatments.

The Opportunity to Bless the Philippines

But even cancer did not stop them. Later they took a three-week evangelistic tour to the Philippines. This was their fourth trip to the Philippines. Their daughter, Teri, an evangelist and musician, asked them to accompany her on an unforgettable tour. They saw things that amazed them. Despite almost unbelievable hardships and inconveniences, the Filipino people—especially the hundreds of Christians they met—were uncomplaining and grateful.

Their first trip was in the late 1970s when Dan and Mary Nell took a two-week vacation to visit some of the countries in Asia. They made stops in Honolulu, Tokyo, Singapore, and Bangkok. The highlight of this trip was to visit with their dear friends Lovell and Ginny Cary who lived in Hong Kong.

They joined Lovell and Dr. Cecil Knight for the dedication of the new Church of God Worship Center in Davao City. As Dan spoke, a young Bible school student, Simeon Valenzuela, interpreted Dan's message into the local dialect. This was the beginning of a lifetime friendship. A couple of years later Simon went to Lee College and spent time on several occasions with the Winters family in Florida. Upon graduation he returned to Davao and later became overseer of Visayis Islands.

Their second visit to the Philippines was in 1983 with the Lee Singers. Teri was a member of the singers, and they stopped in Manila on their way to China.

About 1988 Dan and Mary Nell made their third trip to the Philippines and visited the Faith Bible Institute that was then meeting in the church auditorium over the police station in downtown Iloilo of the Philippines.

A few months after that trip, Mary Nell had ovarian cancer surgery. In 1989, the Winters family made their fourth trip to the Philippines.

The primary purpose of the fourth trip was to accompany Teri as she held evangelistic services in the town of Escalante where she had held a great revival the previous year. It was an honor for Dan and Mary Nell to actually participate in missionary work. They had prayed for and helped finance other people's missionary work for years. Now to go themselves to the mission fields of the far islands of the Philippines was a very moving experience for both of them.

To get from Iloilo to Escalante, they traveled by ferryboat to the island of Negros Occidental where they stayed overnight in the town of Bocolod in what was considered their best hotel. However, conditions at the hotel were rather primitive by United States standards.

The rebels were known to kidnap a person for as little as $2,500 ransom money. They were warned to be very cautious at all times while they were on the island. Most of the local merchants kept an armed guard posted at the entrance to their store to protect the customers and employees. In the hotel, Teri occupied a room on a different floor with one of the native missionaries. It made Dan nervous to realize the risk that existed and to know he was without any method to protect his wife and daughter. It was one of those times in life when he had to just trust in the Lord Jesus Christ for protection.

The Reverend and Mrs. Pol Cabos pastored the largest church in the area and served as district overseer of several other local Churches of God. Their home served as a "hub"—a kind of gathering place for many of the other Christians in the area. Pol Cabos held a city position for many years prior to going into the ministry.

Teri wanted the Winters family to purchase a refrigerator for the Cabos family who had never owned one. Before Dan and Mary Nell went to the hometown of the Cabos, they went shopping for canned meats, staple food, bottled water, and a new electric refrigerator for the Cabos family.

When they arrived in Escalante to unload the refrigerator, about 100 of the neighborhood people gathered to witness and participate as they dedicated it to the Lord, before they even plugged it into the electrical current. Dan felt that there was more prayer, praise, and thanksgiving offered to God over that refrigerator than over some new church buildings when they were dedicated in America.

The next day the Winters replaced the charcoal open cooking area with a bottled gas cook top. Sister Cabos was thrilled to have her very first cook top stove and her very first refrigerator after being married for over 20 years. It was a happy occasion.

The first afternoon they were there, Pastor Pol rode his dirt bike up and down the dirt street with his public address system blaring the news. "Sister Teri is in town and church services will begin tonight." It was worth all the hardships of the trip a few hours later as the open air evangelistic service began out in front of the house in the open area known as the city park of Escalante.

As Teri sang and preached under the one and only 15-watt light bulb hooked up to an automobile battery, the presence of the Lord was there. As soon as the loud music began, hundreds of little children and other people gathered. The anointing fell and many were saved and healed. The people were hungry for God and anxious to worship.

As the healing lines were formed, Dan was amazed at how God healed the sick when he placed his hands on them in prayer. The spirit of the Lord was there and no one seemed to pay much attention to the rocks that were thrown out of the darkness into the worshiping crowd.

The streets were not paved in the town. There were no telephones. No running water. No hot water. The electricity often failed, but the Spirit of the Lord was there in a real way. Dan, Mary Nell, and Teri were on the mission field half way around the world from home and having fun.

While in Escalante, Teri stayed in the home of Pastor Pol and slept on a rice mat. Dan and Mary Nell were houseguests at the home of the former mayor of the city.

An armed guard provided protection constantly for this household. These guards were very welcome considering 18 people had been massacred on the street in front the city hall by the rebels a couple of years prior.

During the next several days the Winters conducted training classes in the local church for about 50 local ministers who had come from several nearby islands. As they taught on faith and putting on the whole armor of God, they witnessed several healings. One afternoon a lady pastor brought her large, teenage son to Dan asking for prayer. His mother said he was demon possessed. Simeon Valenzuela later said, "During prior years the family often chained the boy to a tree because he became uncontrollable." Dan laid hands on the boy and prayed for him, commanding the demons to leave in the name of Jesus. Later Simeon Valenzuela, the overseer, shared with Dan that the boy remained healed and had completed Bible school in the Philippines. He was now preaching the gospel. Dan says, "This is really experiencing going out and having fun."

Before the Winters left Escalante, they purchased a customized 40-foot, fully equipped fishing vessel for Pastor Pol and his brethren to use. Fish were consumed by the members or sold on the local market to help support the work of the Lord. Since the Philippines comprise about 700 different islands, the boat was also used to ferry Christians from island to island to share the gospel.

Dan, Teri and her husband, Ken O'Neil, made a trip to the Philippines in 1992. This was Dan's fifth trip to the Philippines. They participated in the Iloilo Church of God youth camp. They also traveled to Baguio City and held services there.

While there, Dan and Ken were invited to speak at a well-attended meeting of the Full Gospel Business Men's Association in Baguio City.

Opportunity in the Soviet Union

Dan and Mary Nell traveled to Russia in July 1991 and helped plant a church in Tula, which is about 50 miles south of Moscow. This was a glorious experience for them. They stood with Pastor Karl Strader and others on the steps of the Kremlin and sang, "Every knee shall bow and every tongue shall confess that Jesus Christ is Lord."

They went outside the Kremlin wall where together with another couple they laid their hands on the wall and prayed in the Spirit, "This wall shall come down and this Communistic government shall allow the gospel of Jesus Christ to be proclaimed." They felt a mighty anointing of the Holy Spirit. They felt they were expressing this prayer on behalf of multitudes of Christian who were praying in America and other parts of the world. Within a few months the government collapsed and the country was open for the gospel to be freely proclaimed.

In making plans for the trip, Dan had suggested they not just plant a church, but that they also visit the mayor and business officials of the city. They need to hear the gospel also. It was very intriguing when they went with Pastor Karl Strader and a group of 11 other people down to city hall to visit the Communist leader who was mayor of Tula.

They were thought to be the first Americans to spend the night in this city. They sent the mayor of this large city word that there were businessmen from Florida among their group and they would like to visit with him. Upon their arrival the mayor was very cordial; however, another man who sat across the room was very stoic and thought to be a member of the KGB. They witnessed to the mayor as to what they were doing and about the new church being planted. They presented the mayor with a copy of a children's Bible, and a small gift from the Florida Citrus Commission. Pastor Strader testified as to how he had been saved and about his life as a Christian and then asked if they could all have prayer with the mayor. They all held hands around the conference table and prayed. They made a video showing the group praying.

Good food and bottled water were scarce in Tula except that which was provided for a few Communist Party members. The mayor arranged for Dan's group to have plenty of bottled water and to eat excellent food at a special restaurant from that time on. The mayor arranged for them to have a nice lunch with some of the local industry leaders. It provided an opportunity to witness and share their testimonies.

The mayor assigned a member of his staff to escort the group. The Spirit of the Lord was present at every worship service. The guide was a former secretary to the Communist Party. During one of the worship services, she told Mary Nell that she was experiencing a nice feeling about it all and wanted to know if she could be saved. Mary Nell had the privilege of leading this former Communist leader to Christ.

They witnessed the ripe harvest field with hundreds coming to Christ during each service. Dan and Mary Nell gave their personal testimonies and Mary Nell sang for the people. When people were invited to come for prayer, almost everyone came forward. They had about four different prayer lines. After people were prayed for once, they would often go to the back of another prayer line. They were thirsty to feel the presence of the Lord and experience the freedom of His salvation.

When Bibles in the Russian language were given freely to the people, they were eager to get them. Many hands were always reaching out to receive a Bible. Thank God they had enough for every person to receive one. They also delivered Hosanna Praise tapes. This was a life-changing experience. Dan and Mary Nell now knew better what it meant to, "Go out and have fun."

One evening in late 1991 Carl Richardson called to invite Dan and Mary Nell to come to his home in Brandon, Florida, for a time of fellowship with a visiting bishop from Russia. The bishop had come to the United States for a meeting with church officials in Cleveland, Tennessee, and then went to the Richardson's home for fellowship before returning to Russia. The Richardsons decided to invite several friends to their home to meet the bishop.

The 71-year-old Bishop Victor Belykh shared his story of spending 24 years in prison as punishment for preaching the gospel in Russia. Now that the doors were open they were experiencing a great revival. Thousands of people were accepting Jesus. Russian people were being called to preach.

After the exciting testimony, Carl Richardson asked his friends if anybody had a question for the bishop.

Dan asked, "Bishop, what can we do to help you?"

The bishop responded, "You can pray for us."

Dan asked again, "We are praying for you. What else do you need?"

The bishop answered, "Leaders! We need to train our people. It is wonderful that you have Lee College in America. But we have no money. We cannot afford to send students from Russia to the United States. For over 70 years under communism we have not been allowed to train leaders or to own buildings. Now that the government is about bankrupt they are easing up some." He continued, "There is a building in our town of Ribnitza, Moldova, that was half built by the old Soviet government that was intended to be a social hall. Construction was halted when they ran out of money. They have agreed to sell it to us for a Bible school, but we do not have money to buy the building, nor to purchase the materials required to finish it." Dan and Mary Nell both were deeply touched by the bishop's story and felt God was dealing with them about the opportunity.

God blesses people like Dan Winters financially so they can be pipelines through whom He can channel His money. So during the time of socializing and eating, Dan told the bishop he would give him the funds needed to purchase the building from the government and to complete the construction of the building for a Bible school. They immediately felt this was a "God-thing" and were excited about God using them to build a Bible school for the training of ministers in Russia. They processed the transfer of money through Carl Richardson Ministries who later added funds as were needed to complete the project. According to Carl, this was a dollar-for- dollar, matching-fund project and was the first Bible school to have been built in the Soviet Union for over 70 years. It soon became the official training center for the many Pentecostal churches in the 15 nations which comprised the former Soviet Union.

This Bible school meant much to Mary Nell who continued putting the work of God first as long as she lived. She felt that this project in Moldova was a project she and Dan had to involve themselves in. They were unable to arrange for this to be a Church of God institution; however, it is a Pentecostal school doing the work of the Lord, making disciples of young Christians.

How God's Man of Action Dealt With Losing His Wife

Mary Nell continued to battle cancer for over four years. Dan took her to Dana Farber Cancer Center in Boston for consultation, which is considered to be one of the leading cancer treatment centers in the world. However, they were unable to recommend anything other than what was being done at the Lakeland Medical Center. She went through several chemotherapy treatments, radiation, and hospital stays.

They had prayed and trusted God for her healing, but she went to be with the Lord on January 26, 1994. Dan was thankful he had been able to spend much quality time with her, traveling, and sharing many ministries together. Pastor Karl Strader and the Reverend Carl Richardson preached the funeral. Pastor Strader shared during his message of how the good works of some people go before them, and how some people's good works follow them, and that in 1986 Dan and Mary Nell established an endowment fund with his church. Therefore, ministry continues in her name from the endowment earnings. Some of her good works will follow her.

After the funeral, Dan was lost. He missed Mary Nell. She had been by his side in business and ministry during their 39 years of happy marriage, and it was now over. The grieving time was tough for Dan. He did not understand why he lost Mary Nell, but he could not give up and quit. Serving God, and family, was still very important to him.

Ministry Time in China

In May 1994, Carl Richardson invited Dan and a few others to join him on a missionary trip to carry the gospel to some underground churches in Beijing, Shanghai, and some other cities in China. They visited the Great Wall of China and heard some life-changing testimonies from the surviving spouses of Christian martyrs for Jesus. Christians were sharing the gospel at the risk of being jailed and persecuted. Bible lessons in the Chinese language were being hand copied and printed Bibles were treasured. Attending a service in a house church was an experience Dan will never forget. About 40 Christians crowded into a very small two-room apartment on a hot afternoon to share about Jesus. A guard was posted at the door and would admit only those persons who were recognized. The spirit of the Lord was there. The sincerity of their worship and powerful testimonies of how God was working in their lives in spite of persecution greatly impressed Dan. He personally talked with people who had been imprisoned for preaching the gospel.

In another city in China, Dan had the privilege of being present in the home of an elderly saint of God while her testimony was being videotaped by Carl Richardson Ministries. Dan was emotionally touched as she personally witnessed in his presence of how her husband was assassinated 40 years previously for preaching the gospel, leaving her with four young children. She shared how the Chinese government considered her family traitors and, therefore, would not provide food, education, or social support. As she cried and prayed in despair, the Holy Spirit spoke to her in an audible voice causing the hair to move on the back of her neck as He told her not to worry that He would take care of her. God did provide for her and her children, and one of her sons continues to preach the gospel. She had not lost her joy. She continued to serve God and help spread the gospel of Jesus Christ.

She further testified of how she had suffered from cancer and twice was at the point of death. On one occasion the doctor wrote out her death certificate expecting her to die within a couple of days. God healed her, and the doctor did not sign the certificate. She was rejoicing and proclaiming the blessings of knowing and serving Jesus.

In another city, Dan's group also met in a private dining room of a hotel with a small group of Chinese Christians. Their testimonies of how they were distributing Bibles underground and preaching the gospel was thrilling to hear. Dan marveled as he listened to people in their 70s and 80s who were very excited about their evangelistic efforts and talking about taking missionary trips to other nations of Asia.

During this trip, Dan provided funds through Carl Richardson Ministries for the purchase of a newly constructed, two-story building to be used as a Bible school. He also provided funds for a new brick church to be built as a memorial to Mary Nell. George Chinn was coordinating this construction. George is another pastor who survived 18 years of imprisonment and hard labor for preaching the gospel in China.

Larry and Jackie Danley also accompanied Dan on his trip to China. They are his very good friends and former pastor. They also funded a church building during this trip as a memorial to their dear, deceased friend, Mary Nell. To reminisce on these events of eight years ago brings tears to Dan's eyes today.

The Second Trip to Moldova

Near the time Carl invited Dan to go with him to China in May 1994, Cecil Knight had come to his house for a short visit. After many comforting words, Cecil said, "Dan, you have to get out of this house. Why don't you go with me to Romania in June?" Knowing Moldova bordered Romania, Dan responded quickly, "I'll go to Romania with you if you will visit the Bible school in Ribnitza, Moldova, with me." Although classes had been held in the school since May 15, 1993, Dan had not had the opportunity to visit it. Dan was hopeful Dr. Knight could assist in creating connections between the Moldova Bible School and the Church of God Theological Seminary in Cleveland.

The trip in June 1994 was what Dan needed. However, it was rough. In Bucharest, he, Don Price, and Cecil were sitting on the plane getting ready to take off for Moldova, when they learned that two of the plane's engines were on fire. The fire trucks were rushed out and the firemen sprayed the plane while all passengers remained on board and watched out the window. The attendant told the passengers not to be afraid because it happened all the time. The excessive heat caused the fires. Dr. Knight asked what they should do if the fire reoccurred while the plane was in the air. The attendant said, "It never happens after the plane reaches 5,000 feet of altitude because the air is much cooler up there." They were hoping they would reach 5,000 feet without any reoccurrence. This made them question whether or not they would ever fly on that airline again.

When Dan, Cecil, and Don arrived in Moldova at the Bible school, they were extremely pleased with the quality of construction of the three-story building that had been constructed of masonry materials. All of the work had been done by donated labor.

Dan and Dr. Knight witnessed the elderly bishop as he personally taught the class of approximately 50 students from the Bible from early morning until after dark. Dan and Cecil were deeply moved by seeing the building, but even more so by the quality of training being provided to the eager students who had such a hunger to become leaders.

Dan and Dr. Knight observed that the dormitory rooms usually had eight students occupying them. All the rooms including the two large bath facilities were being used to capacity. The students were also using the VCR to play teaching tapes. There was such a sincere commitment apparent among the facility and students to study the Bible and learn about God. The students appeared friendly, well mannered and kept the premises clean.

They were also surprised when they first arrived to find a hole nearly as large as a city block being dug adjacent to the new building. Students from the Bible school were using pick and shovel to dig out the dirt and then shoveling it onto a wagon where it was being hauled away by tractor.

Dan asked, "What is this hole here for?" With tears in his eyes, Bishop Belykh responded, "To triple the size of the Bible school. We need more dormitory space and a larger dining room. God gave us the plan, and our architect has created the detailed drawings for us."

"How much money do you have in the bank?" Dan questioned.

"We aren't allowed to bank in Russia."

"Then how much money do you have to buy all of the material needed for the building?"

The bishop said less than $100 U. S. dollars. When asked about how they intended to finance the construction of the new addition, the bishop replied to Dr. Knight, "God told me to dig the hole, and He would send a raven to provide the money." They would be ready to pour the first concrete that next day. Dan was deeply touched by this level of raw, primitive faith.

Dan wept as he shared with Cecil that he could not leave those people without arranging the funding for that Bible school. The nation was nearly bankrupt. The people earned so little money, yet they were willing to provide all of the labor free. The bishop had spent 24 years in prison for preaching the gospel and now was teaching classes and preaching the same gospel every day. Who would help these people expand their Bible school? Dan now understood why he had felt so impressed the day before they arrived that there was an important assignment for him somewhere in Moldova. How could this need be ignored and left undone? This was another opportunity to "Go out and have fun."

God had given him the gift of doing whatever was in the power of his hand to do. So once again he went into his own checking account and gave the money for the Bible school.

Dan was aware that we are created to be somebody's answer. Dr. Cecil Knight says, "Dan became God's raven for this occasion."

The Man of Action Meets His New Bride

Dan returned home, wishing Mary Nell could share with him what their money was doing in Russia. He had always leaned on Mary Nell, even for things like the clothes he wore, including the color coordination. He was a very lonely man.

When Dan went to the General Assembly in August of 1994, he had never met Mary Boldrey. In fact, he had never heard of her, even though she was executive secretary and administrative assistant to the general director of Publications at the Church of God Publishing House. Dan had been in and out of Cleveland on many occasions, but their paths had never crossed.

He really had no plans for getting married again. However, his children had said, "Dad, you need to get out of the house and do some exciting things again. In fact, you need to take some nice lady to lunch. Have fun." He really did not have an interest. He did not see anyone who caught his eye. Teri teasingly said, "Dad, I have bought you some new suits for the Vision meeting in San Antonio." When he left to go to the General Assembly, he had no idea how drastically this trip would change his life.

Within a couple of hours after arriving in San Antonio, Ken, Dan's son-in-law, first saw Mary in the restaurant at the hotel and pointed her out to Dan. Teri added, "And she doesn't have on a wedding ring." Dan did not respond or turn to check her out.

Then on Saturday as they were leaving the Laymen's Luncheon, Teri exclaimed, "Dad, there's that woman!"

Dan asked, "What woman?"

"That woman Ken saw. Someone needs to do something."

Dan said, "Stop her! Block the aisle." He and Teri blocked the aisle, and as Mary came by with a friend they introduced themselves. She told him where she worked and that she knew his Uncle Bill Winters. It was a casual conversation.

Mary then walked off. When Dan saw Mary, it was love at first sight. Mary's reaction to all of this was, "That was a friendly bunch." She never dreamed the man she just met was her future husband.

Wanting to find out more about Mary, Dan went immediately to the exhibit area looking for Al and Brenda Taylor. He asked, "Do you know Mary Boldrey?" They assured him they did and made several complimentary remarks about her. Al suggested that he and Brenda invite Mary to the Vision banquet that evening. Al and Brenda were able to find Mary and invite her to the banquet. They told her they had a friend who was interested in meeting her. She agreed to go and check him out.

After the banquet, Dan invited Mary to go for a walk on the Riverwalk. They found a small, sidewalk restaurant, sat down at an outside table, and began to talk. They had a great time just getting acquainted. It was exciting to know they had so many mutual friends.

Dan got on the plane the next morning and flew to Florida. He kept thinking about Mary, but did not know what to do. He was busy the following week with house guests. Two Romanian ministers in the states for the General Assembly had gone home with him. After they left, he decided to call the Publishing House to see if he could talk to Mary. This started a series of phone calls which continued for several days. To Dan it seemed impossible that everything could be so "just right."

Being a caring person, Dan had always taken his widowed mother-in-law to lunch on Sunday. She was a strong woman of God and a Church of God minister for many years. She often said to Dan, "There's just one for me and he's gone. One for you and Mary Nell is gone." This one particular Sunday he decided that it was time to tell her about Mary. To his surprise, her response was, "Yes, if you have found a good Church of God girl, that's wonderful." That was a confirmation to Dan. It was important to him that his former wife's mother be happy with his new marriage.

On September 1, Dan made a decision to go to Cleveland where he could spend time getting to know Mary. The more he was with her, the more certain he was that God had brought them together and that she was the one with whom he wanted to share the rest of his life. From the beginning, Mary knew in her heart that there was something very special about Dan.

They made plans for Mary to go to Florida to meet his family. Mary was unaware that Dan had already ordered her engagement ring through a contact in South Africa, and that it had been shipped via New York to a jewelry designer in Tampa. They flew to Florida on September 10 where Mary met the family. The next day, on Sunday, September 11, at one of Dan's favorite restaurants, Berns Steak House, in Tampa, Florida, Dan asked Mary to marry him. It was a beautiful evening, and Dan had everything arranged to perfection. He had planned a seven-course meal. He arranged for the florist to deliver flowers to the restaurant for Mary. Dan had also arranged for the jeweler to deliver the ring to the restaurant. With every course of the meal, Dan read Mary a poem that he had written especially for her. The waiter would then deliver a bouquet of roses to their table. Mary had seven bouquets of roses with a note from Dan written on the card with each bouquet.

After the meal they moved to the dessert room upstairs, where Dan had placed a dozen red roses. After they had ordered their dessert, the manager personally brought the ring on a small satin pillow to Dan. It was then that he asked Mary to be his bride. She said, "Yes." The following day they went to Disney World with the family and then made plans to return to Cleveland.

Upon returning to Cleveland, Mary retired from the Publishing House, after 36 years of service, to start preparing for her new role in life. Dan remained in Cleveland for the next 40 days. They were married on November 5, 1994, at the North Cleveland Church of God, with a host of family and friends sharing in their joy. When Mary walked the aisle of the North Cleveland Church, she got her first husband, three children and four grandchildren with the fifth grandchild scheduled to arrive in about two months. It was a very wonderful time for Dan and Mary. They were so happy to have each other to share their lives with. Dan promised her a life of fun and games. They live part time in Florida and part time in Cleveland, enjoying the best of both worlds.

The Dedication of the New Building of the Russian Bible School

Not long after Dan and Mary were married, the invitation came for the dedication of the new addition to the Bible school in Ribnitza, Moldova. Dan is by nature a very protective husband. He suggested to Mary that the trip might be rough. Mary insisted that it was the will of the Lord for her to go and be with her husband for this important event. Cecil Knight, Carl Richardson, and Don Price joined them for this trip, along with their Russian interpreter, Walter Begrin.

Carl and Dan had decided not to fly again from Bucharest to Moldova. But travel arrangements were difficult because none of the car rental companies would rent cars out of Bucharest into Moldova. So Carl arranged for a friend in Bucharest to send his van and a driver to provide transportation for Carl, Dan, and Mary. Don contacted a friend in Budapest, who sent a driver and a Mercedes to provide transportation for him, Cecil and Walter. The two parties drove along together.

Dan and Mary had read on the Internet a warning about the increased danger of driving in Moldova after dark. The Internet also warned, "Do not go through Transnixia, a small country that had recently been taken over by rebels. There was no official government nor was there a United States consulate there to represent you, so stay out of Transnixia." They did not know where Transnixia was and did not intend to go there. They thought they were only going to the city of Ribnitza via the city of Kishnau, the capital of Moldova.

Dan asked the drivers about how long it would take to make the trip. The reply of both drivers was, "No idea! Never been there." They predicted it would be about an eight-hour journey and they would arrive in Ribnitza around 4 p.m. They agreed that both carloads should leave early the next morning so they would arrive at the Bible school in Ribnitza before dark.

It was a grueling trip through the Romanian countryside where the "conveniences" were almost nonexistent. Young revolutionary soldiers at the border demanded $20 in U. S. dollars. Dan gladly paid it to get away from them and across the border.

As they were crossing the mountains, heavy fog set in. Freezing rain and snow began to fall. It was now dark and driving was treacherous. The trip had taken longer than expected. After they crossed the border into Moldova, local guards sent them on a detour down a side road because the bridge on the road they were to take to Ribnitza had been blown up during the recent uprising. Afterwards a local truck driver informed them they were in Transnixia. Young guards stopped them at check points several times. Each time they demanded a fee. Their driver said the fees were unreasonable, and he was getting angry.

At the last check point, Mary saw one of the young guards walk up to the front of their van and load the bullet into the magazine of his carbine rifle. She, Carl, and Dan began to pray. Their Russian guide was getting nervous. Everyone was anxious to complete this journey. Dr. Knight was on a tight schedule which required them to get to Ribnitza that night. Finally, they were allowed to proceed and arrived in Ribnitza, Moldova, about 10 p.m., very relieved to have gotten through that country during the darkness. Later they were told that during the time they were in Transnixia, they were in real danger because the locals are known to take foreigners hostage to extort ransom money. Praise God they were finally safe! When they left Ribnitza, they were escorted out by the vice president of the Bible school by a different and safer route.

Since they had never driven in Ribnitza, they had no idea where the Bible school was located. Very few people were on the streets since it was late at night. So they stopped and asked the first ones they saw for directions. To their surprise, the couple knew exactly where the school was located. Mary thought they might have been angels placed there by the Lord until Dan observed the smell of alcohol on the boy's breath.

Within a half-hour, the team arrived looking somewhat rugged. The 75-year-old Bishop Belykh was waiting for them. Tears rolled down the old bishop's face. He was so glad to see the Winters family and the rest of the crew. When one has spent 24 years of his life in prison for preaching the gospel, he treasures his friendships. He showed Dan the plaque on the wall at the entrance to the building, dedicating the building to the "Den Winters Family of Winter Haven, FL." The spelling of Dan's name was not correct, but who cared? They had the love of the Russian people whom they loved very much. A wonderful hot meal was still waiting upon their arrival. Dan and Mary were allowed to sleep in the president's suite, which was very nice by Russian standards.

Dan was thrilled with the building. It was like a fortress. It had been finished with student and ministerial volunteer labor. They had dug stones out of the mountains. There was beautiful hard marble tile on the floors and staircases. The kitchen was equipped with all stainless steel commercial fixtures and the dining room seated over 300 people. Not only were they prepared for training the students to become ministers and church workers, they were also involved in community enrichment. Several other groups, including some from Europe, had joined in and helped with the construction of this lovely facility. The German craftsmanship was evidenced throughout the building. They had their own bakery that had been donated and brought from Germany that distributed over 1,700 loaves of bread daily to help feed the local people. The nearby food warehouse facility was stocked with a large inventory of food for the Bible school that was also being shared with the local citizens. This gave them favor with the local government. In the warehouse there was also a room full of sewing machines. The plans were to teach women to sew so they could provide for their families.

Dan wept with joy and humility. No other building he had built or participated in meant as much to him as this building, a building fully operational and training young leaders to preach the gospel of Jesus Christ behind the former Iron Curtain of communism. His financial gift had been stamped with the anointing, and the anointing was bringing in a harvest. This could make a difference in the lives of many people who had been denied the opportunity to worship Jesus for the past 70 years.

The dedication service for the Bible school was a beautiful service. The auditorium was filled to capacity as well as the overflow and hallways with students, faculty, and administration from the Pentecostal Churches in Russia, as Dr. Cecil Knight, Carl Richardson, Dan, and others ministered. Walter Bagrin interpreted the services for the local people who were present. The sincerity and depth of their worship was beautiful and left a definite impression on Dan and Mary.

To Dan, "It was joy unspeakable and full of glory." It was a joyful experience for Dan and Mary as they presented the offering that they had brought to Bishop Belykh. Bishop Belykh immediately announced that the offering would be adequate to cover the unpaid expenses of students who had shown up without any funds for tuition, and that he would use it for that purpose. Everyone rejoiced.

After the dedication service, they were invited to the dining hall for a wonderful meal and a time of fellowship with all the students, faculty, wives, and guests present. Dan and

Mary felt so honored to be among such wonderful and dedicated people of the Lord. They shall always cherish the memories of this very special occasion.

The Opportunity to Assist Other Ministries

Dan has served many years on the board of Emerge Ministries in Akron, Ohio, with Christian psychologist Dr. Richard Dobbins, a renowned counselor and teacher in the Assemblies of God.

He also served on U.S. Board of Directors of Asian Outreach with Paul Kauffman, the founder. Asian Outreach distributed Bibles and established churches in China.

Dan served on the Steering Committee during the capitol campaign at the Church of God Theological Seminary. Today, he is on the Stewardship Committee of the Church of God Theological Seminary, and was recently appointed by the general overseer, Dr. R. Lamar Vest, to serve on the Prayer Team Committee which is part of the Strategic Direction Team. He has also served on numerous boards and committees through the years.

The Man of Action as a Family Man

Family life is a priority for Dan Winters. He has two sons and one daughter. His only daughter, Teri, graduated from Lee University and was a member of the Lee Singers. She has three children, two boys and a girl, Marc, Danielle and Trevor. Her oldest son, Marc, is a very special child with autism. Dan's new wife, Mary, loves and cares for the grandchildren as if they were her own.

Dan's older son, Ed, attended Lee University, and his youngest son Donnie attended Florida Southern University. Dan has two older grandsons, Byron, who is a senior at Lee University, and Brent, who is a junior at the University of South Florida in Tampa. He also has two step-grandsons, Christopher and Cory, living in Central Florida.

Needing help in training her autistic child, Marc, Teri moved her family to Cleveland, Tennessee, in 1998 to be near Lee University were he is in a special education program. Now there are about 20 autistic children involved in the special education program at the University. Dan and Mary enjoy being in Cleveland to share their time with them.

Having an autistic grandson is tough. Dan loves him so much, but he often struggles with the fact that his grandson has such a major problem and is yet to be healed. Dealing with the problems of autism often brings stress to Teri and the entire family.

Dan often says, "It's easier to talk about success than it is to talk about the times you just have to be faithful when things aren't going the way you pray they will go. You just remain faithful in all the circumstances of life. God is still God, and His promises are true."

The Opportunity to Reach the Nations

China has a special place of interest in Dan's heart. On one occasion, he supplied over 1,500 Bibles for Lee College Singers to smuggle into China. His daughter, Teri, was a student at Lee and a member of the Lee Singers. He and Mary Nell were privileged to accompany them when they crossed the border going behind the Bamboo Curtain to deliver the Bibles.

Traveling to Shanghai and Beijing with Carl Richardson and networking with pastors of the underground church has also greatly affected his life.

One day while flying on a plane to Germany, Mary read to Dan an article about China in the flight magazine. She read to him that the Chinese government is concerned about their citizens' frequent use of the Internet. Twenty million of their citizens are on the Internet and the number is increasing daily. The leaders like the Internet for business purposes, but they are concerned about the western influence on their people. The Chinese government was experiencing difficulty controlling the situation. Dan, the man of action, immediately replied, "Mary, why don't we use the Internet to get the Bible into China? We feel very uneasy when we get on the plane to travel into China. Even if we get the Bibles in, we can't share much other information about Jesus and the plan of salvation. But through the Internet, we can share the full gospel. We can make it possible for them to read the entire Bible in their own language plus we could have a prayer page and sermon material for them. This is wonderful!" Soon he was dreaming about the 1.2 billion people that would be able to search the Scriptures in their own Chinese language.

Neither Dan nor Mary had an idea how to develop a web site. They made several trips to Cleveland to convince somebody else they should do it. They discussed their idea with several people who always ended up saying, "That's a great idea. Somebody ought to do it." Finally, it became evident that God was speaking to Dan and Mary Winters.

Dan bought a book on how to develop a web site. He signed up with AOL. After much trial and error, he hired Jeremy Yoder, a student at Lee University, to be his designer for the website. Soon they had www.jesussaves.cc up and running. This site provides information about Jesus Christ, who God is, who the Holy Spirit is, how to pray and how to be saved. It tells about the life of Jesus, the miracles of Jesus. The Bible is there in many languages. There is a prayer page where people can send their prayer requests. Dan or Mary personally answer every prayer request that comes on the board. The prayer requests are also copied and sent to the Prayerborne team at the Church of God International Offices for prayer. The web site is also on the Church of God International Offices web site under "Spiritual Helps."

Today, many lives are filled with problems resulting from such things as divorce, drug addiction, alcoholism, sexual perversion, anger, hostility, stress and greed. Therefore, this site provides spiritual helps plus offers suggestions for people who need deliverance and help in these areas of life.

A model prayer is provided as a guide to direct people in learning how to pray. References or links are provided to the Bible, devotionals, Bible studies, counseling centers, and teaching sessions on RealAudio and RealVideo.

They now have www.jesussaves.cc web site published in the Chinese, Russian and Spanish languages. They hope to add additional languages soon.

All Dan and Mary want to do at this stage in their lives is to help win souls. So they talked to their daughter, Teri, and their oldest grandson, Byron Winters, about designing and hosting web sites for churches and other ministers. The Internet is proving to be an effective method to communicate information about Jesus to a large number of Internet users around the world. Today approximately 600 million people are reported as using the Internet worldwide.

Soon Dan and Teri, along with the technicians, had organized a new company known as WinWorld. "Win the World to Jesus." Several departments of the Church of God quickly recognized the advantage of using WinWorld and its talented team to upgrade their web sites. Winworld now publishes the Church of God International Offices web site. They also designed and publish "Faith News" as well as web sites for several other ministries and local churches.

Internet cafes in foreign countries is a dream of Dan Winters. Through Vision Foundation he has already financed the first computer for an Internet cafe in China. These cafes can be used as businesses in the daytime and provide a source for the underground churches to obtain the gospel message over the Internet after hours.

Winworld is developing an online library known as www.faithlibrary.cc. Teaching sermons and other resources will be available free to Internet users worldwide. This has been a dream of Dan's for sometime. Dr. F. J. May has 1,100 taped sermons in his closet. Dan has started the process of getting them out of that closet, compressing them, and publishing them

on the Internet to change a world. Forty of Dr. May's teaching
sessions on the Book of John have already, at the time of this
publication, been translated into Chinese, Russian and other
languages for Bible school students. They have sermons in
English, Chinese, Russian, Spanish and Arabic published on
www.faithlibrary.cc web site. Further, there are links to web
sites of other great preachers. Dan strongly believes Bible
school students in other countries can utilize good training
material once it is published on the Internet. He is committed to
helping make it happen, free of cost, to the students.

Cooperation with the body of Christ is priority with Dan
and Mary. In April 2002, they agreed to provide a web site for
the Prayerborne team of the Church of God. After they began to
design the site, during the General Assembly of the Church of
God in Indianapolis in August 2002, the general overseer
announced a vision for 50 or more prayer centers connected
around the globe providing prayer 24 hours a day, seven days a
week. Dan felt led to give a sizeable offering to the general
overseer to help start Global Prayer Network for people all over
the world on the Internet. Dan sees this as a true opportunity to
share the gospel as commanded by Jesus. His passion is to
connect these prayer centers around the globe. He is developing
content as a guideline for prayer. He is also developing content
to help hurting people and to teach others in fulfillment of the
commandment of making disciples of others. He envisions
Global Prayer Network web sites as becoming one of the most
important endeavors he has ever undertaken for the kingdom of
God. He is having fun as he helps win the lost and make
disciples for Jesus. He believes he is living in God's will as he
and Mary "Go out and have fun."

The man of action believes that the Internet and the
computer together with CD's and DVD's provide a real
opportunity for Christians to share their faith with multitudes of
people who would otherwise be impossible to reach. During the
past five years the number of Internet users has increased 300
percent, from 200 million to 600 million. Muslims and other
people groups behind various governmental controlled curtains
who are forbidden to hear the gospel message are searching the

Internet for solutions to their problems of life. Anyone searching the Internet has access to what Christians publish on the Internet. Any message can be read. It can be heard, and it can be printed. What Christian will publish the gospel of Jesus Christ in a format that is interesting to the Internet user? The opportunity is ours. Dan prays the world will be told the things Jesus wants us to tell them.

Dan has always believed that God is faithful in every situation of our lives, if we remain faithful to Him. He strives to read the Bible and trusts in the promises of God for every event in his life.

Today at the age of 70, he feels good and has a high level of energy that he is spending to share the gospel on the Internet. While admitting that only God now knows how long he will be able to work, Dan is committed to working as if today may be his last day to live and at the same time expecting to live many more years for Jesus. He is continuing to develop web sites to share the gospel.

It was Henry Ford who said, "Anyone who stops learning is old, whether this happens at 20 or 80. Anyone who keeps on learning not only remains young but becomes constantly more valuable, regardless of physical capacity."

Dan remains strongly committed to the statement of purpose of Vision Foundation adopted in 1977, which includes "...Using the electronic media to share the gospel with the largest number of people at the lowest cost." Although it has been 25 years since the statement was adopted, Dan believes the opportunity is greater today than ever before, and he is applying the talent he has to use the Internet in accomplishing this objective.

Dan and Mary, along with their daughter and three grandchildren, are members of the North Cleveland Church of God.

Dan Winters
1319 Mirror Terrace
Winter Haven, FL 33880

Telephone
863-294-6943 or 423-472-1307
Office: 423-473-8084

Fax
423-478-8011

E-mail
Winters333@aol.com

Raymond Wolf—Minister to the Ministry

Raymond Wolf—Minister to the Ministry

Have you ever felt you had a call of God upon your life? Presumption always says that it is a pulpit call. But not always! Raymond Wolf has a powerful call and a forceful anointing upon his life. God called him to minister to the ministry. God gifts and anoints some people to be affluent so that the ministry of the body of Christ can go forward. Examine the life of this great man of God.

Raymond Wolf's Childhood

Raymond Wolf was born in 1925 on a farm in Shiloh, in Richland County, north central Ohio. His parents were Alvin and Freda Wolf. He had three brothers, Harold, Vergil, Norman; and one sister, Ethel. Their parents were descendants of pioneer Dutch families who moved to Ohio from Pennsylvania.

The school the Wolf children attended was located on the corner of their farm. Their transportation was a horse and buggy and later a model T Ford. Being raised on a farm, they had more than the average child did who attended school. During lunchtime, Raymond would trade his sandwich of homemade bread and thick-sliced ham for a piece of store-bought bread and a piece of baloney. The store-bought sandwich was very appetizing to him because it was different. He was accustomed to food that was made at home.

On the farm, life was simple. There was always a lot of work to be done. Raymond's dad inherited 250 acres from his father. Now, they had 500 acres to farm with livestock and modern equipment. Agricultural products were greatly needed in America. Thus, farming was very important. Help from the Wolf brothers was essential.

One of the things the Wolfs enjoyed was community associations. One association that benefited the community was the Grange. The Grange was organized for insurance purposes. Also, the community would work with cooperation and fellowship when it was time to harvest wheat. Vergil Wolf described the fellowship with the neighbors in his book, Real Life of a Missionary:

Each family cut their own wheat and oats. After it was dry, the neighborhood threshing machine would go from farm to farm, and all the neighbors would join together and help until the job was finished. The eating together, the variety of food, and especially the companionship with the neighbors were the most exciting memories.

At first Raymond and his brothers were only water boys. But as they became bigger and stronger, they became involved in the regular workforce. All of this changed when farmers were able to purchase their own machinery. They were no longer interdependent. Prosperity was creating a fundamental change in the family lifestyle. The fellowship disappeared.

Serving Communion at the Age of 18

The Wolf family were Christians and attended the Shenandoah Christian Church. Raymond became a deacon at this church as a very young man. He helped serve the Communion when he was about 18 years old.

A Crooked Eye Kept Him Out of the Army

When Raymond was born, he had a crooked eye. He has only peripheral vision in the eye. He was always very conscious of that defective eye. His parents tried to get something done, but doctors could not do anything for him in those days. However, this handicap did keep him from being drafted into the Army. He could not pass the physical exam because of the eye, so he stayed on the farm to help his father.

Raymond was Greatly Influenced by Vergil

Vergil had gone into the Navy when Raymond was in his late teens. While there, Vergil accepted the Lord. He wrote home to the family about his experience with God. When he came home, he was such a different person, that Raymond began to watch him very carefully.

Vergil told Raymond all about the call of God upon his life to be a minister and a missionary. Their father just could not go along with the Pentecostal experience with which his boys were getting involved. He insisted that Vergil go to a Church of Christ college.

Vergil went to the Church of Christ school; but his time there was not long. He could not remain quiet about his new experience with God. He began testifying about the Holy Spirit baptism. Vergil describes his experience in his book, Real Life of a Missionary. He wrote:

"One day the professor was saying that miracles had stoppedat the end of the disciples' era, and the presence of the Holy Spirit swept through me and said, 'Testify.' I knew it was the Holy Spirit and I wanted to obey Him, but I was also aware of the disturbance it would make in the class. I hesitated and prayed for help, but the more I waited the more I felt moved by the Lord. Before I realized it, I was shaking so hard that the whole bench and the students on it were shaking. Everybody was staring at me. I held up my hand. The professor recognized me. I had just said a few words when he cut me off, saying, 'Mister Wolf, I know you were in the war, so just calm down.'

"However, the Lord was not through with me yet. I stood up and said, 'You have been teaching us to speak where the Bible speaks.' He allowed me to go on and testify until I got to Matthew 3:11. I told them that Jesus had not changed; that He still worked miracles. The professor stopped me. He said, 'If you are one of them, you ought to go with them.' He was referring to the Church of God Bible Training School at the time located in Sevierville, Tennessee."

The officials of the college then called Vergil in to see them. Since Vergil could not keep quiet about his Holy Spirit experience, he was asked to leave the college. That is how he wound up at the Church of God Bible Training School in Sevierville, Tennessee. All of this was making a deep impression on Raymond.

Career as a Farmer

Vergil went off to Bible Training School in Sevierville and Raymond started out as a farmer, helping his dad. Raymond bought some farm machinery but became discouraged when he did not get any crops planted because of the wet spring. Raymond's father bought the farm machinery from him and suggested that he go to work in the tractor factory to earn some money.

Not Settled into God's Plan Yet

Raymond took his father's advice and went to work in a tractor factory in Greenwich, Ohio. While there, he learned some valuable lessons that shaped his life. Raymond would take broken drills out of the wastebasket and take them to the tool shop. They were ground down and made into good drills— like new. Then he called them his. After becoming a Christian, Raymond got another job. As he grew in Christ, he had to repent over taking the drills. He wrote his former boss a letter, offering to pay for the drills. The man refused and told Raymond he was always welcome to work for him.

After Raymond left the factory, he went to work driving a taxi cab for a short time, then changed to Westinghouse and worked on a laundromat line. It was here that Raymond learned much about how God convicts His children. He was often convicted for listening to stories unbecoming to a Christian's ears.

Raymond Meets His Wife

When Raymond was 22, he met Joanne Altman at a skating rink. She would become the love of his life. While he was practicing to skate backwards, he fell down in front of her. She laughed at him. Later, he asked her to skate with him. When Raymond learned that Joanne could not skate backwards and had a difficult time skating forwards, he was no longer intimidated by her.

Raymond found himself falling in love with Joanne. After their engagement, Raymond started taking Joanne to church with him to the Shenandoah Christian Church. Vergil came home from the Church of God Bible Training School during the summer and invited them to visit the Mansfield Church of God.

The first time Raymond took Joanne to the Mansfield Church of God, he wondered if that would be the end of their relationship because she was a Lutheran. When they walked in the door, the congregation was singing "Amazing Grace, how sweet the sound." They both felt something different from what they had ever felt before.

Raymond and Joanne were married in the Lutheran Church on August 15, 1948, with Vergil as the best man.

The Conversion Experience

A revival was held in the city, a combined effort of many churches. During this meeting, Raymond listened to the preacher and became convicted of his sins. This was a new slant on Christianity for him. The preacher said, "You can know you are saved. You can know God is giving you eternal life. You can know you are going to heaven." Raymond had always believed that whatever happens will happen.

Vergil had written to the pastor of the Mansfield Church of God and asked him to send someone to visit his brother and his wife. Joanne was not at home when two visitors came from the Church of God. Raymond was at home sick. The visitors gave their testimonies of how God saved them from

— 265 —

drunkenness. Raymond felt very self-righteous and told them he was glad they had turned to God and stopped sinning. After they left, Raymond read the Scriptures and was convicted of the things he was doing wrong. He felt the Lord calling him to ask for forgiveness for the sins in his own life. He got down on his knees and prayed through all by himself. He asked the Lord into his heart. Joanne came home to find herself with a saved husband.

A few months after Raymond accepted Christ, Joanne realized she needed to accept Christ while praying with another person at a citywide revival.

Raymond Goes Into Painting

After World War II ended, Raymond was laid off from the Westinghouse plant. He then started his own business. He had cards printed and went door to door telling people that he would like to paint their houses. At first, he did the painting himself. Then he began hiring others to work with him. Vergil had graduated from the Church of God Bible School in Cleveland, Tennessee, and had moved to Ashland, Ohio, to attend seminary. Vergil needed some extra money, so he went to work for Raymond. While they were painting houses, Vergil preached to Raymond and told his brother about the Baptism of the Holy Ghost. As a result, Raymond and his wife went to the revival at the Ashland Church of God, and Raymond received the Holy Spirit baptism. Soon after, Raymond and Joanne began to attend the Ashland Church of God.

Vergil was asked by the state overseer to pastor the Mansfield Church of God. Thus, Raymond and Joanne went to the Mansfield Church of God to help support Vergil in his ministry. The brothers became closer than they had ever been. Many times they would pray until 2 a.m. When it would rain while they were painting, Vergil and Raymond would go inside and find a place to pray. One time, they were praying in a corncrib. A powerful spirit of intercession for the conversion of souls came upon them. They prayed for hours. It was as if they both were being stretched spiritually. Their love for prayer was increasing. They had come to understand the great power of agreement prayer.

Moving Back to the Farm

God began to show Raymond that He had plans for him. Vision is the ability to see God's presence, to focus on God's plan regardless of what it looks like. Raymond felt led of God to move back to the farm. He bought a farm from his dad. However, he took his painting business with him and operated out of an old barn.

Learning to Be a Giver

God was still dealing with Raymond in many ways. He had a debt of $4,600 on the farm he had purchased at the age of 23. God dealt with Raymond to give $100 to missions at camp meeting. Raymond did not have $100. All he could think of was the debt he owed. God was still stretching Raymond. God said, "If you will give this money at the state camp meeting, I will pay your farm off this fall." Raymond had learned to hear the voice of the Lord. He listened, borrowed the money, and gave $100 to missions.

Raymond was blessed abundantly. God gave him ideas about how to make money. He put corn in storage and then sold it for a good price during the off season. He had corn, wheat, oat, and soybean crops and paid the farm off that fall. He allowed his potential to be invaded by God's power.

Giving became a regular part of their lives. Soon the Wolfs were giving 40 percent of every dollar they made. They had learned that tithing gets the heaven above you open, and that giving sends the blessings down from the open heaven.

The Call of God to Raymond

God began dealing with Raymond. Katherine Kuhlman came to town. She and the miracles that accompanied her ministry fascinated Raymond. One night she told about a lady who was bent over, not able to straighten up. God touched the woman and healed her.

During the meeting, God began speaking to Raymond. When they had gone to the Katherine Kuhlman meeting they had sung, "Oh, how I love Jesus" over and over. Then God said to Raymond, "Do you love me enough to preach the gospel?"

Raymond did not know what to say, so he did not answer the Lord. As he and Joanne went into the parking lot he said to Joanne, "I think the Lord is calling me into the ministry." He began thinking seriously about the matter. He thought, I'll have to sell the farm and sell the business I have started. I'll have to go to college and work hard. It will change my whole life.

He began to fast and pray and ask God to help him know His will. Finally, he told the Lord, "I am willing. I'm willing to do all the things I need to do in order to preach your Word."

Then the word of the Lord came back to him, "If you are willing to go and preach my word, then you are ready to do the work I want you to do. I want you to minister to the ministry."

Raymond questioned the Lord, "Lord, what do you mean by being a minister to the ministry?"

God said, "If you will obey me, I will direct you and bless you beyond your imagination."

Many times God has pointed Raymond back to this calling. Many people go through life wishing they had done something different. Raymond knew his calling and has followed through with it.

One young lady, Lucy Gassaway, stood up in church and said, "I must go to Lee College." God spoke to Raymond and said, "I have chosen this for you." Raymond and Joanne paid the girl's college tuition.

A young man testified that God was calling him to preach, but he did not have the money to go to school. Brother Wolf felt led of God to give him an offering. The man later said, "God showed me through that offering that I was to go to Bible school and go into the ministry."

A lady evangelist came along. God said to Joanne, "Give her the new car you just bought." Raymond had just bought a brand new Dodge and had paid cash for it. The woman could not even drive. God convinced Raymond that this was part of his calling and not just his wife's suggestion. Raymond obeyed. When the revival was over, Joanne taught the evangelist how to drive.

God Gives Raymond and Joanne a Son

God spoke to Raymond one day. "You are going to have a son. His eye will be crooked just like yours, but I will heal him." Sure enough, when Raymond first saw his son, he saw the crooked eye. The enemy said, "Just like you." But God kept His promise. By the time they took the baby home from the hospital, his eye was completely straight. What a miracle! God had kept His word.

Not Always Easy to Help People

Helping people was not always easy. While Raymond was teaching his youth Sunday school class, someone broke into the farm and stole gasoline and some of his tools. He and Joanne were crushed when they learned who had done it. It was the boyfriend of the pastor's daughter. The girl had been in their home and knew where the switch to the gasoline pump was in the closet. She had told her boyfriend, and they had plotted to steal while they knew Raymond and his family would be at church.

Ministry to Missions

While pastoring the Mansfield Church of God, Vergil was called to the mission field, and he left to go to Guatemala.

When he was home on furlough, the two brothers prayed together about the ministry. Vergil said, "I think I can build a lot of churches in Guatemala with your help."

The congregations could build a church to the point of getting the roof on. Vergil and Raymond set a strategy. Many churches were built. Each time, Raymond would send money for the roof. He put the roofs on about 20 churches in Guatemala.

Further, Raymond influenced one of his subcontractors, Henry Gassaway of Gassaway Masonry, to go to Guatemala to help with the work of God. Henry drove a motorcycle all the way to Guatemala. He helped Vergil build a long wall on the school property at Quezaltenango.

Raymond visited Vergil while he served in Guatemala. Vergil was the overseer and had to deal with problem situations. He and Raymond traveled a long distance to get to one church where a married pastor was giving too much attention to a young lady in the church.

The pastor was denying all accusations. They began to pray. The power of God fell. Vergil spoke in tongues and Raymond interpreted in Spanish. (He does not speak Spanish.) The preacher fell on his face and repented.

Get God's Direction as You Go

Raymond has a philosophy: "Get God's direction as you go." God gave Raymond direction.

A man wanted Raymond to build a building and lease it to him for $1,000 a month. Raymond was working in the basement of another building seeking God's direction. God spoke to Raymond: "If you will obey my voice, I will lead you in the direction you ought to go."

God brought to Raymond's mind a certain traffic light. God said, "When you get to the light under the underpass on route 30, if it's green, you have a green light for this project. If it is red, stop the project. I will control the light for you."

That afternoon Raymond got in his truck and drove toward the light. Traffic was backed up about 15 cars. As he turned the curve, he saw that the light was green, but knew that by the time he got there, it would be red. He kept driving. The light stayed green. He went through the light, and the light still stayed green.

The enemy whispered, "You mean you are going to borrow money and build a building because a light turned green?" Raymond shouted, "Yes, that's what I am going to do! God said He would control the light. He said that if it stayed green, I had the green light." Raymond borrowed money and built the commercial building for a printing business. The man rented the building for 10 years for $1,000 a month.

Raymond took the money from that building and built the Bible school in Quezaltenango, Guatemala, which is now serving as the Church of God Seminary for Central America. That money was invested in ministering to the ministry.

The Wolfs were now giving 50 percent of every dollar they made to the Lord.

His Daughter Is Healed of Tuberculosis

Raymond taught the youth Sunday school class in his church for 35 years. Before his daughter, Carolyn, graduated, she developed TB. The doctors placed her in a sanitarium. This greatly disturbed Raymond and Joanne. Every Sunday Raymond would go to the sanitarium and teach the Sunday school lesson to his sick daughter. Then he would go to church and teach his youth class. He prayed for Carolyn. He told her that the Lord would heal her. At first, it was hard for Carolyn to believe. But soon it clicked. She began to stand on the Word of God for her healing. The Holy Spirit gave a message that God had heard their prayers and would heal her.

The doctors told the Wolf family that Carolyn had a hole in her lung the size of a quarter and wanted to remove part of the lung. Carolyn decided not to have the surgery, in light of God's promise to heal her. In about three months, she was out of the hospital. Six months later the hole in her lung was gone. She was completely healed by the power of God.

Prayer Brings Good Decisions

The Lord always blessed Raymond and Joanne in being able to make good decisions. They bought property in 1962 on Ashland Road at the edge of Mansfield. Raymond's dad thought the property was worthless. His dad said, "It is foolish to pay $46,000 for that old gully." But Raymond felt the Spirit of the Lord leading him to buy the property.

Raymond took down the trees. He had a friend who owned excavating equipment, and he had his friend move dirt in, fill the gully, and make a nice level parking lot. Raymond built a bank, a post office, a dry cleaners, and later an economy store. He built a shopping center and leased it out. There are numerous businesses in the shopping center today, such as a furniture store, hardware store, crafters store, a barber shop, a pet store, a health food store, etc. Raymond runs the peddlers' market there with about 80 different vendors.

In addition, Raymond built several apartments. His philosophy, then and now, is to build apartments and when that apartment starts getting old, trade it and acquire a new one in place of it. In other words, update what you have done so you don't have so many maintenance problems.

Listening to the Voice of the Lord

At one time Raymond's business installed drain spouting for a large percentage of the new homes in Mansfield. One day he was going up a ladder to clean out the spouting. The Lord spoke to him and said, "Get a rope and tie it around your waist and around the chimney." Raymond did not want to do it, but he had learned to obey.

Raymond went to the ground half disgusted. He got a rope and tied it around himself. He went back up the ladder and was cleaning the spouting. All at once the spouting came loose, and Raymond went over the side. Hanging by the rope tied around his stomach, he looked down at a concrete walk and steps where he would have fallen if he had not obeyed God. He has learned, "You better obey the Lord no matter what the dumb mind says."

On another occasion, Raymond was driving to Texas to the General Assembly. The Lord spoke to him to stop at a certain restaurant. He was not hungry and wondered why the Lord impressed him to stop at a restaurant. At first, he passed on by. Then, he decided he'd better obey. He turned around and went back to the restaurant and had dinner. Later, he found out that farther down the road, a truck loaded with hogs had turned over. There were dead hogs all over the highway. If he had not stopped, he would have been right in the middle of much danger.

There have been many other miracles in Raymond's life. On one occasion, he was digging a deep ditch. He was down in the ditch and heard the voice of the Lord tell him, "Get out and get out now!" He obeyed the voice of the Lord. As soon as he was out of that ditch, the ditch caved in.

Raymond built the housing development where he and his family live. He has named the circles in the development after family members. There is Carolyn Circle (named after his daughter) and David's Lane (named after his son). One day, while putting a sewer system in that development, he was warned by the Lord to get out of that ditch. Again, he obeyed. Immediately after he was out, the ditch caved in. God has always warned him when there was danger.

He Helps Pastors in His Home State

Raymond believes in helping the state pastors. He has freely helped several pastors in their building projects by assisting to build church buildings, church additions, and providing plumbing, heating and air conditioning services. When pastors have an urgent need in building or in finance, Raymond Wolf is there trying to help.

Raymond was the general contractor for the Stewart Road Church of God in Mansfield. He was able to save the church thousands of dollars. He built their building for $135,000. It is valued at $1 million today.

Traveling With Men of Action

Raymond went with the Men of Action to Alaska. While there, he helped install a boiler in a new church and did some plumbing. He, along with 34 others, built a church. He and a Men of Action team went to Zambia, Africa, and started the construction on two churches.

Raymond Wolf Believes in Fasting

Raymond has a practice of fasting one day a week—every Wednesday. As a result, he is continually seeking God's direction. He will have three or four decisions in front of him. He prays. He may say, "This one will give me the most money; but I sense the presence of God on this one. God, direct me and let me know Your will, because I goof up on my own."

He Is Faithful to His Local Church

Raymond is faithful to his local church. He does not miss anything going on at the church. His feeling is: "A great move of God may come. If I am not there, I will miss it." He teaches Sunday school and is also a member of the praise and worship team.

Healing Comes to Raymond and Joanne

Joanne and Raymond have been healed many times. Once Joanne was about to die. She had to have surgery on her bowels, but God healed her completely. She was soon back working beside her husband.

On one occasion, Raymond was having heart pains. He was taken to the hospital and the doctors found that he had blockage in the main arteries. He had surgery to open the arteries. Again, God came on the scene for him. He was healed.

Raymond Ministers in Hospitals and Nursing Homes

Raymond ministers to people in hospitals and nursing homes. He discovered that the Word tells us that whatsoever our hands find to do—to do it with all your might and for the glory of God. Raymond finds needs and fills them. He finds hurts and heals them.

Prison Ministry Is a Love of His Life

Winning souls is a priority in Raymond's life. He took his training from Charles Beach and Leonard Albert. He is involved with jail ministry and underprivileged people. Also, he serves on the National Prison Commission.

Raymond conducts services at three different state institutions: the Mansfield Correctional Institution, the Richland Correctional institution, and the Richland Honor Camp. He often takes people from his church with him. Many times revival breaks out in these services.

Raymond goes back to talk with the tough cases. Many of the men have become bitter because of their circumstances. Raymond gives them hope through Jesus Christ. He also goes into county jails at 8 a.m. on Saturdays and city jails at 10 a.m. every other week. There he talks to people one-on-one through the bars. The prisoners are always happy when he comes. They may be doing other things—playing cards or watching TV—but they usually stop when Raymond Wolf arrives. There have been many dramatic conversions.

Further, Raymond has a program set up so that those getting out of prison or jail can get food supplies for their families. He gets donations from various people and places.

He Is a Member of Vision Foundation

Vision Foundation is a love of Raymond's life. He has been on the board for years and enjoys being a part of financing Vision projects.

Raymond's dream for the future is to keep on doing what he is now doing. God gives him strength to keep working, to keep serving. He is indeed a man of vision. He is also a true minister to the ministry.

Raymond Wolf
1469 Troy Drive
Mansfield, OH 44905-1330

Telephone
419-589-2526
or
419-525-1194

Calvin Wooten — The Blind Man With Vision

Calvin Wooten—The Blind Man With Vision

Calvin Wooten—The Blind Man With Vision

To some men the handicap of blindness justifies a life of begging. With Calvin Wooten, the limitation of blindness produces a man who has great vision. Calvin has a successful piano and organ repair business. He is the owner of 45 rental homes, owner of the largest home in his neighborhood, a man in his senior years who gets up every morning with fire burning in his bones, a man who was chairman of the Alabama School for the Deaf and Blind in Talladega, a man who is a board member of Vision Foundation, a man who has received many awards.

The Day That Changed His Life Forever

Calvin Wooten's life started out like that of most people. The family lived in Dekalb County on Sand Mountain at Rainsville near Ft. Payne, Alabama. His father earned a good salary as a railroad man working out of Chattanooga, Tennessee, for the Alabama Great Southern Railroad.

Calvin's childhood was fairly normal until one eventful morning on May 13, 1931. At the age of 6, he was playing with a straw hat that had a string. Calvin was desperately trying to pull the string out of the vent hole. Then he got an idea. There was a knife on the kitchen table. He ran into the kitchen and got the knife and started working on his project. The knot slipped through the hole, but the knife grazed his eye.

His eyesight was not affected at that time. Calvin describes it: "It was like looking through a clear windowpane." There was a slight little pimple on the edge of the pupil in his eye.

However, the family rushed little Calvin to Dr. Ghobsett, a German doctor who was the best eye specialist in the south at that time. His office was located in Chattanooga on the corner of Zion Street and McCallie Avenue.

At first the specialist thought there would be no major problem because there was hardly any restriction in Calvin's vision. Nevertheless, he took every precaution and started special treatments on the eye.

This was a tough time for the family. Someone had to drive 100 miles every day to take Calvin for treatment and bring him home.

About the same time, Calvin's body was hit by typhoid fever. He and the family had stopped by a spring in Trenton, Georgia, for a picnic lunch on their way home from the doctor one day. Calvin loved to drink from the spring there. Within a short time after that, he became very sick. Typhoid fever attacked young Calvin's eyes. The family learned later that three people from one family died after drinking from that spring.

Suddenly Calvin's eyesight started changing. His father, who was an Alabama Great Southern Railroad man, left home one Sunday and returned on Friday evening. When he left, Calvin seemed fine; but when he returned, his boy could hardly see. Calvin's eyesight went from 20/20 to 0 in less than a week's time. The good eye had sympathized with the injured eye and sight was lost in both eyes.

Good Parents Helped Give the Blind Boy Vision

This was a distressful time for the Wooten family. But they did not know that Calvin was going to see things they never thought possible.

During this crisis, Calvin's parents made all the difference in the world. They kept him out front and kept his life otherwise as normal as possible.

Because Calvin could not go to regular school, he went with his dad on the train to see the doctor in Chattanooga many times. The boy stayed in the hotel where his father boarded while working away from home. Even though the tragedy was hard on everyone in the family, Calvin and his father bonded during these trips. Afraid? Yes! But they faced this crisis with courage.

Calvin Enrolled in the School for the Blind

In the fall of 1933, when Calvin was about 9 years of age, his parents decided to enroll him in the Alabama School for the Blind in Talledaga, Alabama.

This was a very emotional time for Calvin. Talledaga was 100 miles away. That was a long way from home and took an entire day to get there. In those days the roads were not paved en route to Talladega.

The first time the family left him at the school was the most difficult time of their lives. They knew it had to be done, but it was painful. When they drove away from the campus, the last thing they saw was little Calvin with tears streaming down his face. They cried profusely.

About half-way home, they pulled the car off the road to have a family discussion. Should they go back and get Calvin, or let him stay at the school where he could get an education? They finally came to the conclusion that they had done what was best for Calvin and the family.

The family would take Calvin by car and then leave him for several months at a time. The school term went from September until May. He came home for the summer months, as well as holidays, and special weekends. This was very strenuous on the entire family. Calvin said, "It took me three years to stop crying."

God had a plan for Calvin's life. "For I know the plans I have for you declares the Lord, plans to prosper you and not to harm you, plans to give you hope and a future" (Jeremiah 29:11).

The Blind Boy Resolves to Excel

Calvin had every excuse to give up and feel sorry for himself, but even as a young child he was determined to do well. Calvin got it together at a very early age. Blindness became a gift to him. It propelled him forward. This catastrophe changed the course of his life. But it did not make him bitter. It only made him better.

The only blind man he had ever seen was a beggar. This impression haunted Calvin at first. Then he resolved, "I will never be helpless." He lifted his voice and cried out, "God, if you will open the door and help me, I will walk through." To this day Calvin happily testifies, "I have never taken a dime of any kind of welfare. I don't want it."

The Blind Boy Begins to Work

This blind boy had a vision. He could see clearly. School was hard work, but Calvin buckled down to do his best. At the age of 9, he learned how to make leather belts and started earning money. One of the crafts teachers demonstrated to Calvin how to make the belts. Calvin voiced, "I think I can do that." The teacher helped him. They ordered the leather from Robert J. Golka in Brockton, Massachusetts. Calvin could buy the material for about 15 cents and sell the belts for a dollar. Soon he was in business, at the age of 9, helping his family with their finances. This child simply could not be defeated. God infused him with energy.

Vision is not something you are born with. It's something that you have to develop. It's something you have to pay a price for, and Calvin determined to be a person with vision. He was blind, but so was Fanny Crosby, Louis Braille, and John Milton.

Calvin was persistent. The next thing he learned to do was to put bottoms in straight chairs. At first he used cane. Then he contacted with a place in New Orleans where he could get strips of leather. The strips were about 3/8 of an inch wide and 1/8 inch thick. He learned to weave that in the bottom of the chair. This made the chair last forever. (There are chairs in Sand Mountain today that he did 50 years ago.)

Calvin learned early not to conduct his life on the basis of sight. He did not focus on his problem. Had he done so, he might have been intimidated and wound up defeated. He was just a young person in a major crisis with a depressing handicap. But greatness was germinating within him, and he did not know it.

It's what is in your brain behind your eyes that makes you win or fail in life. It's what you do with what you've got that makes you who you are.

Another Crisis Hits the Wooten Family

One day Calvin's father got out of the car and walked around to the back of the car. Suddenly he was hit by another car. Calvin's father's leg was broken. The bone came through the flesh. In that day, that was a bad break. Infection got into the leg and gangrene set up. The doctors gave Mr. Wooten the upsetting news that they had to take the leg off 1½ inches below the hip. Dr. Morgan in Gadsden, Alabama, said that if they had been a day later amputating the leg, he would not have survived. This was a tragedy.

Since the accident did not take place on the job, Mr. Wooten was not able to receive any help from the insurance company. This made the financial situation tough for the Wooten family. Calvin's father was no longer able to work. There were four young children and one of them was blind. Calvin laughingly says now, "The poor folks thought we were poor."

Nonetheless, this became a source of inspiration for Calvin. He decided that as soon as he got out of school he would work and make life easier for his mother. He had a vision and determination.

"For my thoughts are not your thoughts, neither are your ways my ways, declares the Lord. For as the heavens are higher than the earth, so are my ways higher than your ways, and my thoughts than your thoughts" (Isaiah 55:8-9).

Calvin began to take all his classes more seriously. At the age of 14, he trained to work on pianos. He was setting his goals high.

God gave this young blind man a vision to reach out and be somebody and do something great with his life. He said, "We both (God and I) worked on that agreement."

Beginning of a Career

The principal of the School for the Deaf and Blind called Calvin into his office about a year before Calvin graduated. He said, "Calvin, I'm afraid you may have trouble getting along with your employers when you get out of school." Calvin responded, "Mr. Haynes, I plan to be one." He did not have eyesight, but he had vision.

In 1944 at age 19, Calvin graduated from the School for the Blind and started his career. He now entered a negative world that would say to a blind man, "You can't make it." But Calvin said, "I can." He set his mark high and put forth earnest effort to reach it. He had vision and enthusiasm. He looked through the eyes of faith. That eagle personality began to soar.

After getting out of school, Calvin began tuning pianos for people all over Sand Mountain. Like Caleb, he tackled his mountain. Though blind, he was unafraid. He began to envision making money even on Sand Mountain. He was ready to be all that God wanted him to be. He did not allow obstacles to dishearten him. Calvin concentrated on surmounting every obstacle.

Calvin put an ad with his address in the Dekalb Times that stated: "Piano service available." People were happy with the work he did. Soon it was spread all over Sand Mountain that if a piano didn't play at all, Calvin Wooten, the young blind man, could make it play.

Calvin says, "Blind people tend to be the best piano tuners. They are better than people with sight. They hear better and seem to do a better job."

There was something different about Calvin's spirit. He tackled every day with excitement. He was committed to winning.

Calvin's father was never able to work on a regular job after he lost his leg. Calvin was determined to help his father. He began rehabilitating him. Calvin taught his father how to work on pianos, and they worked together for 35 years. What a blessing! A blind man rehabilitates his father!

Developing in Business

Calvin's eyes were always painful. His mother did not want him to have his eyes removed. She lived in hopes that one day his eyesight would come back. When Calvin turned 21, one of the first things he did was have the eyes removed and artificial eyes put in. This way he looked normal. He diligently worked at looking his customers in the eyes as he talked with them. He was very conscientious about business manners. Many people who bought pianos from him or asked for his service had no idea that he was blind.

The Move to Anniston, Alabama

"A man's gift makes room for him." In 1947, W. L. Miller, the manager of Forbes Piano Company in Alabama, went to George Hamm, the instructor at the School for the Blind, and asked for the best man they knew to come to Anniston to handle their outside work. The company wanted someone who would be willing to go out in the county and service pianos in the homes of people who would not travel to Anniston. Mr. Hamm highly recommended Calvin.

Mr. Miller drove all the way to Sand Mountain to find Calvin to ask him to come to Anniston. Miller saw the courage of this blind man. He saw his vision and determination. He realized Calvin was an eagle personality, although he was blind.

The odds may have been against him, but his vision was noticeable.

As they talked, Calvin shared with Mr. Miller that he would prefer to service the public. That satisfied both of them. Calvin moved to Anniston, Alabama, on February 11, 1947, to begin a new life. At first he moved to Anniston without his family. Soon, however, Calvin moved his family to be with him. Calvin and his family were always very close. Blindness had drawn them exceptionally close.

The Man of Vision Expands His Career

God began to bless the piano business. Calvin finally felt that he had worked successfully for the piano company long enough. It was time to go into business for himself. Calvin expanded to his own business for piano and organ tuning and repairs. His father continued with him in his business. Soon he hired another employee and the business was on its way.

Calvin was not content with mediocrity. He often said, "I don't want to be buried in a pauper's grave." He further stated, "I don't want to be average. Average is the best of the worst and the worst of the best." He was not willing to settle for the status quo.

In Anniston, Calvin began to stretch. He had a sleeping giant within him. One day an ad in the paper offered a house for sale for only $1,000 plus monthly payments. What a deal! It was a six-room house. Calvin bargained with the owners to let him make the down payment in installments. He took over the payments on the house for only $46 a month. When that house was paid for, he kept investing in more houses.

The Blind Man Finds a Wife

Marriage was not a priority for Calvin until he was 35 years of age. He was more concerned about his career because he dealt with a fear of starvation much of his younger life.

Calvin started attending the Ft. Payne, Alabama, Church of God in the late 1940s. Thurman G. Pearson was the pastor of the church. His niece Winell came to the church when visiting her relatives. It was at that time that Calvin and Winell became acquainted. However, they did not begin dating until after he moved to Anniston, where Winell also lived with her family. Winell's uncle, who pastored the church in Ft. Payne, had been transferred to Florida, but his daughter was a student at Lee College and came to visit Winell on weekends and holidays. Of course, her cousin knew the Wootens and wanted to visit them. So Winell went with her to the Wooten home.

Gradually Calvin and Winell began to go places together. He would ask her to drive him places. The first place she went with Calvin was to the Alumni Convention for the School for the Blind in Talledaga. It was held in an antique hotel that was famous in Alabama for its food. Winell had never been to a lot of places nor done a lot of things. She was impressed! Calvin was on the alumni board and was highly respected.

Immediately Winell was given some opportunities while being with Calvin that she had never had before. She began to enjoy Calvin's company. He was fun.

Soon they realized they were in love. Winell's father was concerned. He told her that he preferred that she not marry a blind man. He said, "You know you will never have anybody go to the store for you." But Winell says today, "I have sisters that my Daddy has had to help financially; he has never had to help me. Calvin has always provided for me." The Reverend Hoyt Fair performed the ceremony in Anniston at the Sixteenth Avenue Church of God on November 27, 1958.

The Blind Man Grows

Most people with eyesight become complacent and content with a normal life where they can make a living. Our minds are lulled and our wills become eroded. We think we have accomplished all we can accomplish. Charles Kettering once said, "Just the minute you get satisfied with what you've got, the concrete has begun to set in your head." But Calvin Wooten wanted to keep stretching—to keep growing.

He began to buy houses to rent. Today at the time of this writing, he owns 45 houses debt free and collects at least $20,000 a month from the rentals. Calvin keeps the houses in good condition. He works on good relationships with his renters. He is careful to follow through on obligations.

Calvin hired a specialist to tune and repair the organs. But he made the decision to do the piano tuning himself. He tells people, "If you won't let me do it right, I won't do it at all." He further tells them, "You may find someone to do it cheaper, but not nearly as well as I do."

Work has always been a part of Calvin's life . Even though he was blind, he never allowed himself the privilege of self-pity. Every day he got up with the feeling, I am going to work today. He has no plans of ever retiring. Calvin says, "When you're blind and out here dealing in business, toe to toe every day with a sighted world, if you're not a little aggressive, you'll get run over. You'll get stepped on and left. So I have always been kinda' aggressive." His vision replaced his lack of eyesight. His vision overstepped laziness and self-pity.

Calvin has no patience with people who want to be on welfare. He testifies, "I have never asked for one cent that I did not work for. I have never asked for any kind of disability."

Family Life of the Man of Vision

People may think a blind man is helpless. But his family lives in the biggest house in the neighborhood and has never had a mortgage payment. After children came along, the Wootens decided to build another house—paying for it as it was built. It is a 7,000-square-foot brick house with four levels which sits on five lots. They have never had a mortgage payment.

Winell wanted Calvin to teach her how to tune pianos, but he wanted her just to be by his side. She goes everywhere with him. She can drive any vehicle she wants. She is his "eyes," and they have a very close relationship.

Travel and fun have been a part of this marriage. Winell says, "I have had more advantages than most of my friends. I have gone more places, done more things and met more people than any of my friends. There has never been a problem married to a blind man." They have traveled to all 50 states and have gone to Israel, Canada, Mexico, and many other foreign countries. Much of this travel was to conventions for the blind.

Winell lives a very fulfilled life of her own also. She is involved in Republican Party politics. She serves on the state committee. She was alternate delegate for two national Republican conventions—in Philadelphia and San Diego. She has been an elected member to the state Republican committee for at least four years at the time of this writing. She has been in Republican politics ever since she was 21. Further, she served on the county school board from 1972-78.

Calvin and Winell gave birth to four children in five years—three daughters and one son. Calvin passed his philosophy down to them, "You can make it!" By the time their children were 12 years old, they had been in 46 states.

The toughest battle of their lives was when their son developed AIDS. Joe was very close to the family. He was very family-oriented. He was present for every family gathering. He never forgot birthdays, etc. He had been selected as the outstanding student in high school and received an award at graduation. Also, he was a drum major. He graduated from Birmingham Southern College and worked in research at Baptist Princeton Hospital in Birmingham for 12 years of his life.

When Joe got sick, he came down with pneumonia. The doctors did a series of tests and found that he was HIV positive. The Wootens were devastated. On Sunday, Calvin and Winell went to see their son. They had a heart-to-heart talk about when and why. This is when they learned of his lifestyle. They told him, "We don't approve of this lifestyle; but we love you and whatever you go through, we will be there for you." The Wootens did not discuss their hurt with even their closest friends. Their son continued to work for the research hospital for two years.

After Joe had a major seizure, he went to the hospital in Birmingham. Calvin and Winell called Paul Henson on the phone. Paul left his home in Cleveland and went to the hospital in Birmingham to counsel with Joe. Joe completely surrendered his life and future to the Lord. Paul said that he had never experienced such a move of God in his life as he did when talking and praying with Joe.

Joe lived with the family for the last months of his life. He had a wonderful testimony. Winell had much apprehension at first, but God gave her the knowledge and strength to be his nurse during those last days of his life. It was a good experience for the family.

Before he went to be with the Lord, Joe told his mother, "I am ready to go." The last few hours were spent back in Birmingham in the hospital. When Joe was dying, the family found much comfort. He just stopped breathing and went to be with the Lord. There was crying, but there was victory. They had no doubt that Joe was with the Lord.

The only regret Winell and Calvin had was that they did not allow their friends to share their pain during the long months of suffering. They only told friends when they had to. The suffering for them would have been less if they had leaned on their godly friends and counselors.

Now they continue to enjoy their three daughters and seven grandchildren. The Wootens take great pride in the successes of their family.

Member of Vision Foundation

Calvin was one of the early members of Vision Foundation. Other board members were happy to have a man with such great insight share their times together.

Board for Alabama Institute for Deaf and Blind

Calvin was originally appointed to be a member of the
Board of Trustees for the Alabama Institute for the Deaf and
Blind in 1978 by Governor George Wallace. Three successive
Alabama governors then reappointed him. At the time of this
writing, he has served them well for 22 years. In all those years
he missed only one meeting and that was when he was in Israel.

Calvin was elected Chairman of the Board in 1989 by
Governor Hunt and then served for eight years in that office.
He is the only alumnus who ever served as chairman.

Governor Hunt said of Calvin: "Calvin is one who
reflects all the key ingredients of success: determination,
integrity and ability. His friends have long since forgotten that
he is blind. In my opinion, he is a man of vision." The president
of the Alabama Institute for the Deaf and Blind, Dr. Jack
Hawkins, added to the governor's comments: "Mr. Wooten
represents what America is all about—success through hard
work. He has accentuated his strengths and in doing so he has
risen above the obstacles of blindness."

The school has a budget of over $38 million. It is the
best-equipped facility in the country for training and equipping
the sensory impaired. Calvin considers it a privilege to reach
out to other people who are sensory impaired. He has been an
inspiration to thousands who are handicapped.

American Foundation for the Blind

For a number of years Calvin served on the Southeast
Regional Advisory Board for the American Foundation for the
Blind. This took him and Winell to New York City on many
occasions. He is presently board member emeritus. He has
served on the investment committee of the AFB. When the
board was interviewing candidates for financial advisor, the

Wootens went to New York City every two weeks for a number of months.

Calvin was at one time president of the Alabama State chapter of the American Council of the Blind.

Migel Medal Award

In New York City on October 27, 1988, a standing-room-only crowd of family, friends, colleagues, and other well wishers gathered to applaud the achievements of Calvin Wooten, a recipient of American Foundation for the Blind's Migel Medal for achievements that have significantly improved the lives of blind and visually impaired people.

The late M. C. Migel, the first president of American Foundation, established the Migel Medal in 1937 for the Blind. Two medals are awarded annually—one to a professional and one to a layperson. Calvin was the lay- person in 1988.

Calvin was introduced by Alabama Governor Guy Hunt and Jack Hawkins, Jr., president of the Alabama Institute for Deaf and Blind in Talladega and member of the AFB Board of Trustees.

Governor Hunt and Hawkins spoke about Wooten's excellent track record in business and strong commitment to community service. They noted that in spite of economic hardships, Wooten displayed a strong determination to succeed early in life. Governor Hunt continued, "Wooten is blessed with a world of knowledge and has made his life amount to something." The governor continued, "He serves as an outstanding role model for all Americans."

Calvin Wooten Hall

In September 2002, Calvin received one of the thrills of his life. The Alabama Institute for the Deaf and Blind was naming a dormitory in the E. H. Gentry Technical School in Calvin's honor. The 14-room handicap-accessible dormitory is for the very handicapped deaf or blind adults. The name is Calvin Wooten Hall. Because it was a state building, the Alabama State Legislature had to give their approval before it could be named in honor of a person.

The building was dedicated on September 19, 2002, at 10:30 a.m. Winell was thrilled by this honor. She related, "Most of the things that were said and done at the dedication ceremony are usually done only at somebody's funeral. The recipients seldom get to hear these kind of remarks in person."

There was a beautiful ribbon-cutting ceremony, and the Wooten's grandchildren cut the ribbon at the building. Not only did the children cut the ribbon, they unveiled a plaque. On the plaque was a picture of Calvin in front of the building. The plaque read:

Calvin Wooten's energy, drive, and dedication have led him to a lifetime of service that has helped propel AIDB forward in its mission to serve deaf and blind children and adults. Since his graduation from the Alabama School for the Blind in 1944, he has been appointed a member of the Alabama Institute for the Deaf and Blind Board of Trustees and has served as chairman of the board, and served as chairman of the finance and development committee and member of the planning and policy and executive committees. He has donated his time and effort for the AIDB foundation board of directors. He has been recognized at a local, state and national level for his many contributions. Through his lifetime of service and with the support of his wife Winell, he has proven that blindness is no obstacle in the road to success. Winell and Calvin have paved this road with the love of their children and grandchildren. In appreciation for your lifetime of service to the Alabama Institute for the Deaf and Blind, presented to Calvin Wooten, September 19, 2002.

Ambassador Award

In 1987, the American Council of the Blind named Calvin the outstanding blind person in the country. He was given the

Ambassador Award, the Council's highest award. This award was given to him for integrating well into a sighted community. This award was presented in Los Angeles at the Airport Hilton Hotel.

One of Calvin's greatest thrills was when he received a telegram from President Ronald Reagan. The Western Union Mailgram read:

Dear Mr. Wooten,

I've just learned that the American Council of the Blind has chosen you to receive the 1987 Ambassador Award, and I want to join your many friends and Governor Guy Hunt in congratulating you.

Your tireless efforts and your gift of self over the years in behalf of the blind have been sources of hope and inspiration to countless men and women. Moreover, your own success as a businessman, civic leader, and trustee of the Alabama Institute for the Deaf and Blind serves as a shining example of the triumph of the human spirit. This award is truly well deserved.

Nancy joins me in extending best wishes to you, Winell, and your children for every happiness and success.

God bless you.

Ronald Reagan

Civic Clubs

Calvin has 18 years of perfect attendance in the Rotary Club of Anniston, Alabama. He is also a Gideon. He is also a member of the Calhoun County Chamber of Commerce. Being a blessing to the community is important to Calvin.

The Senior Years of the Man of Vision

At the time of this writing, Calvin Wooten is in his senior years—late 70s. Retire? He has no such word in his vocabulary. Slow down? He is doing more today than he has ever done! The world is held back by people who slow down, who decide to rest on what they have already done. Too many people in their senior years quit. The church and the world suffer. The glory departs. Calvin Wooten presses forward.

Hear Calvin as he almost exults, "If I could have only one prayer answered, eyesight would be way down the list." Stop? He could have; but he didn't, and thousands of people are grateful.

Calvin Wooten
820 Old Gadsden Highway
Anniston, AL 36201

Telephone
256-236-6092 (Home)
256-236-1397 (Office)

Printcorp. LP # 347 of 11.05.99. 40 Staroborisovsky Trakt, Minsk. Ord. 03128. Qty 3 000 cps.